# Springer Series on
# LIFE STYLES AND ISSUES IN AGING

1993  **RETIREMENT COUNSELING**
**A Handbook for Gerontology Practitioners**
*Virginia E. Richardson, PhD*


1994  **AGING AND QUALITY OF LIFE**
*Ronald P. Abeles, PhD, Helen C. Gift, PhD, and Marcia G. Ory, PhD, MPH*


1995  **THE IMPACT OF INCREASED LIFE EXPECTANCY**
**Beyond the Gray Horizon**
*Mildred M. Seltzer, PhD*


1995  **GEROCOUNSELING**
**Counseling Elders and their Families**
*Virginia S. Burlingame, MSW, PhD*

**Virginia S. Burlingame, MSW, PhD,** earned her Master's degree from Boston University and a doctorate in counseling/psychology from Northwestern University; her dissertation was on the History of the Family Therapy Movement in the U.S. She has worked in many areas of social work for over 40 years and is now a Board Certified Diplomate. She is presently in private practice with Southeastern Wisconsin Medical and Social Services, where she specializes in marriage and family therapy and gerocounseling. She is a clinical member of the American Association of Marriage and Family Therapy.

Dr. Burlingame received a Certificate in Gerontology from the University of Wisconsin–Oshkosh and was a 1990 Fellow with the Midwestern Geriatric Education Center. She currently teaches at and is Director of the Wisconsin Gerontology Institute of the University of Wisconsin–Parkside and Whitewater and the University of Wisconsin Extension. In 1994 she was awarded a Mini-Fellowship in Ethnogeriatrics from the Stanford Geriatric Education Center. She writes a column, "Artful Aging," and produces and hosts "Senior Racine" for cable T.V.

# GEROCOUNSELING

## Counseling Elders and Their Families

---

Virginia S. Burlingame, MSW, PhD

Springer Publishing Company

Springer Publishing Company, Inc.
536 Broadway
New York, NY 10012-3955

*Cover design by Tom Yabut*
*Production Editor: Pam Ritzer*

95 96 97 98 99 / 5 4 3 2 1

---

**Library of Congress Cataloging-in-Publication Data**

Burlingame, Virginia S.
    Gerocounseling : counseling elders and their families / Virginia
  S. Burlingame.
       p.   cm.—(Springer series on life styles and issues in
aging)
     Includes bibliographical references and index.
     ISBN 0-8261-8820-6
     1. Aged—Counseling of.  2. Aged—Family relationships.
3. Caregivers—Counseling of.  4. Family counseling.  I. Title.
II. Series.
HV1451.B875   1995
362.6'6—dc20
                                                        94-43090
                                                            CIP

---

Printed in the United States of America

# Contents

*Foreword* by Marilyn J. Bonjean, EdD      *vii*

*Preface*      *xi*

*Acknowledgment*      *xv*

**Chapter 1**    The Gerocounselor      1

**Chapter 2**    Gerocounseling      21

**Chapter 3**    Gero-Clients      45

**Chapter 4**    Gero-Assessment      75

**Chapter 5**    Gerocounseling Goals      105

**Chapter 6**    Gerocounseling Modalities      127

**Chapter 7**    Gerocounseling Interventions      147

**Chapter 8**    Gerocounseling: Specific Disorder Interventions      161

**Chapter 9**    Gerocounseling Terminations      179

*References*      *203*

*Index*      *209*

# *Foreword*

As the longevity of humankind increases, new opportunities become available for each of us. For example, living in a four- or five-generation family is becoming ever more common. This experience allows members to know each other through the eyes of grandparents and greatgrandparents, hearing firsthand the family stories and history which define the unique characteristics of each group. It also challenges members to care for each other as frailty and dependence increase. Stressors in the lives of elders often proliferate. A person becomes more frail and can no longer drive a car safely, which makes social contact difficult and leads to isolation and depressed feelings. Moderators of stress, such as coping repertoires, social support, and certain elements of self-concept such as mastery, regulate the impact of stress on well-being. Careful assessment and intervention may prevent the proliferation of stressors and help elders not only meet challenges but also make contributions to family, community, and society.

In *Gerocounseling*, Dr. Burlingame points out that elderly individuals are faced with issues of meaning and definition of useful social roles. Elders can contribute their skills and energy toward volunteering for worthy causes, serving as models for younger generations, and sharing the wisdom gleaned over a lifetime of experience. Age-related changes can call into question the underpinnings of self-definition and evoke questions about the purpose of life. Exploring these ideas may emphasize the importance of spirituality and offer a model for aging not yet available.

Longevity brings both opportunities and challenges to elders and their families. Gerocounselors, professionals from many areas of expertise but knowledgeable about the mental health of elders, can help elders and their families to focus their problem-solving abilities, overcome the challenges and take advantage of the opportunities aging brings. Human beings are never too old for change and growth. Like a plant moving toward the light, humans have an innate tendency toward curiosity and adaptation. My oldest client was 100 years old. He had come to make changes in the relationship with his 75-year-old daughter. Both were able to successfully change their communication and stop the constant arguments. They set a useful example for the future generations of their family and were able to enjoy each other for however long the future would allow.

Dr. Burlingame provides an important resource for the training of gerocounselors through the development of this volume. She knows from her years of teaching and clinical experience that assisting older adults takes special knowledge and expertise. Understanding the developmental issues of late life, the influence of chronic illness and medication, the importance of family relationships with established behavior patterns, and the influence of ageism on the elder, family, and professionals is important to successful outcomes. Counseling elders requires professionals to utilize themselves as change agents. They need to identify their own images and issues about aging because work with elders brings them into direct experience with frailty, dependence, and death, as well as strength, commitment, and transcendence. Ageism is a peculiar response to elders in our society. It means that all of us have absorbed certain myths and stereotypes about aging that are expressed in our behavior. There is an important difference in working with elders as opposed to other populations. Counselors will need to recognize their own ageist responses and be able to choose different, more helpful behavior.

This volume approaches gerocounseling from a systemic perspective, acknowledging that both problems and solutions are formed in relationships. Dr. Burlingame assists readers in thinking about problems and solutions in complex, multiple-level, interacting human systems. This approach will help readers provide useful consultation to elders as they appreciate the ecology of the client's context and the impact of every small intervention.

Ample documentation exists that most elders do not use mental health services, due in part to the stigma attached to seeking such help. Therefore the role of a gerocounselor is of primary importance to the emotional well-being of elders. These counselors will provide service in such alternative settings as health care clinics, neighborhood centers, senior centers, community organizations, and religious and educational institutions. Those attending can define themselves in very normal terms and still receive assistance with mental health issues. When counselors are able to help elders identify personal problems and form a trusting relationship will it prove to be the first line of prevention and early intervention. Because stressors tend to proliferate, elders receiving help early may never need to go any further for mental health assistance. However, if problems are more severe, the gerocounselor can make a referral for more in-depth service. Many clients will need the support of their counselor to utilize other help, and the therapeutic relationship with the counselor will often be a part of their aftercare and relapse prevention.

Community-based service programs that make accessing help for personal problems more appealing to elders will require well-trained gerocounselors to assist the increasing numbers of elders who can benefit from early intervention. There are financial benefits to elders who avail themselves of the services of gerocounselors, since counselors can perform many roles and may keep elders from entering the more formal mental health service systems. Dr. Burlingame has made a useful and timely contribution to the training of gerocounselors and the overall well-being of elders through her identification of the importance of community-based counseling—a textbook which will aid many in developing their counseling skills.

MARILYN J. BONJEAN, EdD
*ICF CONSULTANTS, INC.*
*MILWAUKEE, WI 53202*

# *Preface*

The aging population is increasing—rapidly. That is nothing new. What is new is the slowly dawning realization that we must recruit and train the health and social service providers needed to serve this constantly growing group. Up to now, caregivers in all disciplines have had to face this large elder population with little preparation. The clergy, for instance, touch the lives of more elders on a regular basis than any other group besides the family, as evidenced by the fact that one-fourth to one-third of the memberships in the major faith groups are over 65, while the elderly comprise only 12% of the total population. Nevertheless, the clergy as a group have little gerontological training to prepare them to minister to these large segments of their congregations. Many seminaries do not include gerontology in their curricula, and few treat concerns about aging in their continuing education workshops or courses.

But it is not only the clergy that is behind. Nurses in my gerontology classes report that suddenly 80 to 90% of the beds they serve are occupied by the very old. They want to learn about this population, not only in terms of nursing but with respect to counseling skills as well. If they are to effectively teach, advise, and counsel elders, these nurses and caregivers in other medical specialties must learn a lot more about the aging personality and intellect. Now there is a vital need to develop new sensitivities toward the elderly population—to rethink ethics and professional courtesies, as well as spiritual issues.

To this end, many clerical, geriatric, and gerontology specialists are right now broadening their skills and knowledge bases with the latest information on aging. They will be joining the 40,000 to 50,000 new social workers estimated to be needed to serve the elderly by the year 2000. Even now they can see that to meet the needs of the eldercare crisis in an effective, dignified, and cost-efficient manner, there will be a need for more teamwork and even a cross-over of some professional boundaries. As more caregivers pursue a holistic approach, the one that has now emerged as the most logical, they find that the earlier system of rigid specialties is no longer appropriate. Today, professionals from various fields teach each other at workshops and conferences nationwide.

Counseling is a good example of this trend. Every service provider to the elderly serves as a gerocounselor—be it with information, advice, understanding, or emotional support. Classes and workshops on counseling the elderly are very popular now as trained counselors share their knowledge and skills with those from other fields. But oddly, the fact is that professional counselors who have training and expertise in this field are doing very little of the actual counseling of older adults. For one thing, most elders are reluctant to seek professional counseling (despite the data regarding stressful aging years), and, for another, it is apparent that whatever counseling the elderly do receive comes from professionals in various other fields.

Obviously, a better balance has to be struck, and this book is just such an attempt. And it *is* needed. As I was assembling materials for courses on counseling the elderly or recommending independent reading to others, I learned how very little has been published recently—or even earlier—about the subject. Where does a professional caregiver go to learn more about aging? Good articles do exist, but they are often hard to come by. As an instructor, I found most of my preparation time eaten up searching for materials to use as handouts—costing both the university and me considerable time and expense. The students themselves were equally hard pressed to keep up with this increasingly important discipline because it was not their primary field and they were not attending the workshops or reading the relevant journals, etc. Most college libraries carry few gerontology works; for those students in rural areas, the offerings are nonexistent. Another problem is that few eldercare workers can afford the luxury of national conferences, workshops, and journals that lie outside their immediate field of interest.

To ameliorate this situation, I intend in this book to walk the gerocounselor through the various steps of elder and family counseling. These are not giant steps, in that I avoid extensive theory and do use many common examples. But they are not baby steps either. An advanced education is not required of the reader, but a certain amount of knowledge and experience in caregiving and counseling is assumed. Moreover, the steps in this counseling process, although described in linear language, form a circular system because gero-clients and gerocounseling necessarily involve circular, interactive processes. The steps covered here are also eclectic because, as the book makes clear, there is more than one way to view and serve the elderly effectively.

The reader may not use all the information presented, but certain interventions are applicable to all disciplines. A general knowledge of the generic counseling process is necessary to *all* elder providers if only for purposes of referral and for interpretation of the service to clients. For example, to be at all effective, a social worker, who is not professionally responsible for physically treating a stroke patient, must nevertheless know some basics about the stroke process—its course of rehabilitation, the meaning and effect of the stroke on the patient and family, ways of coping with it, and appropriate resources to use when referrals are needed. Likewise, the primary physician, although not expected to be fully cognizant of the patient's and the family's emotional responses to the stroke, still must be able to assess powerful emotional and social problems that would necessitate a referral to appropriate counseling and other resources.

Useful across a wide range of senior services, this book is especially designed for elder care providers, students in courses on counseling the elderly, or participants in counseling workshops. Thought–discussion questions, which follow major points, allow the reader to interact with the material directly, and the exercises may be worked through independently or done as class assignments. Case examples cover a multitude of common gerocounseling issues from a variety of service-provider fields. The names of all clients, families, and gerocounselors have been altered to perserve confidentiality.

I would like to thank several people who contributed to the preparation of this manuscript. Nowadays a writer is blessed if one can find a patient, accommodating typist who is competent in grammatical skills as well as computer technology. I found that in Dee Miller, who squeezed me in despite a big family wedding. One is fortunate to find a talented artist such as Theresa Schiffer, who designed my graphics in between having a baby. One is also lucky to find a discerning editor, as I did in Patrick McGuire, who got the job done even though there was a tragic family death. And one is always blessed, as I was, to have friends, colleagues, and mentors such as Carol Ruxton, Carol Woosley, and others too numerous to mention, who edited and proofread various parts of this book. Thank you all.

VSB

# *Acknowledgments*

I want to thank my parents: my father who taught me how to die well and my mother who is teaching me how to age well. At 89, she is teaching me firsthand about the aging process through her successful adjustment to the nursing home and her dealing with the vicissitudes of aging. I also even thank her for pushing her eldest child in the role of "family achiever," for without that I never would have gotten a PhD at 51 or written a book at age 64.

# Chapter 1

# The Gerocounselor

This book examines the practice of *gerocounseling*—dealing with the physical, social, and emotional concerns of older people, especially as they relate to the counseling process. To do this, gerocounseling draws on both *gerontology*, the study of normal human aging, and *geriatrics*, the study of the medical problems of aging.

Gerocounselors are those who help older persons and their families help themselves. This help can take the form of active questioning and listening, clarifying a problem, providing necessary information, or discussing options and consequences. It includes giving advice while leaving the final decision-making to the one being advised. It is usually done with emotional support and, sometimes, with confrontation. The list of gerocounseling practitioners includes: physicians; nurses; physical, occupational, and rehabilitation therapists; nursing assistants; social workers; employment counselors; activity specialists; directors of senior nursing facilities, centers, and housing complexes; Medicaid, Medicare, and Social Security workers; benefits specialists; clergy; respite volunteers; caregivers; and anyone else who is left out of this long list but who administers to the elderly and their families. Henceforth, if you are among the above, you will be called a gerocounselor here.

## Is Gerocounseling Important?

The elderly comprise the fastest growing segment of our population, and their numbers will continue to grow in the coming decades. To provide the medical and social services needed by this group, the National Institute of Aging (NIA) conservatively estimated that the number of social workers serving the elderly in 1987 must more than double by the year 2000 (Peterson, 1990), and that the ranks of other fields serving them must swell accordingly. The need for caregivers trained in gerocounseling is obvious; the problem lies in training such numbers in a relatively short time.

Fortunately, there *is* time, as the majority of older persons today generally do not approach trained counselors for help. It was estimated in 1987 that only 4% of the elder population availed themselves of public outpatient mental health clinics while only 2% received treatment in private psychiatric care. This occurred, despite the fact that service to the elderly has been a requirement for federally funded mental health centers since 1975, and, more importantly, the fact that up to 25% of older persons have been estimated to have significant mental health problems (Gelfand, 1988).

Where have the elderly and their families gone for counseling help? The literature suggests that the majority of older persons receive whatever counseling they get in what can only be called "by-the-way" or "doorknob" fashion, meaning that mental health questions come up only when the departing health provider's hand is on the doorknob and he or she is suddenly hit with a psychologically loaded question in an offhand, "by-the-way" manner. This is not an efficacious method of counseling.

There are several explanations for why older persons are diffident about seeking professional counseling. Sometimes it is simply a matter of finances. Reimbursement for outpatient counseling has been minimal, and most elders living on fixed incomes do not feel they can afford it. In other instances, generational attitudes play an important role. Many of today's elders were raised with strict rules about family privacy, and do not feel comfortable talking about such matters with strangers. Some other seniors avoid counseling because of familiar myths and stereotypes. They fear they will be labeled "crazy" or, even worse, "perverted." As far as these people are concerned, counseling is for "those other folks." Finally, many elders have not benefited from professional counseling because there has been little outreach by the profession. Counseling providers have been said to suffer from the YAVISS syndrome, a personal bias for those clients who can be labeled Young, Attractive, Verbal, Income-producing, Success-making, and Speedy-recovering.

In other words, today's older persons routinely turn to church, family, physician, pharmacist, or others for counsel and/or support—often with mixed results. Along with a few seasoned, and some fledgling, trained counselors, this is the group that makes up the bulk of today's gerocounselors.

## You as Gerocounselor

If you are in a situation providing care to one or more elderly people and/or their families, you are a gerocounselor. As you are reading this book it is safe to assume that this describes your situation. Still, you all come to this book from varied backgrounds. Many of you who lack specific training in the health and social service fields may wonder if you are even qualified to call yourself "a counselor." Well, if you are providing some of the services of a counselor, the only question is whether you are doing it well or poorly. This book will help you do it well.

Others of you, with sophisticated counseling skills, may question whether this book is up to your level. It will certainly be of value to you because of its treatment of the special problems of the elderly and the tested techniques for dealing with them. Others of you may wonder if such a book can fit your particular orientation. It probably can because it is written for gerocounselors *and* for the widening group in areas of education, business, leisure, finance, insurance, entertainment, and others who wish to improve their ability to relate to older persons through increased understanding of proven gerontology and counseling skills.

Remember, "counselor" in this discussion is not to be confused with "psychotherapist." Psychotherapy and family therapy are disciplines that include concepts similar to those treated here, but they also address unconscious processes to a greater extent. Advanced psychotherapy is not the sum and substance of this book—nor, presumably, of your situation. The following discussion is designed to help you examine that situation in relation to your own personal experiences, education, ambitions, attitudes, etc. so that you can more readily determine just how you fit into the world of gerocounseling.

---

**THOUGHT–DISCUSSION QUESTION**
In what ways do you now engage in gerocounseling in your work or avocation?

---

## Your Life Experiences

A gerocounselor, it is hoped, uses a holistic, not a "part-of-the-elephant" approach. The following adaptation of that old story will explain what I mean:

At the zoo, blindfolded children were asked to describe an elephant. Each touched the animal from his own vantage point and reported. Touching the ear, one child said, "An elephant is like a fan." Touching the tail, another said, "An elephant is a rope." Another, touching the leg, responded, "It is a tree trunk." And so the story goes. Each child got a sense of one part of the elephant but none experienced a sense of what the whole animal was like.

As gerocounselors, you need to see the people you are trying to help in all their diversity and individuality. This is what we mean by a holistic approach. However, your own personal histories and experiences may blind you to some important traits of the people you are caring for. Even if you feel this is not the case now, you should consider such a possibility. Read over the following examples.

*Annie Mae, age 26.* Annie Mae, a nurse at Oaks Home, never knew her father, and her mother was available only now and then as she was growing-up. Her grandmother was the stable, nurturing person in her life, and they are still close. A diabetic, Grandmother raised Annie Mae and her four siblings and cared for Grandpa who developed Alzheimer's disease when Annie Mae was twelve. The family lived on welfare. Annie Mae went to nurse's training through a grant after her second child was born.

*Juan, age 35.* Juan, a casemanager for Human Services, did not know either of his grandfathers. One died before Juan was born, and another moved back to Texas when Juan was two. The families did not communicate due to a conflict Juan never understood. He did know his widowed paternal grandmother, whom he described as "a bitter, crabby old woman who cheated him at cards." He recalled her being greedy with money; she kept her prized possessions in a locked cedar chest. When Juan was ten, she had a stroke and Juan's mother (who hated Grandmother) became the caregiver. Juan's parents fought over Grandmother. Dad, a recovering alcoholic, resumed drinking and mother blamed Grandmother. Juan remembered his grandmother being called "vieja," an uncomplimentary term for "old lady."

*Mary, age 56.* Mary, director of a senior center, had middle-class grandparents who were well-educated, devoted to their grandchildren, and in good health for many years. They entertained and traveled. They moved to the South and Mary visited them every spring vacation. Grandfather developed cancer, and Grandmother nursed him until his death. Later she resumed traveling and moved to an expensive life-care community. She had many friends and the money and opportunities to visit and phone relatives often.

*Ernie, age 27.* Ernie is a new resident in family practice at University Hospital. His father and grandfather, professional men, were described as competitive males with much charm and charisma who stressed excellence and were often critical of others with lesser standards. Grandfather financed Ernie's Ivy League schools. "Hurry for success," "Find future cures," and "Make lots of money," were some of his messages.

The bios are short, but if the four depicted above tended to stereotype, what do you imagine each might feel about older people? Might they be guilty of ageism? (Ageism is systematic stereotyping of and discriminating against people because they are old.) (See Butler, 1969.) Even if they did not openly discriminate, do you think the early impressions of older persons that have been embedded into their subconscious could/would influence their work?

The answer is most probably yes. Such a process is called *countertransference*, a Freudian term describing the totality of feelings experienced by a counselor, attributable to past and present experiences, which are activated in counseling and therapy. Countertransference influences how we act toward those we are helping, so we should be aware of it as a shaper of our responses to them.

---

**THOUGHT–DISCUSSION QUESTIONS**

How might each of the gerocounselors in the above four case studies regard and respond to older persons because of countertransference? Can you think of how your experiences with your grandparents and older significant others have colored your feelings about older persons? (See Genevay & Katz, 1990.)

---

## Knowledge Base

Gerocounselors also come with various specific but limited knowledge bases about aging processes and services. Annie Mae, age 26, Ernie, age 27, and Juan, age 35, may have had some helpful aging courses in their training, but, being mostly in the health fields, they took courses in geriatrics rather than in normal human aging. Of the four, Mary, age 56, had the broadest background in normal aging studies, but even most of this is of limited value. Most of the major advances in aging research occurred after her schooling.

The four also have had on-the-job training. Annie Mae attends in-service programs to keep up with the medical care of her patients. Juan, distributing Medicaid funds, knows about financial services. He learns how the economy and housing crisis affect his older clients, and he is sensitive to the ethnic aspects of their situations, too. Mary, at the senior center, networks with other eldercare workers to keep up on senior activities, education, and services. She is quick to spot social isolation, loneliness, and signs of depression in her group members. Ernie is learning the latest techniques in geriatric assessment. All four know a part of "the elephant" well, but they must be careful of how limiting their experiences can be. Annie Mae and Ernie must not think of all older persons as sick; Juan must not think all elderly are poor; and Mary must not think of them all as well-to-do and gregarious.

You probably have your own unique sense of what the elderly are like, derived from your own experiences. And, naturally, you must build on what you already know (Waters, 1984) if you are to take a holistic approach. But you must not be confined by your experiences. You must try to understand your older clients through the prism of your experiences and training, but you must also be able to make sense of your clients' total personalities, their past and present and their correlations with normal development. In other words, you will need a knowledge of human growth and development across the life span. Some counselors attain this by living it. Others begin by counseling adolescents (your client was an adolescent once), then move to young adults and marriages (where your older patient was at one time), and on to midlifers (not too far away from your client's present state), and, finally, to older people. However, this does not have to be the prescribed route; many younger counselors have the enthusiasm, talents, and commitment to be successful with older persons at the onset. You will need to prepare yourself in a number of different areas, though, if you are to effectively serve those in your care.

As a gerocounselor, you should learn about the biological changes that occur in aging so that you can recognize a problem or a normal change. You may have to differentiate between reversible and irreversible dementias and between normal bereavement and clinical depression in order to know how to help and when to refer. You should own and consult medical and psychiatric manuals to help you communicate with other providers. You will also need to know about public and private programs for the elderly and how they affect (or should be affecting) your clients. You should have information about the Older Americans Act, Social Security, Medicare, Medicaid, SSI benefits, pension and retirement funds, elder employment and volunteer opportunities, widowhood, relocation, and retirement issues. You will need to know how any new national health insurance programs will affect your older clients and you will have to know about services in your community and how to make referrals and to whom. You may sometimes become frustrated in your activities about how uncoordinated many service programs for the elderly are. You may wish to become an advocate for older persons' causes. This will entail becoming savvy about how public policy is formed and how one can effect changes in community, state, and national programs.

It is difficult to find enough resources to learn about counseling older persons. Because elders have for so long been few in number and shy or fearful about counseling, there is a lack of documented research about what works best with them. Also, you will have a hard time finding existing books and journals on gerocounseling unless you live near a university that offers courses on aging. You will have to subscribe to the important journals yourself, share articles, start your own personal library, or encourage your facility to do so. As professionals who can pass on their accumulated wisdom about counseling elders have also been few in number, you will again have to pioneer and adapt what you already know.

You can pick up much just by listening and learning from each older person, the families of clients, healthcare specialists, social workers, clergy, and others. You can also learn from workshops and training programs, and by participating in community groups that serve the elderly. You can take courses in continuing education. Your greatest teachers will, however, be your older clients themselves. Let us look at a learning experience that Mary had at the senior center.

> Mary was puzzled about a new drop-in at the center. Mr. Smith was nice enough when he arrived, but soon he became irritable and almost disoriented. One day he spoiled an activity with his belligerent manner. Mary learned that he was a recent widower who said he was "having a lonely time of it." His physician recommended the center. He said he was "all thumbs" in the kitchen. Mary also learned that Mr. Smith had diabetes.
>
> Mary knew that often depression can express itself as irritability, so she consulted one of the leading books on late-life depression. She was unsure that this was the whole problem, so she next looked at a medical manual and read about diabetes. She learned that diabetics can experience a personality change with decreased blood sugar levels because of inadequate nutrition.
>
> She asked Mr. Smith for a private session and described his conspicuous personality changes from pleasant to irritable. Was he feeling unwell? Mr. Smith noticed the changes, too. As a diabetic, he knew that he should eat well, but he didn't feel like cooking or eating.
>
> Mary told him about the Meals-on-Wheels program and called the agency for facts about it and other meal options. Meanwhile, Mr. Smith consulted his physician who, after seeing if improved nutrition could solve the problem, put Mr. Smith on a low dosage of anti-depressant medication that would stimulate mood and appetite.

Soon Mr. Smith was feeling more upbeat and became one of Mary's best volunteers. Without playing doctor, Mary had helped Mr. Smith and, along the way, learned additional information about diabetes, depression, and the community senior meals programs— all helpful additions to her first-hand knowledge about aging.

THOUGHT–DISCUSSION QUESTIONS

Can you think of elder clients with whom you have worked who enriched your knowledge base about aging processes? What did you learn?

## Skills

Although gerocounselors possess specific expertise (medical, financial, religious, etc.) to use with elderly clients, many need help in expanding these skills to fit their elderly clients. Gerocounseling places more emphasis than regular counseling does on support and practical applications to life in addition to helping clients maintain control, mobilize support, and effectively cope with their problems. Basic counseling rules such as respect all clients and avoid arguments, over-involvement, side-taking, speaking for another, rescuing, and breaking silences still apply, of course. You will also observe the old guidelines such as start where the client is, help the consumer find solutions, empower the patient with information, allow self-determination, respect confidentiality, and demonstrate empathy and genuineness.

Handling defense mechanisms, however, may be different in gerocounseling. Some behavior considered dysfunctional in younger people might be encouraged in older ones. Some elderly people's suffering is too great; denial and repression become saving graces. You may encourage your younger client to give up self-pity, but your older client may need sympathy from you. Your younger client may need confrontation to face reality; sometimes your older client needs to rationalize about life experiences in order to come out ahead on the integrity-versus-despair task (Erikson, 1950). Older people have a lifetime behind them. They may be working their way through old guilts and past wrongs by using mild forms of *reaction formation* (overdoing the emotion opposite to that one feels). At this stage of life, they do not need such behavior analyzed unless it is harmful. This is not to suggest a reverse ageism wherein one overprotects the elderly and denies help when it is clearly needed. But sometimes gerocounseling requires a different emphasis.

*Transference* (another Freudian term, meaning the totality of conscious and unconscious feelings from the past and present experienced by the client, which are activated by the counseling) is different in gerocounseling, too. Some older clients may want to bask in your accomplishments and treat you as an idealized child, but others will be in awe of your credentials, and still others may treat you as if you don't know a thing because of your tender years. It takes a new kind of skill and humanness to remain professional, helping, accepting, and caring in these circumstances.

These specialized gerocounseling skills are covered in detail in later chapters. Chapter 2 deals in depth with how these skills are both similar and different from normal counseling skills. Chapter 4 discusses the assessment of older persons' strengths, deficits, and problems—a process posing some unique challenges. Chapter 9 treats the always delicate problem of terminations. You will also have to learn to say good-bye in a new way. For one thing, you will be saying good-bye to many clients because of their deaths. In other cases, they will be moving to another level of care. One of Juan's goals, for instance, is to keep his clients out of the nursing home, but sometimes that doesn't work, and he must help them with relocation. Handling these farewells requires special strengths on the part of the gerocounselor.

## *Settings and Structures*

Gerocounseling can take place almost anywhere. Much good work is done at the client's kitchen table, and it is generally a good practice to have at least one early session in the client's home. Naturally, home visits should be offered to the homebound and to those with transportation problems or who are inhibited by ethnic shyness. Other forms of outreach can utilize neighborhood centers, emergency rooms, or even a session at a coffee shop after a doctor's visit or in the doctor's waiting room. Gerocounselors also work in formal settings such as senior centers, community mental health centers, family service agencies, private practice clinics, long-term facilities, and bilingual program offices. (See American Society on Aging, 1990.) Referrals to gerocounselors for intangible services are still minimal. They usually come from geriatric assessment centers, physicians, and relatives. Other referrals can result from articles in local papers, workshops, educational programs, support groups, and other places. Such resources could be used for more community awareness of the benefits of counseling elders and their families.

## *Orientations*

There are almost as many theories of gerocounseling as there are gerocounselors. That is good because we know older persons are not all alike, and different counseling styles offer clients options—an important counseling intervention. Counseling theories in general are usually age-related. Most were developed for children and young adults. Early studies of older persons were often done in institutions giving only a one-sided account of this many-sided population. Because the older a cohort becomes the more heterogeneous it is, there is a definite need to research and expand the psychological theories about all older adults.

Early leaders in psychology were not optimistic in their views about working with the elderly. Freud (1924), "the father of psychoanalysis," did not treat older adults because he believed that their personalities were too rigid to change. James (1890), one of the early pioneers of scientific psychology, made a similar statement: "Outside of their own business, the ideas gained by men before they are twenty-five are practically the only ideas they shall have in their lives. They cannot get anything new" (p. 402).

As a gerocounselor, you will find your philosophical orientation taking on an importance you may not have imagined it had. The philosophy and psychological theories with which you feel comfortable guide your thinking and, to a large extent, determine your gerocounseling goals and style. It is most useful then for you to take a moment now to examine the philosophical orientation that underlies your approach to yourself and your profession, in short, to get to know who you are and who you are becoming. The following briefly describes a number of philosophical orientations, designed to help you formulate consciously the thinking that has up to now, perhaps unconsciously, shaped your behavior.

## The Psychodynamic Orientation

Freud's (1924) later followers modified his pessimistic beliefs about treating elders. Among them were Alfred Adler (1927), Carl Jung (1933), Erik Erikson (1950), and Robert Butler (1974).

Adler (1927) believed that people defined themselves in relation to others, and he saw older persons as threatened and feeling powerless from the inevitable loss of their former social roles. Because he counted social involvement and a meaningful lifestyle as critical to mental health in later years, he believed substitutes for interaction and intimacy should be created if necessary.

Jung (1933) focused on the middle and older adult and was not deterministic like Freud. He wrote, in a somewhat evocative vein, "It is not productive in the fall of adulthood to rummage through the spring and summer of childhood" (1933). His individuation theory holds out an optimistic prospect for older persons in that he saw an inner orientation to life and a coming to peace with oneself in later years.

Writing "the wine of youth does not always clear with advancing age; oftentimes it grows more turpid" (1933, p. 105), Jung showed he did not shrink from the realities of aging despite his underlying optimism. He instructed older persons to have "a duty and a necessity to devote serious attention" [to themselves for . . .] "after having lavished its light upon the world, the sun withdraws its rays in order to illuminate itself" (p. 109). His idea of pursuing the other sides of the self has since been developed by Gutmann (1964) and others.

Erikson's (1950) theories are widely quoted in gerontological literature. His social psychology emphasized lifelong development through the accomplishment of psychosocial tasks. Each "age-stage" along the way presents a particular task to be accomplished through the balancing of two opposite developmental goals, the result of which leads to developing the qualities of hope, will, purpose, competence, fidelity, love, care, and, finally, wisdom. The older person's final task is to find a sense of integrity about his or her life and to develop an acceptance of approaching death rather than despair over what might have been. This final achievement then is wisdom. Eriksonian applications to gerocounseling are many, especially in the notion that one can develop a sense of one's life as meaningful and that the way one lives at the final stage gives meaning to, and helps complete, previous stages. His empowerment concept is a defense against depression and is a builder of self-esteem. His theory has been used for the assessment of life strengths (Kivnick, 1993).

Butler (1974) adapted Freud's ideas of free association and catharsis to develop *Life Review Therapy*, probably the most popular gerocounseling tool today. Butler, a former director of the National Institute of Aging (NIA), coined the term "ageism" (1969) to dispel negative stereotypes about aging. He wrote, "Old age is the only period of life with no future. Therefore a major task in late life is learning not to think in terms of the future"—or, conversely, learning not to retreat into the past (p. 245). He recommended an emphasis on the present, balanced by the life review, a process inaugurated by old age itself. Life review involves a return to consciousness of past experiences to help the older person survey, resolve, and integrate old conflicts. Taking stock of one's life enables the individual to determine what legacies he/she will leave behind. It can be done privately, in life-review therapy, or in life-cycle therapy groups. Since Butler's earliest articles, others have developed versions of life review, using various terms like reminiscence therapy, oral history, validation therapy, and others. (See Chapter 7.)

## The Humanist Orientation

Humanists hold that the way one perceives life's circumstances (e.g., aging) is often more important than the reality itself. This is a helpful concept to geriatric specialists because it works to explain how a patient may view and respond to illness (Siegel, 1986). Chopra (1993) wrote that we not only construct our own world reality but our aging reality as well. Paying close attention to clients' individual perceptions is critical because otherwise gerocounselors may do too much logical, rational work to talk a client out of a feeling instead of validating it. In addition, clients are apt to feel misunderstood or angry if their emotions are considered silly or inappropriate. A cardinal rule is: Never say, "You shouldn't feel that way."

Frankl (1977) emphasized the idea of *transcendence*; it is not what happens to us in life that counts as much as what we make of it, how we transcend it. Understandably, many hospital chaplains use his approach in counseling patients when they deal with issues of suffering and death. Frankl's psychology has helped older persons marshal strengths of the human spirit to transcend suffering through secular as well as religious means. He postulated that many people experience an "existential vacuum" or suffer from a "deficit of sustaining values." Such inner voids, he felt, could be filled by a "will to meaning."

## The Behaviorist/Cognitive Orientation

Behaviorism, a more avowedly scientific model, includes cognitive and reality therapy approaches. Behaviorists postulate that our behavior, what we do, creates our feelings and assessment of the outcomes. By changing our behaviors, we can change our feelings and even some pathological states. For example, a person who says, "I don't remember very well anymore," is advised to reword that to, "I don't pay attention very well anymore." A person who says, "I can't" may be encouraged to change that to, "I won't," implying more of a choice. A person who is afraid is advised to "try it anyway" . . . at least to a point slightly beyond one's present limits. Many adaptations of behavioral therapy can be used effectively with the institutionalized, but they must be done with respect for the patient's personality.

Beck's (1976) work in cognitive therapy for depression has been used widely with older adults. Meichenbaum (1974) also worked with behavioral change through principles of cognitive therapy. His Stress Inoculation Training is used to retard functional aspects of mental deterioration. Skinner (1983), who in his 80th year wrote *Enjoy Old Age*, stressed the importance of role-playing "old person" with positive self-fulfilling prophesies and appropriate behavior modification.

## The Family Systems Therapy Orientation

Family systems is an important component of counseling older adults. It is a superstructure theory that views and treats a person as an individual and also as an important part of an interactive system.

Family systems therapy requires intensive training, but most gerocounselors do include the family in informational, planning, and supportive sessions. The inclusion of "family" goes beyond traditional definitions and can include your elderly client's physician, attorney, clergyperson, neighbor, lover, or live-in. Your scope may also go beyond your local area; for example, "What does your daughter in Iowa think you should do? Let's get her opinion." And sometimes it includes the dead, "What would your deceased husband have wanted you to do with that promise you can no longer keep?"

Some believe that family systems work is too mechanical but it can be especially helpful in situations that appear overwhelming. An axiom of systems theory is, "A change in one part will create changes in all other parts." When even a small part of a family system is changed, the whole system must change. Therefore, your smallest intervention (say an hour of respite services) can make a big difference in a stressful family situation.

While working with the family system is complex, it is easier than *not* getting the family involved. We can convince a Toledo daughter that, "Your mom really wants to remain in her home and, with some assistance, can manage quite well," or "Your dad has decided he wants this operation now," but if the son in Houston calls, exerting power in an opposite direction, you could be back to square one. So family counselors say it is better to get everyone involved (even out-of-towners) for their input. Reframe it this way: You can see family work as a problem of logistics and time, or as a method to gain more helpers for your care plan.

## The "Grandmother" Orientation

Common sense, or "Grandmother psychology," has triggered a 180-degree turn in today's psychology. Home remedies are returning as we escape from *polypharmacy*, the practice of using often too many expensive, synthetic drugs, and fancy interventions. We psychologists and social workers used to discourage people from talking to themselves. Now we say, "Talk to yourself. Put good messages into your subconscious." We used to say, "Take a sleeping pill." Now we say, "Try a leisurely walk, warm milk, some pleasant music, or meditation." Many of the old remedies advocated by our grandmothers worked to relieve what we called "nerves" or "nervousness." Originally, we were sanctioned to stay out of a client's religion. This "down-home" approach tells us to respect diversity and to view a client's spiritual or religious convictions as a source of strength, coping, and solace.

We certainly do not want to turn our backs on advances in modern medicine and psychological research, but if using these older, simpler interventions seems beneficial to our clients and work in today's economy, it is a perfectly valid practice. Such interventions may be reminders to clients of old coping mechanisms from bygone days. They act then as interventions within interventions because they affirm and validate the clients' experiences.

---

**THOUGHT–DISCUSSION QUESTIONS**
What theory or theories most describe what you have experienced in terms of how persons change and how they can age with good mental health? Why? What theory would you like to learn more about?

---

## *Orientation of This Text*

This book is based on two general principles:

1. The most practical way to view older persons is as circular, interactive, multidimensional entities (with more variability than any other age group). The biological, psychological, and sociological facets of each elderly person do interact with each other so that it is difficult to see where one begins and one ends. An approach based on treating a single facet of the client's personality is likely to prove ineffective.

2. It follows then that any gerocounseling should also use a like circular, interactive, holistic systems approach in dealing with the client. Gerocounselors must be mindful of the interacting bio-psycho-social factors involved in each client's systemic problem.

Chapter headings in the book may imply a rigid procedure of intake, rapport-building, assessment, and so forth, but this is misleading. Good counseling is never linear or rigidly structured. For example, assessment and rapport-building begin with the first phone call and continue through termination and follow-up. Intervention, in the forms of hope and action, starts with making the first appointment and continues after termination. Even though language and textbooks are necessarily linearly conceived, it is possible to conceptualize circular processes in models that are easy for the reader to visualize. Two such models, in diagram form, are included in this book. The first diagram is a circular, holistic, interactive model of the gero-client (Gero-Chi-Model; Figure 1.1). The second diagram is a circular, holistic, interactive counseling model (Gero-Chi Counseling Model; Figure 1.2). Please refer to these illustrated models as you read the rest of this chapter. They are intended not only to conceptualize the circular, interactive processes, but also to provide organizational devices for the whole of this book.

## The Gero-Chi Model

### *The Self-System*

Countless writers have attempted to define the self. A safe synthesis of their efforts seems to be that the self is that unique composite expression of all that one is and all that one is becoming or has

Psychosocial Tasks

1) Hope
2) Will
3) Purpose
4) Competence
5) Fidelity
6) Love
7) Care
8) Wisdom

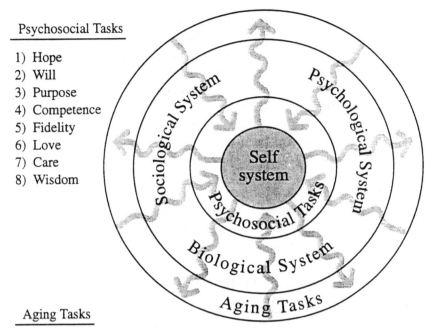

Aging Tasks

1) Efficient use of medical, social, emotional supports
2) Adjustment to declining physical strength and health
3) Maintenance of satisfactory living arrangements
4) Coping with retirement and financial changes
5) Independence, assertive control of life
6) Assumption of new community responsibilities
7) Revised relationships
8) Adjustment to loss of significant others

*Gero-Circular ° Holistic ° Interactive

FIGURE 1.1   Gero-Chi* Systemic Model.

potential to become. Simply put, psychoanalysts describe a healthy personality or "self" as a dynamic between id (instinct) and super-ego (conscience) that is mediated by the ego. In the Gero Self-System, we will look specifically at two facets of the self because of their special importance to aging. They are gender, which is important to note because it is experienced differently by men and women, and spirituality, which is also noteworthy because it helps to shape one's aging condition and it can be used as a coping tool to abet it.

*Gender* provides the energy and is all-invasive of other systems. It is more than biology or sexual instinct; it defines the core, says who we are, and to a high degree determines how our life will be—particularly in late-life. *Spirituality* is more than superego—it provides the organization and is also invasive of other systems. It is also more than religion. Like gender, it too defines the core and also influences how one views the self, the world, and any after-life existence. It too is a determinant of who we are and how our life will be—particularly in late-life. (Note that the term "ego" which is another word for the self-system, and "libido," another term for sexual energy, were *not* chosen here. This was in order to avoid confusing the Gero-Chi Model with a psychoanalytic model and because the Gero Chi Model expands on both concepts.) The goal of the Self-System is continued development and preservation of the self (Tobin, 1988).

### The Psycho-Social Task System

Next comes the psychosocial themes in life that affect, and are affected by, other systems (Erikson, 1950). Although influenced by biology and environment, and psychosocial in nature, these themes can be seen as constituting a system in themselves because they, like gender and spirituality, are all-invasive. They will be incorporated in your gerocounseling assessments, goals, and interventions. The themes are hope, will, purpose, competence, fidelity, love, care, and wisdom.

### The Major Subset Systems

There are three major subset systems:

1. *The Biological System* includes one's genetic background, sex, physical growth and development, history of illness, trauma, and diseases, treatment and remediation, drug history (if any), current health status, activities of daily living (ADL), and disease prevention and maintenance of wellness.

2. *The Psychological System* includes one's cognitive, affective, coping, and personality characteristics—whether conscious or unconscious.

3. *The Sociological System* includes one's ethnicity, status, social relationships, housing, finances, work, and so forth. The family system is of prime importance here, and elsewhere as well.

## *The System of Aging Tasks*

The fourth circle on the diagram represents the circular, interactive tasks of the core and subsets to be accomplished in the aging years. These are interactive with and largely determined by issues from the above subsets. They are important in goal setting.

# The Gero-Chi Counseling Model

Counseling is the art of helping people help themselves. Gero-counseling is the art of helping older persons and their families help

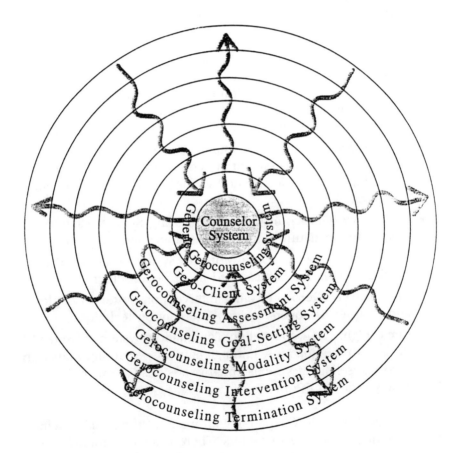

*Gero-Circular ○ Holistic ○ Interactive

FIGURE 1.2   Gero-Chi* Counseling Systemic Model.

themselves. It is a tenet of this book that all effective counseling requires a circular conceptualization.

## The Counselor System

As the Self-System is at the core of the Gero-Chi Model, so the Counselor System is at the core of the Gero-Chi Counseling Model (Figure 1.2). It includes such factors as the gerocounselor's countertransference, knowledge and skill bases, and psychological and philosophical orientations.

## Remaining Systems

The remaining circles in this model are treated in depth in subsequent individual chapters of the book.

- Circle Two (Generic Gerocounseling Systems, Chapter 2) includes ethical, relationship, and communication skills. They are interactively related to all other systems in this model.
- Circle Three, (Gero-Client System, Chapter 3) and Circle Four, (Gerocounseling Assessment System, Chapter 4) deal with normal aging of the elder client and the assessment of the elder and family.
- Circle Five (Gerocounseling Goal-Setting System, Chapter 5) is systemic in nature and discusses the importance of goals.
- Circle Six (Gerocounseling Modality System, Chapter 6) covers the various modalities used in gerocounseling.
- Circle Seven (Gerocounseling Intervention System, Chapter 7 and Chapter 8) covers various intervention techniques.
- Circle Eight (Gerocounseling Termination System, Chapter 9) deals with terminations. Endings have a special importance in gerocounseling. More existential issues arise at this point than at any other in the process.

We have dealt here in Chapter 1 with many of the special characteristics required of gerocounselors. There is also an abundance of challenge, pioneer satisfaction, and career opportunities for those at work with the elderly. The rest of the book will cover them in depth.

# Chapter 2

# Gerocounseling

*Counseling* is the art of helping people help themselves gain a better understanding of a stress or problem situation in order to mobilize strengths and resources toward a change or a more effective management of that stress/problem. The nature of the counseling depends on many factors, for instance, the setting (biomedical, psychological, social) or the modality (individual, conjoint, group, environmental). The nature of the counseling may also take into account the counselor's orientation (psychodynamic, cognitive, humanist) or credentials (peer, paraprofessional, MSW, PhD, MD). Finally, the counseling may be based on "who is the client?" (identified patient, married couple, family, agency, society), or on the client's age group, transitional stage, financial status, or medical diagnosis. Counseling can be long- or short-term or what is now called "brief counseling." It may also be "by the way counseling," peer counseling, general counseling, or psychotherapy.

## Gerocounseling Structures

The structure of all counseling encompasses beginning, middle, and end stages. The building of a relationship (rapport, therapeutic alliance), assessment, and goal- and contract-setting usually take place in the beginning stage. Working through the solution (interventions) occurs in the middle stage, and termination and follow-up comprise the end stage. Although these distinctions are widely used, they are to a certain extent misleading; counseling, as we saw in Chapter 1, is neither static nor linear but, like the Gero-Chi Model, a circular process.

The counselors introduced in Chapter 1, Annie Mae, Juan, Mary, and Ernie, are all gerocounselors. But because of different training, orientations, and settings, they are counseling differently on different levels and about different issues. As most are without counselor training or certification, they are all careful to keep their helping within the range of their capabilities and to use consultation, supervision, and referral when needed. The examples below expand on the four you already know and add two others. These examples will be referred to throughout the book.

Annie Mae, RN, works in a medical setting where admittance is determined by medical diagnosis. Her primary discipline, training, and work tasks are in the medical field, but she often finds herself "counseling" residents. She tries to become more adept at grief counseling because many of her patients are experiencing multiple losses, and they turn to her because of her empathetic nature. The nursing home has a social worker who advises Annie Mae and takes over when she feels she is "over her head."

Juan, case manager, has a BA in social work. His consumers are over 65, considered medically frail or at-risk, and often in financial distress. His goal is to keep them out of the nursing home. Providing emotional support, information, and referral assistance as well as concrete services, Juan utilizes many counseling skills. He says he always needs more, particularly in assessment, in order to know when and where to refer. His supervisor, a MSW, talks over cases with him.

Mary, with a BA in sociology, is working on an MA in art therapy while she is director of the Senior Center. There, she plans and leads group activities and an aging support group which grew out of a program that she planned for senior members on the cognitive aspects of aging. While she has no formal training in group work, she is learning as she works and is studying group dynamics. Joan, the counselor from the Counseling Center, gives her consultation as needed.

Ernie, an MD, is a resident in family practice at the University Hospital, which has a fine psychiatry department. He often prescribes psychotropic drugs for anxiety and depression and tries to offer some stress management and support to these patients. He also gives the Folstein Mini Mental test to all geriatric patients. He provides information and counseling about medical conditions and counsels when there are unsubstantiated medical complaints. If his counseling is unsuccessful or if the condition is too severe for brief treatment, he refers the patient to the psychiatric unit. The nurse, who works closely with him, operates in a similar manner.

Joan, a MSW, is taking courses toward a gerontology certificate while working at the Counseling Center. Most of her elderly clients are referred by local physicians, patients' families, or other professionals. A small percentage are self-referrals in keeping with a national average. (Also, as seen nationally, only six percent of the Center's clients are over 65.) Joan has supervision from a PhD psychologist and consults with a psychiatrist and peers. She refers clients for psychological testing or alcohol or drug assessment (AODA) and/or treatment if indicated.

Pastor Martin Johnson's family counseling has lately been centering more around adult children and their elderly parents. While he had some counseling and gerontology courses at the seminary, much of his information is outdated. He tries to attend one-day seminars and ministerial retreats that offer such training. He still, however, does not feel comfortable with many of the psychological issues. He refers clients often to a Lutheran Social Service agency and consults with LSS or Rabbi Jean Goldman when necessary.

These gerocounselors are without doubt helpful, but they are careful not to extend their counseling beyond their individual expertise and certification, and they are mindful to secure professional supervision or consultation. This is important for several reasons: (a) to insure that the client receives the most appropriate treatment; (b) to reinforce the client's trust in the provider, who takes pains not to make false claims about his/her abilities; and (c) to protect the provider (and the provider's facility) from legal action for performing professional services without necessary qualifications.

## Gerocounseling Skills

This book, while providing information about counseling older persons, has repeatedly admonished readers not to attempt psychotherapy without adequate, advanced training. But a dilemma exists here. The requirements of your work and the nature of counseling are such that many of you are counseling now whether or not you call it so. It behooves you then to acquire some counseling tools so that you can be more effective at what you do.

Likewise, trained counselors can contribute much to helping older persons today by sharing their information, training, supervision, and consultation with beginning gerocounselors. Just because gerontology, geriatrics, and gerocounseling are multidisciplinary fields, the various disciplines should be able to still teach one another this holistic approach while respecting professional boundaries. This chapter identifies and discusses the requisite skills in the areas of ethics, relationships, and communication, as they apply to counseling older persons and their families.

## Ethics Skills

The American Association for Counseling and Development (AACD) has identified three ethical principles as guides to all good counseling: *autonomy*, *beneficence*, and *fidelity*, which are seen as "prima facie" binding principles (1981). The three also interact in a circular way, and the integrity of each should be maintained unless there is a stronger overriding moral obligation.

There often are extenuating circumstances. For instance, the three ethical principles are sometimes in conflict. Fitting's (1986) discussion of ethical dilemmas in counseling asks if these principles need to be reconsidered with respect to older persons. Which principle comes first when there is a conflict? How can one remain "ethical" to elder clients (respecting their confidentiality or autonomy) when they are not able or willing to take care of themselves and need outside help? Older persons suffer more chronicity and dementia and are more at risk. Must their counselors assume a more aggressively protective role? When does protection become infantilizing, demeaning, paternalistic, or an infringement of civil rights?

There are some helpful guidelines to these sticky questions. Unless older people suffer from a condition such as depression, delirium, or end-stage dementia that so alters their decision-making abilities as to render them incompetent, they should be allowed to make their own decisions. A counselor can help them weigh risks against benefits, but the final choice is not the counselor's. Additionally, it is not always clear that the older person really is at risk. In such a case, a home visit by the gerocounselor to determine the elder's living conditions and decision-making capacities, plus an assessment of the home and family system, is vital. If the person is not suicidal or profoundly impaired, an adequate solution can often be found by working with the client and family to reframe and resolve the issues.

Proper assessments of the older person's capacities by a well-trained professional are critical so that: (a) older persons capable of making decisions are not denied this right, and (b) elders incapable of decision-making are given the protection they require. When persons are adjudged incompetent, they still have rights, but someone competent is selected to speak for them regarding those rights. Sometimes adult children may pressure the gerocounselor to "make their stubborn parents shape up" (e.g., move to a safer neighborhood.) Such pleas may range from serious and urgent to seemingly trivial, but none should be disregarded. Sometimes there are hidden agendas.

Mr. Jack Allen and his sister Alice requested an appointment with Joan at the Counseling Center for help with their 75-year-old father whose "inappropriate actions were endangering his life." At the family session, they told Joan that Mr. Allen was a menace to himself. He drove a motorcycle, drank beer, and smoked marijuana. He saw loose women. Father–son conflict was obvious and father told Jack to "bug off." Jack didn't want father injured and to be more trouble for them. Mr. Allen replied that he was sane and could do what he pleased. He refused an AODA (alcohol or drug assessment) and a Mini Mental Test. It was the counselor's opinion that he was not cognitively impaired, but she did suggest that he consider his children's request to adopt a more conservative life style, for his own safety and for family harmony. In the end it was determined that he had the right to do what he chose.

Natalie Brown called Pastor Johnson to complain that her mother was becoming increasingly incompetent and living in unsafe conditions. She visited recently and the apartment had boxes scattered about, which was very unlike her mother's tidy ways. Pastor Johnson visited Mrs. Brown, who explained that because of recent cataract surgery, she was instructed not to do heavy lifting for awhile. She placed the boxes along the wall until she could tackle the job later.

Aline Roberts revealed (in confidence) to her case manager, Juan, that she consumed a pint of vodka daily. A follow-up with a sister confirmed the fact that Aline had been a closet alcoholic for many years. Aline also smoked heavily. While she required a residence with more assistance, none would accept her if her smoking and drinking habits were known. Juan was in a quandary. One day Aline was admitted to the hospital with a suspected heart attack. Fearing that she might go into withdrawal, Juan called the hospital to inform them of Aline's closet behaviors. When Aline recovered and learned that Juan had "told on her," she expressed anger about the betrayal and refused to see him again.

---

### THOUGHT–DISCUSSION QUESTIONS

Some of the above case examples ask the question, "Who is the client?" Others ask, "Which principle should be upheld if there is a conflict of ethical principles?" Before proceeding to the ethical guidelines treated below, think about or discuss what you, the gerocounselor, would do in these circumstances.

---

## Autonomy

*Autonomy* is the right of individuals to make their own choices and decisions about their lives. It assumes that the individuals are rational and therefore capable of independence, an important goal in working with older persons.

Self-responsibility for health care is to be encouraged among the elderly—and others. Assertiveness with one's physicians, the right to refuse medication, and the ability to ask for second opinions in regard to medical tests and aggressive medical treatments are all now part of an older person's options. There is much current discussion on the right of older people to make individual decisions about living and dying, as witnessed by such recent events as the "right-to-die" movement, the Nancy Cruzan case, the efforts of Dr. Jack Kevorkian, and the book, *Final Exit.*

Senior power has emerged in the political arena, too, as groups such as the Gray Panthers, Older Women's League (OWL), and the large membership in the American Association of Retired Persons (AARP) make their impacts on legislation and social policy-making. Such "empowerment," the taking charge of one's life and one's affairs, is invaluable for older adults who wish to maintain their autonomy and self-esteem. Unless an older person is helpless, it is better for you as a counselor to encourage the elder and/or family to actively pursue their personal and group needs themselves, rather than to act on their behalf.

There are other ways that you must recognize your client's autonomy. You may not share your client's political, religious, or world views, some of which in your opinion may go against what you believe are the best interests of the client. For example, your dying homebound patient may be following the oncologist's orders, but also drinking large quantities of vegetable juices as a home-remedy prescription. A client in pain may not be doing everything possible to relieve an arthritic condition or another may do nothing to get out of a bad marriage because they believe that suffering now will provide everlasting peace later. Or a client may be fighting legislation for family leave or catastrophic health insurance, which that same client badly needs. Even so, you must think of your client as a consumer who has the right to accept or deny services (including your own). You must not take such autonomous actions personally.

Marion was unhappy with the nursing home from the start. After leaving her apartment with no preparation, she was subjected to painful treatments for psoriasis and a stringent diet for obesity. A son lived too far away to be of comfort, and they were "never close, anyway." The staff tried to handle her verbal—and physical—abuse with as much TLC as they could muster. Marion refused further treatments and simply demanded bananas. A counselor, called in to encourage her to comply, decided that her nastiness and refusals were mainly a means of maintaining control over herself and her environment and to avoid further depression. She was encouraged to express her negative feelings in less self-defeating ways.

Meg was the grouchiest client that Juan ever had. She complained constantly about her new residence, though he tried every means to win her over. She played "yes, but" with any positive suggestion he made. Finally in desperation, he told her that she enjoyed being miserable. Meg fired him. Juan felt angry and sad that he had spoken impulsively and failed. He was afraid to discuss the firing with her daughter and his supervisor. When he finally reached her daughter, she chuckled and said that her mother had just "fired" her the previous week. Meg was just expressing her anger and her autonomy. They decided to continue to show her that they cared, but to give her more space and let her complain when she felt like it.

The principle of autonomy also comes into play when one asks the question, "Who is the client or consumer?"

Dr. Nesbitt called Joan, the counselor, and almost ordered her to get Mrs. Sims to change her stressful life style, ". . . divorce the bum if she has to, and tell her daughter to find someone else to babysit." He wanted a progress report. All this was not within Mrs. Sims's plans for her future. She was angry that the doctor made the referral and did not want her personal issues discussed with him. Dr. Nesbitt was one of Joan's best referral sources.

Allison, Juan's friend, called requesting help. She feared that her grandmother was being abused by a son. Allison was upset and Juan wanted to help her. He made two home visits and gained grandmother's trust. Allison called to ask what was going on.

The family brought in Mr. Lee after his stroke. Despite good progress, he had depression compounded by the usual labile affect seen in frequent, uncontrolled crying. The daughter, Amy, felt that Dad should be rational and concentrate on the positive aspects of his recovery. Amy wanted the counselor to see Dad alone and get his attitude changed. The wife, needing Amy's support, sided with her as her husband's depression was depressing her, too. The father only wanted to cry and get out his feelings of worthlessness. Who is the client?

Issues of autonomy run through all of these cases, and there are some helpful guidelines. With respect to the first example, when you accept referrals and work with other professionals (which you must do in this multidisciplinary field), it is better to say initially that you will get back with a report when you have written consent from the client. Agencies usually have forms for this purpose. If the client refuses consent, you may ask if it is acceptable to tell the referring source that the client wishes no information divulged. If the client refuses, you must comply with the client's right to autonomy and confidentiality.

In the second example, it is better not to accept clients who are your friends or are related. Such a refusal can be reframed into a compliment. "You are too close a friend for me to be of help. Let me refer your grandmother to a well-respected colleague who can do a more objective job."

The third example presents another problem that can occur when you are working with a family. Although family counselors say, "The family is the client," this is sometimes easier said than done. A family member may not want another to know what has been said, and sometimes, as in the Lee family, everyone has a different agenda. The family wanted Mr. Lee to be seen alone, but the counselor thought that the family should work on this systems issue together. Most families do not think in terms of systems; they are more comfortable with an individual approach. A certain amount of systems education for the family may be necessary to point out that all members are vital links in Mr. Lee's recovery process.

## Beneficence

*Beneficence* is the responsibility in counseling "to do good" or in medicine, "at least do no harm." Beneficence can conflict with the other principles, autonomy and fidelity, as seen in the cases of the alcoholic Aline Roberts and others. Otherwise, it is easy to think of very many ways that gerocounselors "do good." We do good, don't we, when we help a patient get on the john at the nursing home, establish Medicaid eligibility, plan an informative program at the Center, help a patient get well, assure a parishioner that God is forgiving? We also do good when we listen, pat a hand, bend down to be at eye level with a person in a wheelchair, when we try to understand confused talk at the day center, when we laugh at a joke together. Sometimes we do best when we don't interrupt, don't argue, don't gossip about our clients to colleagues, and don't judgmentally raise an eyebrow when our client reveals a shortcoming.

We can also do harm. We do harm, of course, if, through carelessness or ignorance, we make an incorrect assessment about a suicidal or homicidal person, someone seriously demented or dangerously psychotic. We do harm if we do not carefully investigate clues about elder abuse. These are situations in which all conscientious counselors must exercise caution, respect, and compliance with the law.

There are inadvertent ways of harming clients, too. We harm by not being knowledgeable or competent, by not recognizing when we don't know enough or, as Annie Mae put it, "when we are over our heads." We harm by not referring when we must, not seeking supervision or consultation when we are stuck. We harm inadvertently when we don't know ourselves, and countertransference causes us to overprotect, avoid, or be angry with our clients through displacement or projection. We harm when, unhappy with our agency, supervisor, family, spouse, or grandmother, we let our frustration interfere with our work. We harm if we overwork and accept a too-large caseload and don't take the necessary R & R. We harm when we do not seek help for our own psychological problems, including drug and/or alcohol abuse, and therefore do not function at our best or with good judgment. We can do much harm when we express our ageism by words, actions, or silent sanctions, when we let our opinions and biases interfere with necessary objectivity, or when we violate a confidence, take on friends or family as clients, or otherwise act unprofessionally and unethically.

## Fidelity

*Fidelity* focuses on the counselor–client relationship and includes faithfulness to obligation, trust, and duty. It means that the client has trust in you and you will be trustworthy. It says that the client comes first over your tiredness, your cousin's party, the monthly report, or a court subpoena.

It is not unusual for a counselor to hear, "You're the only one to whom I've told this." That includes the spouse, parent, best friend, priest, or rabbi. It implies that, "You won't judge, tell, laugh, over-worry or fall apart, and/or won't think I'm crazy or a bad person when you hear this." This is a high honor for your profession and for you, but it is also a great responsibility. You must live up to that trust. It's important for your client, too, because having a trusted confidant is a prime requisite for good mental health in the elderly, and in others. You must assure your client of confidentiality unless there is danger of suicide, homicide, or abuse (which legally must be properly reported). The AACD Preamble (n.d.) also states that a counselor must be "dedicated to the enhancement of the worth, dignity, potential, and uniqueness of each individual." This is the backbone of good relationship skills.

---

### THOUGHT–DISCUSSION QUESTIONS
Review the case examples given in the previous section on ethics. What ethical principles were involved in each? Which principles were in conflict? How should the counselor proceed in each scenario?

## *Relationship Skills*

All relationships need a commitment to stand by the obligations incurred by the relationship. Such a commitment is called *faithfulness*. In gerocounseling, faithfulness requires the counselor to undertake that, no matter what occurs, within reason, the client will not be abandoned, that the stated function of the agency or facility will be upheld, and that the client–counselor contract will be honored. Following are several other crucial skills and qualities for a successful client–counselor relationship.

## Empathy

*Empathy* is the ability to mentally enter into the feelings of others, for the moment comprehending the world the way they do. It is a "feeling with" as distinguished from a "feeling for," which is sympathy. When we feel with, it means that we are trying to understand what the client's experience must be like. When we are feeling for, the client may sense he is pitied or devalued. When we feel just as our clients do, we run the risk of becoming as mired and overwhelmed as they are. The quality of empathy is valuable because older persons often live in conditions that cannot be helped, and the mere presence of another who cares and understands has great comforting powers. Sometimes counselors just bear witness. It is one of their gifts.

## Boundaries

New counselors, desiring to be helpful or important to their clients, will sometimes exaggerate the importance of the relationship between themselves and their clients. Even if inadvertent, this may lead a client into becoming too dependent on the counselor, so that if the counselor leaves, the client may experience yet another in a series of painful losses. Although the counseling relationship is important, it is critical that the client be encouraged to form a relationship with the facility in question as well as the counselor, because the former is bound to be more stable and durable.

Gerocounselors also may encourage too much dependency by spending an inordinate amount of time and energy on the case in the beginning. Clients, however, will continue to expect what they have become used to, and if a gerocounselor at first allows frequent home telephone calls, many drop-ins, requests for rides, and the like, that is what clients imagine they are entitled to. Counselors, on the other hand, usually cannot keep up these gallant efforts for an extended period, and they would do well to think ahead and set limits on the relationship early to avoid later misunderstandings. Crisis intervention is, of course, an exception. Here, great effort is expended in a compressed time. Let the clients know, however, that while you are readily available to them for the moment, your contacts with them will be less frequent as the situation improves. This is a positive approach, as you are holding out the hope that improvement is likely to occur. In addition, limits and boundaries are not only conveniences for the counselor. By maintaining them we often help our clients firm up their own personal boundaries, and such discipline, on our part, is a form of teaching through modeling behavior. Your facility has rules, boundaries, and limits. Help the client learn them early in the relationship. People feel more comfortable knowing what the boundaries are. This can prove difficult sometimes in informal settings where drop-ins occur and are even encouraged. In such a situation, you may want to structure a certain part of the day for drop-ins so that you will not show frustration at being interrupted when you need to do paperwork.

## Courtesies

*Courtesy* is the common sense application of rules of behavior to a relationship. It implies respect on all sides. Keeping appointments on time, always showing up as promised (or calling if there is an emergency), never stopping in without an appointment, not taking telephone calls during sessions, are among the courtesies that all gerocounselors can and should demonstrate to their clients—and expect from them.

Sometimes older persons sense that they are obliged to wait longer for appointments because the caregiver assumes unemployed persons have unlimited time. To give such second-class treatment is ageist and unprofessional and lowers self-esteem. (Also, you may not know the schedule, responsibilities, arthritic spine, medication regime, or bladder capacity of the elder client in the waiting room.) It is only fair to give all clients similar treatment (and perhaps ageist to give elders special treatment if their conditions do not require it). There are, however, special considerations that older persons should be given. For example, the present older generation grew up using people's last names as a gesture of formality and politeness, or in circumstances where first names would sound too familiar and intimate. Many elders feel decidedly uncomfortable being on a first-name basis in professional and business relationships. You can handle this with, "Hello, I am Mrs. Jones, and I hope you will call me Mary. What would you like me to call you?" Younger counselors will find a little thoughtfulness and courtesy can go a long way toward winning acceptance from their elderly clients. Being respectful, using polite language, and acknowledging the experience and learning that their years have acquired, will enhance your elderly clients' acceptance of you and your services. A peer approach may engender hostility or lower self-esteem, as elders may wonder what this young whippersnapper has to teach them. In line with this, present a personal appearance and office demeanor that are pleasant and professional, and avoid language that is cluttered with professional jargon or, worse, everyday slang or profanity. A good rapport is founded on mutual respect.

## Communication Skills

Good communication is of special importance in elder work. As aging and illness can be isolating, the elder must be able to communicate in order to maintain contact with the world, preserve alertness, fend off excessive egoism or disengagement, prevent the somatization of feelings, convey what is troubling them, and reach out for affection.

All people need to do these things, but aging can bring physical problems that hamper communication. Along with diminishing function of the sensory organs, the neurological effects of strokes, and other traumas, there are many medical disturbances that cause communication problems. Memory impairment and, hence, faulty communication can be caused by the dementias, anxiety or depression, thyroid problems, anemia, arrhythmia, alcohol, drug and prescription overuse, and so on. When such disturbances to communication become apparent, it is important to have a frank discussion with the client to expedite referral.

Moreover, the extrovert communicates expressively (talking, writing) and the introvert, receptively (listening, reading). In our zeal to teach communication, we should make it clear that we do not expect each client to communicate with us in a certain way. Some will be good expressers and others good receivers all their lives. You, likewise, communicate with your clients through many modes. These include your environment, non-verbal communication, humor, silence, voice quality, and your questioning and listening styles. Each should convey, "I have time for you; you are not bothering me."

## Your Environment

Your physical setting communicates much about you. Your office should be handicap-accessible, well lighted, quiet, private, neat, and comfortable. At the Counseling Center, Joan has tissues handy to show that feelings are okay here. If you take notes, use a tape recorder, or employ a two-way mirror; you should explain their presence and obtain your client's acceptance before you use them. Counselors do not work with the problems of transference as many psychotherapists do, so it is acceptable and often an icebreaker to display a family picture. If you manage a senior residence or center, you should find a room where you can counsel privately and without interruption. Mary uses a "DO NOT DISTURB" sign on the door, and that works.

Some of you, like Juan, the case manager, see clients in their own homes. Home visits communicate acceptance and outreach, and with proper counselor discretion, the client will not see this as a social call. When Juan senses that the client is "getting social," he turns the talk immediately to points in the agenda of the meeting.

Here are some helpful general guidelines about your counseling environment. Alzheimer's patients do best in settings that employ "white noise"—a neutral background of quiet music and restful, unstimulating colors and patterns. Color-coded pathways help residents to find rooms. Do not move furniture around or have things lying on the floor. Keep the environment safe. Often an older client will not want to face the glare from windows and may prefer a straight-backed chair. If your client is in a wheelchair, you should sit or squat at eye level. Having to look up is fatiguing and demeaning. Ask about hearing problems. If one ear is better, where would the client prefer you to sit? It is often difficult for the hearing-impaired to hear in a group session. Mary suggests that Bill beckon or cup his hand over his ear when he has trouble hearing. Whichever side you are near, sit facing the person to allow your lips to be read and facial and body expressions to be noted.

Don't take telephone calls (other than emergencies) during the session. Making this clear to all your clients demonstrates your respect for their hour with you and explains why you aren't always immediately available for calls. When you telephone your client, let it ring many times; don't be impatient. Use a slow to medium speaking pace and pronounce each word clearly, especially with the hearing-impaired, aphasic, or disoriented person. Ask the aphasic patient to repeat the message. Clearly identify yourself and your relationship and give any necessary background for the message. Confirm the call with a letter. When you do send letters or printed material, use large (bold, not script) print on off-white paper. White shiny paper has a distracting glare; blue on green is difficult for the colorblind to read, and yellow is hard for those with cataracts. All of the above will save you time.

## Non-Verbal Cues

Non-verbal cues such as body language give you and your client important clues about each other. Does either person appear relaxed, on edge, worried, fretful? Do *you* give hope by appearing optimistic? Do you appear comfortable, offering eye contact frequently but not continually? Eye contact is probably the first non-verbal cue signaled. Often, little eye contact signals a wish for avoidance, but too much can trigger discomfort and suggest aggressiveness. Closed or shifting eyes can convey a desire to escape; looking down from your glasses can imply that you are looking down on the client.

When working with someone from another ethnic group, be aware of different cultural meanings of certain body movements. Americans, for instance, tend to recede a step from a close encounter; some Asians see this comfort mechanism as a form of rejection. What may be inconsequential to you, may be offensive to another. Facial expressions, folded arms, tapping fingers, crossed legs, jiggling feet, and the like may often convey messages about internal states.

You will also be interested in congruity. Why does Carol say that she is worried or angry with a pretty smile on her face? Why does

James deny anger even though his teeth are clenched, his voice harsh, and his fists clenched? Do these folks give double messages to others, too? Check on such incongruities, which will convey your wish to understand. A good approach is to start by avoiding confrontation and blaming yourself for any confusion. You can say, "I'm sorry, but I'm mixed up. You say you're not angry, but you look and sound as if you are." Facial expressions may be incongruous or difficult to read because of the flat affect caused by depression, strokes, medications, and other medical conditions. In such cases, one would not take a confrontational approach or read too much into the demeanor.

Family therapists watch where people sit. A granddaughter who sits closely to the elder while other family members are united across the room is physically describing the splits and alliances in the family. A couple who sat far from each other in the first session but who are now on the same loveseat may be revealing that progress has been made. Pay attention to the signs, including posture and gestures. Stooped shoulders and a hanging head may indicate low self-esteem (or improper medication), while leaning forward in a chair may indicate interest and encouragement. Hand gestures can enhance or detract from communication. Likewise, squirming, clock-watching, or shaking a finger can be signs of negative reactions.

Generally, the therapeutic effects of touching older clients cannot be overemphasized. Gently holding a hand, squeezing an arm, hugging affectionately—all such appropriate touching can convey positive feelings. With some clients, who have certain forms of dementia and lack impulse control or judgment, however, you may decide that touching is inappropriate and not use it as a communication tool. This is also true when dealing with certain ethnic and religious groups where physical touching may be regarded quite differently from the way most of us see it.

## Humor

Humor is a problematic issue. Laughing together at a good joke can be an ice-breaker or a sign of healthy rapport. Laughter is regarded as a constructive tool in the healing process, but in many cases, humor is used to veil hostility, despair, discomfort, ageism, racism, or sexism. The 60-year-old whose husband is having an affair with a 40-year-old may joke, "Why wouldn't he find someone younger what with my sagging boobs and flab?" but she's not feeling funny on the inside. Don't laugh. Also, even though older persons tell ageist jokes, it is better for you, the gerocounselor, to avoid them. They are demeaning and could be interpreted as laughing at another's pain. Teasing and ageist greeting cards, too, are to be avoided.

## Silence

Silence is the golden non-verbal communication. It allows time to think and reflect and show acceptance. Sometimes sitting silently with a person in emotional pain is more helpful than trying to be glib. If you are uncomfortable with silence, you might say, "I wish there were some magic words to help you feel better, but there are none, so perhaps we can just sit quietly together."

## Voice Quality

You can improve your voice quality. First, slow down. This will help clients who need to relax, those with hearing loss, and those whose rhythm beats out a slower tempo than yours. Pause often and speak distinctly and without exaggeration.

Volume is tricky. If after a session you find yourself shouting at the next client or a colleague, you were speaking too loudly. Shouting raises the pitch of your voice, and most people with hearing loss have more problems with high-pitched sounds. Try lowering the pitch of your voice rather than raising its volume. Shouting creates anxiety and annoyance, especially if you shout in the listener's ear. It also takes your lips out of eye range. Keep your lips easy to read and your words clear; do not cover your mouth with your hand, pipe, or other object. Check your voice tone as it evokes different states in the listener: for instance, being listened to, ignored, confused by conflicting messages, or annoyed.

You will notice speech differences among your older clients, also. Elders' voices differ from middle-aged ones; they are often tremulous, hoarse, weak, or more low- or high-pitched. Imprecise consonants and slow articulation rate are common because of lessened speed and coordination. Dental problems and poor fitting dentures affect speech and may lead to social isolation. The speech of the hearing-impaired or stroke victims undergoes certain physical changes that can make communication much more difficult. Dreher (1987) offered helpful suggestions for communicating with older persons suffering from speech or language difficulties. With the dysarthric (persons with Parkinson's disease), expect poor articulation and read gestures and nonverbal cues, "listen for the slow motion of intelligibility." With the laryngectomee, one should listen for shortened phrases without melody and "listen with the eyes" (lip read cues). Slowed, accepting communication gives the aphasic person enough time to grope for words and ideas and to transmit "telegraphic messages" (p. 74). With the Alzheimer's patient, you should remain calm and adapt communications flexibly and creatively. Simplify with touch, warmth, and affection and reassure and validate feelings. Avoid negatives, teasing, scolding, and arguing.

## Active Questioning

Active questioning involves more than eliciting information or feelings. Used skillfully, it can help the client focus, establish counseling goals and termination plans, think in terms of solutions, learn systems, modify behavior, gain hope, recognize validation, and even get unstuck. Let us look at some active questions to see them at work. Bonjean (1991) suggested the following solution-focused questions to be used by gerocounselors:

- *Focused* questions help the client maintain a focus. "What is the problem?" "How long has it been happening?" "How do you feel about it?" are the mainstays of first-session counseling.

- *Solution-focused* questions help the client to think creatively and become solution- (as opposed to problem-) oriented. Examples are, "When is the problem a little less intense, frequent, better?" "What would you need to have happen for more of this exception to occur?" "How will it affect you? Your spouse?" This is behavior modification wherein the counselor rewards or pays more attention to solution-based behavior rather than the problem behavior.

- *Circular questions* can teach systems. "When Mary does that, what do you do?" And then, "When you do that, what does she do or say?" And then, "How do you feel?" "What do you say?" "How does Mary respond to that?"

- *Exception sequence questions* combine solution and circular questioning with more detail. Examples are, "When is the problem a little less intense or not there?" "What is different about those times?" "How can this difference happen more often?" "Who will have to do what?" "How will you know when change has occurred?" "How will significant others know?" "How will you know when the problem is solved?" "How will others know?"

- *Miracle questions* creatively give hope and help the client get "unstuck." Examples are, "If, by magic, your problem was solved, what would be different?" "How does that happen a little now?" "How can this happen more often?"

- *Coping questions* validate clients' feelings. The gerocounselor acknowledges the immensity of the problem and helps the clients appreciate their own coping capacities. "I'm surprised that the situation is not worse. What do you do to keep it from getting worse?" "How could this coping mode continue?"

- *Pessimistic questions* accomplish the above goals and are useful with pessimistic or negative clients. Examples are, "If things do not get better, what do you fear may happen?" "What is your worst fear?" "What will you do if things don't improve?"

---

**THOUGHT–DISCUSSION QUESTIONS**

Alone, or in small groups, role-play and practice the seven forms of active questioning with the case examples at the end of this chapter. What are your reactions to each? What kind of client responses might you expect from each?

---

## Active Listening

Good listening is the backbone of counseling, and it includes three essentials: hearing, understanding, and reflection. Active listening demands conscious energy to ensure that you maintain (a) attention and a corresponding posture; (b) a suitable environment; and (c) the setting aside of your own self-interest to focus on the client. When you attend to these factors, your memory will astonish you. Good listening produces good recall.

Dreher (1987) identified three forms of listening. In "listening with the brain," you acquire facts about the client and lend your own brainpower to help the person compensate for losses by suggesting creative forms of communication. "Listening with the eyes" involves watching body language and providing non-verbal communication tools (magic slate, communication board, etc.). In "listening with the heart," you listen with empathy and without sitting in judgment (pp. 70–74). Reik (1949) wrote of "listening with the third ear," a skill that interprets psychodynamics as one listens. Systemic listening attends to process instead of content; the systems listener is asking, "What is going on?" instead of "What is being said?" Counselors who are good listeners pay attention to all levels of communication: words, tone, non-verbal cues, psychological meanings, and process.

Because we are individuals, we all listen through our individual cognitive sets, and this can sometimes create listening problems. Herr and Weakland (1979) warned, "The message sent is not always the message received" (p. 33). Cognitive sets are based on experiences people may not have shared. Mary, for instance, was angry that John did not ask about her IRS audit and saw his avoidance as uncaring; John didn't ask because he believed that inquiring about finances was impolite. Different cognitive sets created a misunderstanding that required active reframing. Thus, active listening is listening and also prompting, that is, attending to communication and encouraging more. Strelow and Specht (1986)[1] identified eight positive listening techniques in a listening skills pyramid. At the base are techniques 1 through 8:

1. *Minimal encourager* ("hm hm, go on") agrees, understands, acknowledges, and encourages,
2. *Restatement* ("You seem to be saying . . .") rephrases with no meaning change,
3. *Reflection of feelings* ("You seem to be feeling . . .") is similar to restatement (2),
4. *Supportive response* ("That's normal . . .") shows positive acceptance and encouragement,
5. *Clarification response* ("Let me see if I have this right . . .") requests more information,

---

[1]From Strelow, A., and Specht, H. *Peer Counselor Trainer Workbook* (Rev. ed.), © 1986. Permission granted through copyright 1986 University of Minnesota, per Minnesota Peer Counselor Alumni Association.

6. *Non-verbal referent* ("I see . . ." or "I hear . . .") asks about/points out nonverbal cues,

7. *Confrontation* ("I'm confused. It doesn't fit.") sensitively addresses incongruity between statements, history, or nonverbal cues; and

8. *Self-disclosure* ("I feel that way sometimes, too."), appropriately and sparingly done, shows the counselor to be a real person who relates to the client's problem,

9. *Direct guidance* ("You ought to consider . . ." or "If I were you . . ."), and

10. *Shift of focus* ("Let's talk about . . .").

The two skills that may be harmful if not skillfully handled can occur at midpoint, 9 and 10 above, in the active listening pyramid. Direct guidance may imply that the client cannot think independently or is not unique. Older persons tend to prefer a direct approach, but you should explore all avenues that the client has already considered first. Less patronizing or demeaning is the approach, "I wonder what would happen if you did . . . ," or "What do you think of . . . ?", or "Have you ever tried . . . ?" Remember, shift of focus can be a move to change the subject or emphasis from a factual topic to feeling material. It is appropriate if done for therapeutic reasons, but not if it is due to countertransference problems. The peak of the listening skills pyramid contains two harmful behaviors in Nos. 11, 12, and No. 13.

11. *Denial* ("You really don't mean that . . .") indicates that the listener does not take the speaker's content, values, or feelings seriously. It implies that they are improper or unreal, and this can cut off further communication and harm self-esteem.

12. *Judgment* ("You shouldn't feel that way.") shows negative judgment of feelings or behavior verbally or physically (raising an eyebrow, etc.) and also does harm.

13. *Argument* ("I disagree.") We have added argument, a combination of denial and judgment, which is a final unproductive response. Argument, in counseling, is belittling. It also does not work. If the person is ambivalent, argument only reinforces the side not taken by the counselor.

> **THOUGHT–DISCUSSION QUESTIONS**
> Alone, or in small groups, role-play and practice the thirteen forms of active listening with the case examples at the end of this chapter. What are your reactions to each? What kinds of client responses might you expect from each?

## *Some Communication Guidelines*

The following guidelines are suggested for communicating with elderly persons and their families.

*Communicating with anyone*
1. Concentrate on what is being said.
2. Allow completion of thought or sentence.
3. Clarify what was said before responding.
4. Make nonjudgmental responses.
5. Be certain that all has been said.
6. Don't use put-downs.
7. Maintain good eye contact.
8. Respect the speaker's space and pace.

*Communicating with the withdrawn or depressed*
1. Talk about real things.
2. Give realistic praise about things well done.
3. Talk about past and possible future pleasures.
4. Suggest activities that will bring success.
5. Accept sad or fearful feelings as real.

*Communicating with the angry*
1. Don't take the anger personally.
2. The angry words require no response from you.
3. Show caring by repeating what you heard.
4. Don't raise your voice.
5. Show understanding before resolving the problem.

*Communicating with the confused*
1. Speak clearly.
2. Demonstrate if necessary.
3. Use eye contact and touch.
4. Remain calm and reassuring.
5. Don't pretend understanding or agreement.
6. If you don't understand, ask the person to stop, take time, and repeat.
7. If misunderstanding continues, don't criticize. Show that it is your problem.
8. Use intuition and guesswork to get the message.
9. Comment on the feeling behind the message if you can't get the content. "I'm sorry this is making you angry/sad."
10. Touch or stay with the person to show acceptance despite your lack of understanding the content.

## *Examples*

1. Mr. Adams told the counselor that he could not talk to his doctor about the fact that since retirement, he has not had an erection. He wants help but fears others will think he is a dirty old man.
2. Mabel Petsky told Mary that Alicia Perez did not fit in group because Hispanics could not be trusted. She worried about her purse being stolen when she went to the bathroom and couldn't always take it with her.
3. Charles Jones told Pastor Johnson that he wanted to take a lady out for dinner. Was it too soon after his wife's death? His daughters were objecting.
4. Hilda Greenwich, home health aide, was assigned to Janet Ferguson. All Janet did was cry, and talk about her dead husband. Hilda couldn't work.
5. Henry Martin told Joan that he was embarrassed about his suicide attempt and felt that his family was angry with him.
6. Janie Martin accompanied husband Henry to his second ap-

pointment. She was angry for the suicide attempt as daughter Kimmie needed their help now.

7. Sally Rogers, daughter of Clara, one of Annie Mae's patients, seldom visited. Annie Mae felt sorry for Clara and knew that she needed her daughter's support. She suggested that Sally visit more. Angrily, Sally spat out negative feelings for Clara and Annie Mae's intrusion into family affairs.

8. Pearl complained about being unable to do anything. She forgets, can't do housework, and wants to sleep all the time. It is all too hard. Her husband must care for her. He shrugs his shoulders questioningly.

9. Joyce is angry because her husband is not supportive about her colostomy. He doesn't help and drinks nightly. He denies alcohol abuse. She wants a divorce.

10. Sam, resident manager at Elmbrook, thought that his tenant, John, was depressed. He isolated himself and didn't mix. John said that he was just a sad old loner.

# Chapter 3

# Gero-Clients

The basic needs of the elderly are like those of all other age groups. Older people, though, differ from other groups and resemble each other in that they all experience, to a greater or lesser extent, a weakening of their bio-psycho-social systems. Moreover, this weakening is compressed into a short period of time, making them more vulnerable to stress-induced problems. The elderly also differ as a class because of cohort effects. A *cohort*, you remember, is a group of same-aged people going up the escalator of life together and who, therefore, are likely to experience events at the same time and develop similar attitudes. For example, as a group those who grew up in the Great Depression of the 1930s may value money differently from those who grew up during an economic boom. Because a cohort involves an age span of about ten years, there can be five or more cohorts over age 65.

> **THOUGHT–DISCUSSION QUESTIONS**
> What are some characteristics of your cohort? Compare them to your grandparents', parents', and children's cohorts.

At the same time, each older person also constitutes an interactive system within many systems as seen in your Gero-Chi Model. Those of you who have known older persons, have probably noted that there are very great differences among them. In fact, there is more variability among this age group than any other. Why is this so?

Generally, we are all more similar at birth than at death, even though there are many prenatal conditions that tend to distinguish us from one another at birth. As we develop, our varied personal experiences shape us into our own unique selves. Always experiencing, the longer we live, the more different from each other we become. The continuity theory reminds us that we don't change when we age, we just get more like we were at a younger age (Neugarten, Havighurst, & Tobin, 1968).

Because of these variability and cohort effects then, this chapter begins with the warning: We cannot and must not lump all older persons together. Having made that point, let us go back to some similarities seen in normal human aging. As we saw in Chapter 1, The Gero-Circular, Holistic, Interactive Model suggests that the gerocounselor understand and work within the elder's contextual systems. Although the family system holds a middle place in this classification, it by no means plays a minor role in gerocounseling.

## *The Self-System*

The core of the Gero-Chi-Model is the Self-system, which was described in Chapter 1. Among many other facets, it includes one's gender and one's spirituality. These have been highlighted because they often make a profound impact on aging outcomes. The literature often refers to aging as mainly "a woman's issue." One's spirituality, a vehicle of perception, influences not only how we perceive our aging, but it also can help to support it. Elements of the self-system are often expressed through one's self-concept and one's self-esteem.

Self-concept is the cognitive definition of the self's identity and includes one's social roles. It must be redefined, however, with each role loss. You will often hear an older person say, "I don't know who I am anymore," or "I don't know how to be now," indicating role confusion. Self-redefinition is easier if one bases self-concept on internal rather than external states. Older clients, therefore, can be counseled to focus on their internal qualities.

Self-esteem is the emotional counterpart of self-concept. It is determined by one's emotional evaluation of self based on an acknowledged standard or value. Thus, if one's self-concept is dependent on a spousal role or if one's self-esteem is reinforced by one's valued self-sufficiency and independence, can you see how the inevitable aging process may come to jeopardize both?

# Gender

The source of energy for the self is often credited to sexuality, but gender is more than sex. Closely tied to both self-concept and self-esteem are the roles and opportunities that one's gender provides. Gender helps us to determine "who I am" and "what life will be," and it also helps us to define the self, especially in the later years. Despite recent societal gender and role modifications, gender still holds a signal place in our lives, particularly to older cohorts.

You will probably counsel more women than men because older women are more (a) numerous, (b) prone to consult a doctor or counselor, (c) vulnerable to poverty and chronic poor health due to lower Social Security benefits, inadequate health care, and other factors, and (d) often the caregivers and hence subject to emotional stress.

Older women also are more often single, isolated, lonely, caregiver-deprived, and feeling no longer valued sexually. They were usually more subject in their early years to discrimination in education, employment, income, health care, and other areas, particularly if from a minority race. Often older women were not socialized to be assertive, an important mental health component. Despite this, most older women evidence strengths and resilience through their ongoing relationships and homemaker skills which aid them in maintaining a relatively normal life.

Older males fare differently. On the average, they die seven years earlier, of more acute causes but enjoying the benefits of more insurance, covering more hospital and caregiver costs. The older male's depression and suicide rates (particularly for whites) are alarmingly high, and rise with age. Causes point to incongruities between the older male's ideal self (high-status worker, in control, physically adept) and the losses brought on by advancing age. Male widowhood is often added to these narcissistic insults, creating a situation wherein the male often finds himself lacking in relationships and homemaking and self-care skills. Other societies dealt with these conflicts by elevating males in religious orders, for example (Gutmann, 1977). This has not happened here. But gerocounselors can help older men, particularly ones who are infirm, to recognize and honor new values for the self.

On the plus side of gender and aging is the theory that says we get in touch with the other sex in us as we age (Gutmann, 1977; Jung, 1933). Women seem to become more assertive (finding employment, adjusting to widowhood, etc.); men, conversely, are noted to become more "feminine," stern fathers turn into teddy bear grandfathers and the like. But the idea that males become more what used to be regarded as "female-like" (passive, gentle, spiritual, etc.) has been cited as one reason for the high elderly male depression rate. Tobin (1988) warned, "Passivity leads to adverse outcomes. . . . Aggressiveness, therefore, is a way to cope with adversities over which one has no control" (p. 552). Gerocounselors can help elders of both sexes learn to channel aggression into assertiveness and to help families and caregivers reframe how they look at an elder's assertive behaviors. For example, "Marion's not a grouch, she's just coping."

> The nursing home staff consulted Joan about Marion, who was refusing treatment for her psoriasis, not complying with her diet, and acting generally abusive. The staff tried TLC, logic, and reasoning with Marion to no avail. When Joan arrived, the anger at Marion was so excessive that Joan felt its displacement on her. She tried to explain that Marion was not a "nasty woman" but one experiencing much pain and many losses, and this was her way of remaining in control. She gave them Tobin's article (1988) and tried to help Marion develop new relationship skills with the staff, while also maintaining the assertiveness to say "no."

> Henry Martin, age 64, was referred to the Counseling Center following a suicide attempt. He retired at age 62 from the Acme Company as a middle-manager. An introverted man, he anticipated an easygoing retirement that was to begin with the construction of his "dreamhouse." Soon the dream became a nightmare as the lot developed unusual drainage problems. He had water damage in his basement and his new neighbor sued him. Concurrently, his youngest daughter, Kimmie, returned home after a job loss, a divorce, and with an alcohol problem.

> Feeling helpless and out of control, Henry attempted suicide and was hospitalized. At discharge, he was no longer at risk but still passive and unable to cope with his problems.

> Henry's wife, Janie, was another matter. After playing the "June Cleaver 50s role" for 25 years, she went back to school when Kimmie married. Then she landed an excellent job as an executive secretary. She blossomed in her academics and job and was elected to an im-

portant church position. When Janie discovered Kimmie's alcohol problem, she planned an intervention with her minister's help. Kimmie entered residential treatment and Janie initiated family sessions there.

In working with Henry's depression, Joan was quick to see family systems' issues along with the psychiatric problem. She wondered where to begin.

---

**THOUGHT–DISCUSSION QUESTIONS**
Were Marion and Janie being assertive or aggressive? What is the difference? How can the staff be helped to cope with Marion? How can Henry be helped to deal with Janie? Should Marion and/or Janie change? Should Henry? How?

---

## *Spirituality*

---

If gender provides the energy to the self, spirituality provides organization. Frankl (1977) saw spirituality as a part of personality and a process by which one organizes all that one is. Many older clients wish to talk about their spiritual concerns, and many believe that a spiritual outlook enhances adaptation to aging.

What is spirituality? Like gender, it is largely defined by one's self-concept and, in turn, helps to define the self. Spirituality is different from religious affiliation. Here, it means how one views life and all of its meanings, and older persons naturally experience spirituality in a variety of ways. As one's spiritual and religious views are often foundations for coping, relating in families, and handling suffering and death, they are relevant in gerocounseling.

A common myth is that religiosity increases in old age. There is no evidence to support this. Older persons today may be more religious than younger ones, but it is more probably a result of cohort effects and the continuity theory. Today's older persons were socialized when religion was paramount in life, and this practice (for them) has remained stable or increased in importance over time. Originally, counselors were trained to stay out of clients' religious views. Frankl (1977) opened the door to more permissible dialogue, writing that he aimed to make patients stronger in their particular faiths. Many believe there is a recent trend from a secular society to a more spiritual one. If so, gerocounselors must be more able to discuss comfortably spiritual concerns with clients. In the example below, even though they were not her own, Annie Mae sensitively used Leola's spiritual language and concerns to comfort her dying patient.

> Annie Mae knew that Leola would die alone. Her few relatives lived far away and seldom visited. Annie Mae observed Leola's terminal drop as all organs seemed to gradually give up. The two had a special relationship and Annie Mae promised that she would be there for her at the end.
>
> At the end and still conscious, Leola asked Annie Mae if she believed. Annie nodded. Leola said that she knew this was her end but still did not believe in God. Did Annie Mae think her bad? Annie reassured her that she didn't. Although a strong Baptist, she would not impose her faith, but picked up on Leola's words . . . that it was not "her end." She would always live on in Annie's heart. Leola smiled.

---

**THOUGHT–DISCUSSION QUESTIONS**

Can you recall an episode in counseling when your spiritual views were in conflict with your clients'? How did you feel? What did you do? In retrospect, are there ways you might have responded differently?

---

Recall now the major subset systems of the Gero-Chi Model. Successful aging requires the realization of certain psychosocial goals and the completion of practical tasks. These relate to three systems: the Aging Biological System, the Aging Psychological System, and the Aging Sociological System. Each can be assessed and converted into goals and interventions. (See Chapters 4 and 5.)

## The Aging Biological System

If you were told that 80-year-old Arthur Brown would be your new client, what would you expect? A tanned, vibrant senior with a golf bag over the shoulder or a pale, wrinkled oldster writhing in pain and leaning on a walker? The truth is, you couldn't predict; there is that much biological variability among older persons.

In this discussion, the biological system includes one's genetics, gender, physical growth and development, treatments and remediations, current functioning (ADL), disease prevention and wellness maintenance, and history of illness, trauma and disease. Today, theories of biological aging abound. Early ones used metaphors from physics, viewing the aging body as a machine wearing out or as a programmed quantity of energy being depleted. There are more recent sophisticated theories, but they often resemble the blind-folded children at the zoo, each exploring the elephant from his/her own perspective.

What can be agreed on is that normal aging, the process of senescence, is the increasing vulnerability of an organism processing through life; normal aging also refers to the changes in later life after the reproductive period. It is a multidimensional process. Beyond this, there is no single theory that predicts aging or the rate of aging in individuals. Because there are so many variations within a single individual, it is believed that biological aging is a result of a wide range of processes created by the interaction of physical, mental, and social systems. Effects of genetics, nutrition, medical care, sanitation, stress, support, life styles, and social circumstances must all be considered important, giving testimony to how we lived (and live) are how we age (and die).

Let's examine how this typical, if fictional, elderly gentleman, Arthur Brown, and his cohorts experience normal biological changes as they age. Your older clients may be concerned about the physical changes brought on by aging, and you will need to know if such changes are normal or problematic and worthy of referral. Even if they are normal, your client will need to adjust to them. Let us look at some of the changes as manifested in Arthur Brown and friends.

## Appearance Changes Occur

A look at Arthur's family photo album traces his aging development. Because his skin lost subcutaneous fat, it has less elasticity. That and his devotion to sunny golf courses created wrinkles. His skin is more friable, easily bruised, dry and itchy. His hair is white, but not balding like some of his golfing buddies.

## Mobility Changes Occur

While Arthur is on the golf course daily, he notices a slower pace due to stiffness and pain. Slower reaction time makes it take longer for him to respond physically and mentally. He can be advised to compensate for this slower reaction time by avoiding situations with excessive pressure, limiting activities, delegating tasks, and getting help when needed. When pressure is too great, he feels anxiety or fatigue. Others may feel resentment, blame themselves, or be depressed about something quite normal for age 80.

## Sensory Changes Occur

Arthur and friends noticed losses in sensory acuity around age 70. Most are part of the normal aging pattern but some are due to injuries or diseases.

### Sight

More than half of those over age 65 have some vision loss; many need glasses and use magnifying devices. Losses in peripheral and night vision and changes in depth and color perception evoke anxiety about loss of driving privileges and, hence, independence. Confusion and misinterpretation of the environment can be caused by lessened ability to distinguish pastels and react to light. Arthur's eyelids droop, hampering his sight and appearance. Gerocounselors may help some of these problems in their clients by providing well-lighted offices without glare. To avoid night driving, schedule daytime events. Use heavy black print and enlarged figures on non-glare paper handouts.

### Hearing

Hearing aids are still unacceptable to many elders despite the fact that one third of persons over 65 (more men) have some hearing loss. When a hearing problem is unattended, paranoid thinking or excessive shyness can result. This is important in assessment.

### Taste

When Mary, at the Senior Center, tried to learn why Mr. Jones was not eating, he complained that nothing tasted good anymore. By one's seventies, there is an 80% loss in sensitivity to taste, creating a desire for more salt (especially in men) and sugar, ingredients that conflict with the management of high blood pressure and diabetes. (Note: A loss of interest in eating can also be an indicator of a nutritional deficiency, depression, or periodontal disease.)

## *Smell*

The olfactory senses suffer a decline after age 70, which also influences the appeal of food. Smoke or fumes can go undetected. People who live alone should have smoke alarms and be advised to watch hygiene more closely because smells and body odors may go unnoticed by them.

## *Touch*

At the center, Mary noticed that some members' fingertips were less sensitive, causing them to drop utensils, or to have other mishaps. Because accidents upset them, she offered reassurance and gave a program on "Sensory Losses in Aging."

# Skeletal Changes Occur

Arthur Brown is slower on the golf course due to stiffness and pain, which could be arthritis, a chronic disease of aging, or some other problem. Also, bone density lessens, joint and ligament elasticity decrease, and there is a thinning and loss of elasticity of intervertebral discs. Muscle fibers are replaced by fibrous tissue. These can lead to weight loss, kyphosis, stiffening of the joints, osteoporosis, and loss of strength and endurance. Since these are mostly attributable to life style changes, Arthur is wise to continue golfing. Because falls are a high risk for older persons, all home and counseling environments should provide adequate lighting, proper thresholds, and nonskid mats and bars at toilets and showers.

# Neurological Changes Occur

After age 30, nerves begin to die, creating a loss of neurons and nerve endings. This decreases one's sensitivity to pain, sense of position, and vibratory sense. Changes in brain mass lower fine motor coordination, which, along with failing eyesight, causes older women to find earlier hobbies, like needlework, difficult. Your older clients will probably complain about lightened sleep and frequent arousals. Reassurance and advice to avoid sedatives, reduce calories, improve posture, and continue exercise can decrease neurological problems.

## Gastrointestinal Changes Occur

Production of saliva, digestive enzymes, and gastric acid secretion is less, causing dry mouth, which can lead to difficult chewing and periodontal disease. Loss of gastrointestinal juices can also impair iron and calcium absorption, which may lead to protein and vitamin deficiencies, constipation, fecal impaction, diverticulosis, and cancer. Advise elders to eat smaller but well-balanced meals, chew more slowly, and seek help about problems.

## Oral And Dental Changes Occur

Problems include periodontal disease, decay, and loss of teeth. Of the one-fourth to one-half of today's elderly who have lost their teeth, only half of them have dentures. The elderly and poor resist preventive dentistry. Gerocounselors may want to encourage flossing, regular dental visits, and become advocates for improved dental financial assistance.

## Respiratory System Changes Occur

Fatigue and difficulties in effective coughing and shortness of breath when exercising are seen. Common problems are pneumonia and emphysema (now called COPD, **C**hronic **O**bstructive **P**ulmonary **D**isease). Elders should improve posture; learn abdominal breathing, relaxation and coughing exercises; and avoid indoor and outdoor air pollution.

## Cardiovascular Changes Occur

Arthur Brown was wise to consult his physician about the advisable extent of his exercise regime because of changes in cardiac reserve and pulse rate after he golfed 18 holes. Those patients with orthostatic hypotension, common with low blood pressure, are advised to change position more slowly with mild exercise before standing. Gerocounselors should see that the phone is placed near the patient's bed and advise the family to ring a long time to prevent the elder from getting up abruptly. Programs advising the modification of smoking, drinking, tight clothing, and the use of iron-rich foods and sodium are advisable.

## Renal System Changes Occur

Urinary incontinence is a problem to many older clients and a million-dollar business to others. It is a common source of embarrassment, and frank help should be offered. Both sexes note an urgency to void. Elders with urinary abnormalities should seek medical advice because problems can range from medication toxicity and urinary cancer to nocturnal incontinence. Often help is given through simple exercises, panty liners, and advice to avoid multiple drugs and to drink the right fluids.

## Endocrine System Changes Occur

As cells and gland size decrease, intolerance to cold and thyroid disorders increase. A reduction in adrenal activity slows stress response and inflammatory processes. Lowered estrogen levels cause female hirsutism and dry vaginal mucosa and dyspareunia. In males, lowered testosterone causes a longer refractory period for erections.

## Sexuality Changes Occur

Observable sexual changes can alter self-esteem. The penis decreases; the testes lower; the prostate and male breasts increase in size. Female breasts sag and pubic hair thins. Coitus is more difficult but not impossible. Ejaculations are slower with less seminal fluid. Females experience less muscle tension, lubrication, and intensity of orgasm. Prolonged foreplay is recommended, and intensity is determined by frequency, again supporting the adage, "If you don't use it, you lose it." The positive side is that performance tends to improve with increased activity.

Couples who cannot participate in normal coitus due to medication, medical problems, or the like can be reassured that individual or mutual masturbation is acceptable. When gerocounselors regard sex as a taboo subject, older persons, already burdened by a cohort repression of sex, often have nowhere to turn. Elders should be encouraged to overcome ageist attitudes about late-life sexuality and to voice concerns to physicians and others. Often help is available.

# Common Medical Problems

On average, women live seven years longer than men. More than three-quarters of deaths of men over age 65 are attributed to heart disease, cancer, and strokes. Women suffer longer with chronic diseases and have more arthritis, high blood pressure, strokes, diverticular diseases of the colon, hiatus hernia, incontinence, osteoporosis, and senile degeneration. They spend more sick days at home or in nursing homes with less financial assistance. Women probably experience less quality in their last years of life. Men spend more total days in the hospital (usually Medicare and insurance covered). Most men die with benefit of caregivers; many women do not.

Other medical problems reduce mobility and social participation. You should know your client's particular medical diagnoses and also their intensities, prognoses, costs, and how they are perceived and handled by patient and family. Frank communication with your client, the physician, and the family together with geriatric and prescription drug manuals will help you. Even though your client has Medicare, or other insurance, certain medical conditions can destroy financial security in uncovered medicine bills alone. Your clients consequently will be worried about medical economics. They will in any case be talking about their diagnosed and undiagnosed medical problems with you. It is important that you know about the biological signs of normal aging so that you can encourage your client to seek medical advice when something appears abnormal. Too often, a real problem in need of attention will be attributed to "aging." Learn about the common medical problems of aging so that you may listen to them intelligently. In addition, special considerations should be given to how members of various ethnic groups deal with health and medical problems.

## *The Aging Psychological System*

At Mary's Senior Center, a Tuesday support group meets to help its seven members with the "changes of aging." While issues, personalities, cognitive skills, and coping devices vary, the seven share two characteristics: They are all over age 65 and they are motivated to help themselves and each other.

> Marge Adams, a 75-year-old retired nurse, says that she is too busy for groups due to volunteer jobs, but she started coming to provide

"wheels" for a member, Mabel Petsky. Now she has friends in the group and comes to see them. Mabel, age 81, met Marge when she moved to Ellis Home six months ago. She was relieved to finally be with congenial people because living with her sister "didn't work out and her children did not want to take her in." She worries about her memory as her mother had Alzheimer's disease.

Carol and Arthur Brown are the group's only couple. Carol, age 78, says that she does not enjoy the group but her doctor and husband encouraged it. Lately she has had many physical symptoms and is continually complaining because Arthur golfs so much. Arthur, age 80, a retired business manager, likes being in control and says that Carol should "get on with her life."

Bill Smith, age 70, became widowed a year ago, and is struggling with housekeeping chores and a diabetic regime. Alicia Perez, 68, was an efficient financial manager but now worries excessively about money. Sara Crimmings, 71, sees the group as her morning out. She is caregiver to husband Tony, who is in mid-state Alzheimer's, and she is heavily burdened even though a large family helps out. Clarence, a respite volunteer, relieves her on Tuesdays so that she can attend.

Mary's group presents a variety of personalities and issues. In general, how does gerocounseling deal with varied concerns like these? As might be expected, various gero-theories from the paradigms of psychoanalysis, humanism, and behaviorism are used. Except for the behaviorists, most counselors base their theories on empirical work with patients. These may not have undergone scientific testing, but they are helpful.

In addition, developmental and social psychology and sociology contribute to our understanding of aging personalities. Some see personality as evolving through life. Instead of homing in on psychopathology, they concentrate on successful aging and study adaptation, adjustment, surviving stresses, coping, life satisfaction, and other parameters. A new trend is emerging—it is a movement toward the identification, assessment, and marshalling of strengths and resiliencies of the aged instead of concentrating on the "misery perspective" (Tornstam, 1992). Thus, Mary's group had a number of jumping-off places for their discussions. In addition, they examined the aging psychological system in a number of contexts.

## Personality Contexts

*Personality* is a "unique pattern of innate and learned traits that influence the manner in which each person responds and interacts with the environment" (Hooyman & Kiyak, 1993). Birren (1969) saw it as "the characteristic way in which an individual responds to the events of adult life." Individual responses are both inner (thoughts, feelings, perceptions), and outer (behaviors). A major research question is whether personality dispositions endure or change through life. Costa and McCrae (1980) and Neugarten, et al. (1968) concluded that personality endures across adulthood and is a formative influence on life. The latter, in describing the continuity theory, saw four enduring personality types: The Integrated Type (Marge Adams?), the Armored–Defensive Type (Arthur Brown?), the Passive-Dependent Type (Carol Brown?), and the Disorganized or Unintegrated Type (Mabel Petsky?).

Cummings and Henry's (1961) disengagement theory postulated that a mutual withdrawal of the older person and society occurred. Because it allowed for individual gratification and societal continuity, this disengagement benefited both. This has been debated. Activity theory supports the opposite, that is, keeping active should be the aging goal. Correlations do exist between morale, adjustment, and activity levels (Havighurst, 1968). Maybe Carol Brown is disengaging and Marge Adams is the activity theory in vivo. Other areas are of crucial importance in this debate between disengagement and activity.

### Mental Health

A new approach stresses thriving instead of surviving. The mentally healthy older person has positive self-attitudes, continues to grow, self-actualizes, synthesizes, and integrates aspects of the self (Sherman, 1993). Kivnick (1993) sees late-life mental health as "an attempt to live meaningfully in a particular set of social and environmental circumstances, relying on a particular collection of resources and supports." It is a three-part effort of (a) developing internal strengths and capacities, (b) identifying and using external resources, and (c) compensating for weaknesses and incapacities.

### Life Satisfaction

This, a popular study in gerontology, was found to include (a) adopting a wider view of life, (b) sharing and leaving legacies, (c) enjoying positive health, marital satisfaction, and financial status (power), and (d) having a confidant or similar relationship.

## Stress

Stress was originally seen in very general terms as "the nonspecific response of the body to any demand made upon it" (Selye, 1946, 1970). Some stress is helpful. Negative or positive stress is determined by one's cognitive appraisal of stress, the number of concurrent stressors, and their timeliness and desirability. For Carol, the group is stressful; for Marge, it is fun. Because of aging, the bio-psycho-social stressors are compounded in a compressed time; subsequently, their negative effects are more pronounced and more coping is required to deal with them.

## Coping

Coping, the manner in which a person responds to stress, can take many forms: instrumental, intrapsychic, affective, escapist, and/or defeatist. Coping mechanisms and styles vary among and within persons. In the Kübler-Ross (1969) coping-with-grief model, one moves back and forth through denial and isolation, anger and resentment, bargaining and postponing, depression and acceptance. Coping mechanisms are conscious and are different from unconscious defense mechanisms. (Common defense mechanisms are denial, projection, repression, reaction formation, and displacement.) As gerocounselors, you will see older clients use both coping and defense mechanisms, but you will only be working with the coping mechanisms.

Elders use more mature coping styles than younger persons. These include problem-solving, seeking advice, distancing, reframing, turning to faith or religion, and using less escapism and confrontation. Women tend to use more expression of feelings and neurotic responses such as wishful thinking or sedation.

Coping mechanisms remain stable throughout life. They depend on cognitive skills, personality traits, health, and access to a support network. Learn about your client's coping responses so that you can help resurrect, reinforce, or replace them. Mary helped Mr. Smith cope through expressing his feelings, problem-solving through seeking information and the advice of experts, and accessing services. Mary's group members bring their own unique personalities, stresses, and coping strategies. They are also reporting some cognitive changes and fears about aging cognition.

## Cognitive Contexts

In fact, the teasing about cognitive functioning in the group became so problematic that Mary ran a short series on cognition. Her members needed to curb anxiety, dispel myths, access accurate information, and also learn techniques to maintain cognitive skills. Mary reported, "In terms of cognition, there is good news and bad news." With the help of a retired psychologist, they reviewed some common definitions.

*Cognition* refers to the way we process knowledge, and it involves intelligence, learning, memory, and problem-solving. *Intelligence* is a multifaceted, multidimensional, composite, statistical measure of distinct but interrelated capacities. It is generally seen as the ability to combine available information to pursue a specifiable goal—such as the effective utilization of environmental resources. Performance limits of intelligence are determined by genetics and biology, and they are very much influenced by environment. Intelligence Quotient (IQ) tests, which measure mental capacity, are seldom used with elders but are used to make predictions about academic and career potentials.

*Learning* is the process of encoding (entering data), storing, and retrieving new information meaningfully. Older persons learn, but there is some decline in test scores after 65. However, some tests are biased and may include tricky memory assessments. Lower scores may also be due to elders' cautiousness, anxiety, lack of strategy, less or less-recent schooling, slower reaction time, mental stimulation deprivation, or other factors. Learning involves retrieving data from the brain's memory bank.

*Memory* is the process of storage and retrieval. The group was given a handout that discussed three kinds of memory.

1. *Sensory Memory*: Iconic (shapes we see) or echoic (sounds we hear) stimuli enter the sensory memory. This is a temporary, short-term holding tank capable of remembering at most six or seven digits for about 60 seconds. Sensory memory can be aided by hearing the name spoken several times (by others or yourself) and by seeing a face associated with a name.

2. *Primary Memory*: This is another temporary tank for holding, organizing, and processing information. Unless the new ma-

terial is manipulated here in a meaningful way, it will not be remembered. Older people often need instructions here in rehearsal, mnemonics, and uses of imagery to improve primary memory functioning.

3. *Secondary Memory*: This is a file cabinet of unlimited capacity over time, and it does *not* become overloaded with age, as many believe. It is sometimes called the mind's junk drawer. Often older persons complain about some difficulty in retrieving information from secondary memory. This is often accompanied with anxiety about dementia, sometimes resulting in a self-fulfilling prophecy and/or depression, and hence, more memory loss.

New information is received through one of the sensory organs to become a part of *sensory memory* for a few seconds and then moves to *primary memory*. If manipulated, the information goes to *secondary memory*. Aging reduces the efficiency of processing information in sensory and primary memories and retrieval from secondary memory, but it does not influence the storage capacity of primary or secondary memories.

Your older client will bring memory concerns to you. Simple knowledge of the aging memory process and how to keep it functioning helps. Sensory deficits, anemia, arrhythmia, heartbeat irregularity, thyroid dysfunction, alcohol abuse, or use of hallucinogenic drugs can all contribute to memory problems and are correctable.

The classic aging pattern is seen in cognition. Older persons score lower on the performance part of tests but verbal scores remain stable. If we add performance scores (fluid intelligence) to verbal scores (crystallized intelligence) and divide by two, the scores for older and younger are similar. (Elders' scores on performance are lower, but verbal scores are higher because they have often acquired more information). Older persons do better with items that are familiar, relevant, meaningful, concrete, true-to-life, do not involve speed, and which are presented in a supportive rather than a challenging manner.

"There are pluses, too," Mary said of aging. "There is *wisdom*, a combination of cognitive and emotional qualities seen in many (not all) elders." The group listed qualities they felt exemplified wisdom: mastery over emotions, experience, introspection, reflection, empathy, deliberation and avoidance of the impulsive, and transcendence (unconcern with trivia), and cautiousness. From the dictionary, the group found wisdom to be "knowledge of what is right and true coupled with just judgment as to action."

---

**THOUGHT–DISCUSSION QUESTIONS**

Are all elders wise? Can you add characteristics to the above wisdom list?

---

"What about *creativity?*" they asked. "Would the continuity theory inhibit the new development of creativity in older persons?" If creativity can be defined as the ability to devise new, unique solutions to new problems, and if one has been doing that throughout life, one will be creative in old age. People like Grandma Moses and Winston Churchill, who later took up painting, were very likely creative and inventive in their earlier years. Others were genetically or culturally programmed to be "uncreative," Mary told them. "Still others," she said, "have suppressed creative urges due to the pursuit of everyday necessities and may find new available time in retirement to uncover creativity." There have been few studies on late-life creativity and there is much to learn. Mary concluded, "Normal healthy adults should expect good mental function to age 80, when mild changes will occur. Only four percent over 65 have a form of dementia that indicates a reversible or irreversible disease that warrants attention."

Personality, too, should not change dramatically unless there is a disease process (affective disorder, organic brain disorder, etc.). One sees less affective, anxiety, or substance-use disorders, but more severe cognition problems among late-lifers. The few psychotic conditions seen stem mostly from earlier problems. Older persons are usually admitted to psychiatric hospitals for depression, anxiety, confusion, and paranoia. Women are more at risk for depression and anxiety; men have more substance and antisocial personality disorders. "Most older persons maintain a satisfactory level of mental health, but for those who do experience changes in their psychological status, appropriate and accessible treatment is essential" (Wykle & Musil, 1993). Good treatment depends on accurate assessment.

As your Gero-Chi Model suggests, your elderly person's biological system interacts with the psychological one in a circular fashion. A third system is also important in this holistic model, the sociological system—comprising your client's social contexts.

## *The Aging Sociological System*

Ernie sees patients from many social contexts in his family practice. Situational and family issues and differing cultural ways of addressing health, illness, and dying affect his medical model. Juan, at Human Services, considers cultural and relationship issues in his care plan, too. Both find that how clients feel about treatment is a fair prognosticator of whether it will be successful. To determine the real effect of cultural and social practices on an individual, though, is not easy. There are a number of contexts in which society and culture interact with people, and we will examine here some of the most important.

## Historical Contexts

Historical contexts, the actual world conditions people lived through at various times, are good clues as to how social forces help shape notions of who one is and how one views self and the world. They can be helpful but not definitive. Arthur and Carol Brown may have lived through the same historical era, but they see what they have experienced differently. Arthur once wrote the following essay for the local senior paper.

Imagine coming from "the old country" in 1910 with barely the shirt on your back, to making it big in the 20s, to losing it in the 30s, to having financial ups and downs in the 50s to 70s, to worrying about Medicare and Social Security cuts in the 80s, and national health insurance in the 90s?

Imagine going from horse and buggy to the streetcar to the automobile to the Concorde? Imagine being raised by the switch in the woodshed, to being retaught to raise kids by Freud's antirepression theories or Dr. Bundeson's rigidity, to watching one's grandchildren being raised by Spock's permissiveness?

Imagine a childhood tightly bound by religion and traditional values, to having one's children leave the church, to seeing them divorce, to learning of grandchildren having premarital sex, and then worrying if one's grandchildren are getting abortions or HIV? Imagine learning from the chalk and slate and McGuffy Reader to seeing your children go to a big consolidated school with Sesame Street under their belts and being taught by fancy electronic equipment?

Imagine going to World War I, sending a son to World War II, sending a grandson to Korea or Vietnam, and worrying about losing a great-grandson in the Middle East. Imagine a life wherein alcohol and tobacco were socially encouraged for fun and "calming your nerves" only to find fifty years later that you were dying of lung cancer, your daughter lost her job due to alcoholism, and your grandchild was in drug rehab.

Some hold that such dramatic changes gave older persons strong survival skills. Arthur does evidence much resiliency. Other survivors, like Carol, became more cautious, anxious, and troubled. Remember, personalities tend to remain stable over time, and experience often does not alter as much as confirm existing personalities. There is a danger in thinking of older people as frail because of biological changes or sturdy because of their historical survival records. There are many variations in each elder's experiences, and there are many variations in how they were perceived and processed. Arthur pridefully says, "Wow, look at me and all the changes I've been through. What exciting times." Carol says, "Poor me. So many changes, I can't trust."

## Cultural Contexts

Cultural contexts include among others one's ethnic/racial group, socioeconomic class, and majority-minority status. Both strengths and strife come from these contexts. Culture ". . . refers to the fact that human groups differ in the way they structure their behavior, in their world view, in their perspectives on the rhythms and patterns of life, and in their concept of the essential nature of the human condition" (Devore & Schlesinger, 1991, p. 22). This includes one's patterns, art, symbolic language, and the everyday comings and goings of life. Your clients' cultures will influence how they view and respond to present experience and also how you are accepted.

### Ethnic/Racial Group

Ethnic groups are defined by or set off by race, religion, or national origin. Members share a sense of peoplehood, a past, and a future. Pride in ethnic diversities offers a richness to American life and helps to maintain the integrity of the immigrant and succeeding generations. The mores of a group determine such things as childrearing and elder care, and they are deeply entwined with the family.

New arrivals to the country, faced with the dangers, discrimination, competition, and crises of their new society, tended to resist assimilation, drawing their old ways about them as a safe, protective blanket. Native ethnic language, food, religious rituals, humor, and social retreats such as lodges and singing groups served to preserve one's earlier roots. Conversely, the societal message to people like your clients was that it was shameful to have ethnic roots. If one was White and Anglo, one tried to pass as native born, but others could not employ this option, and they felt prejudices more deeply. Arthur, for example, legally changed his name from Brounowski to Brown. In the 1960s ethnic and racial pride were encouraged. By the 1990s debate again centered on whether an ethnic group should melt or maintain its diversity. Gerocounselors and clients will be on both sides of the fence.

The tasks of birth, death, adolescence, and senescence are executed differently by each ethnic group. The Chicano and Chinese came from agrarian societies where every family member had an important role in the extended family. Chicano adults worked in the fields while elders raised the children and passed on the culture. Chinese young adults supported their elders and turned to them for advice. In both societies, old age enjoyed a proud station in life.

As ethnic groups became urbanized and acclimated here, the status, security, and self-esteem of the elders diminished, but they stayed intact in various ways. For example, Chinese immigrants (a) continued to expect their children's financial support, (b) resided in neighborhoods where clannishness maintained a sense of Chinese peoplehood, (c) placed high significance on family celebrations, and (d) identified themselves as "Chinese in America" (Cheng, 1978). Other groups took similar steps.

As the preservation of self and self-esteem are two major aging tasks, the work ethic of your client's ethnic group is important to retirement adjustment. Middle-European males may view retirement as a threat to manhood and overdo physical labor, employ aggressiveness in relationships, or become depressed. To many ethnic males, retirement means loss of authority and power. Most women, however, do not share that problem because their basic roles do not change. Middle- and upper-class white women continue to look after domestic affairs, administer to family needs, and indulge grandchildren. This is also true for Native Americans, Italians, and African Americans (Devore & Schlesinger, 1991).

Although grandparents are often accorded a function in the family, it does not necessarily follow that all families reciprocate with emotional support and physical and financial security. Many elders must live near or with kin in high crime areas. Others feel burdened and tied down by the rigors of child care. Italian and Polish women, primarily family caregivers, often become angry and depressed, seeing this ongoing role as abusive (Devore & Schlesinger, 1991). Many African-American elders report high life satisfaction. They generally enjoy family outings, visits with family and friends, and church, which is a basis for social life, leadership and spirituality.

### Social Class

Social-class status includes occupational orientations, educational backgrounds, economics, and life experiences. It is reflected in attitudes regarding work, money, and tasks such as elder care. Clients in the *underclass,* for example, are usually uneducated, unskilled, homeless, and live in a ghetto or alone in an area characterized by poverty, unemployment, and danger. Many, today, are African American or another minority.

*Working class* clients may have experienced a narrow world with little mobility and stereotyped ideas. Many are "meat and potatoes" people, wanting counseling that is highly structured and that offers concrete services. Used to dealing with authority, they may be distrustful of service providers. Depression memories bring anxieties about the cost of services. They stress "getting by" instead of "getting ahead," which may affect your gerocounseling goals.

*Middle-class* clients may bring concerns about the demise of middle-class values such as the work ethic, sexual morality, and paying bills on time, with funds, not credit. Because male identity was bound to work and female identity to child raising, clients may be mourning such losses.

*Upper-class* clients fare better in aging as good bio-psycho-social well-being is often connected to increased education and income, which can afford better preventive and remedial health care, and other amenities. Upper-class clients are used to delegating and purchasing services and may think of your services as no different from others they are accustomed to buying and administering.

### Minority/Majority Groups

Minority groups are "the underprivileged in a system of ethnic stratification, and are people of low standing—people who receive unequal treatment and who therefore come to regard themselves as objects of discrimination" (Shibutani & Kwan, 1965, p. 23). Most affected in the United States are African Americans, Native Americans, Asian Americans, and Hispanics—primarily people of color. Others included are women, gays, the handicapped, and the elderly.

## Relationship Contexts

Relationship contexts, which include a broad range of human relations, have special bearing on an older person's physical and psychological functioning.

### Family

The place of the family is critical. The oft-pictured lonely elder, neglected by self-centered adult children, is *not* the reality (Sterns et al., 1984). Of those over 65, 67 percent live in a family setting; only 5 percent are in institutions. Of those alone, half live within ten minutes from kin. Others, miles away, check in by phone to maintain "intimacy at a distance." And elders reciprocate: 7 out of 10 report helping children and grandchildren with services, money, and gifts. Most dependent are those over age 75. Although most families manage these dependencies well, there are also some strained relations, abuse, and negligence. Such cases must be carefully watched by service providers and referred for help when necessary. Sometimes the abuse is subtle and difficult to detect, as the following two examples illustrate.

> Since Sylvia Jones died last year, her 78-year-old husband, Charles, has not been "himself." In April, a daughter, June, called their minister for counseling help. Pastor Johnson agreed to meet with the father and his two daughters. June, unmarried and closest to Dad, initiated the story.

It appeared that Charles had been dependent on his wife for many things, including the handling of finances. After her death, he let some bills go, did not deposit checks, and overdrew his account three times. He also sent for unnecessary items from TV shopping and went to the dog track twice. Alarmed, June acquired power of attorney and had his mail and finances shifted to her address. His phone, too, was shifted to her number so that she could monitor his calls. Passive and somewhat confused at the time, Charles acquiesced to his daughter's help.

Presently he began to assert himself about another matter that brought them to the session. Soon after the death ("too soon," the daughter added), he met Karen. She cleaned and cooked for him. ("She even scrubbed my floors, which my knees couldn't manage," he said.) She also offered needed companionship. He wished to continue seeing Karen, and some day live in with or marry her.

The disapproving daughters tried to break off this "unholy relationship" that was dishonoring mother. After reasoning, they threatened to pull out of Charles's life and take the grandchildren with them if he did not stop seeing her.

Charles was at a loss. He cared about and needed Karen; she was a good woman. But he also feared losing his family. And he would not assert himself with his daughters. The dilemma was causing more depression, but he remained unconfused.

Pastor Johnson, later alone with Charles, administered the Folstein Mini Mental Test which would substantiate his impression that Dad was cognitively sound. While the depression gave Charles some difficulty with concentration, his cognition and judgment were not impaired. Charles agreed to consult his physician about the depression. He also agreed to try to assert himself.

It was harder to deal with the daughters. The minister believed that their behaviors bordered on elder abuse, and he told them so. At least they were infringing on Charles's rights. He said that their father was depressed but cognitively "intact." If father wished to go to the dog track, order products from TV or have Karen as a friend, it was his money and his life.

As the daughters argued with him (and he erred in letting an argument occur), he learned that June recently had been rejected by a lover about whom the family knew nothing. Pastor Johnson thought that this may be related to her need to control her father now. Pastor Johnson wasn't sure where to go from there.

Juan, from Human Services, was assigned the case of Juanita Juarez, age 82. Mrs. Juarez was hospitalized for several somatic complaints but after medical tests proved negative, a diagnosis of anxiety neurosis was made. Because Juanita and family were so guarded about history and current living conditions, and because of financial need, a referral was made to HSD.

After several unsuccessful attempts to make an appointment by phone, Juan wrote Mrs. Juarez that he would visit. No one was at home at the main farm house, but a small cottage in back gave evidence of life. Amidst barking dogs and nursing cats, Juan was admitted by Mrs. Juarez to the small uninsulated unit. She hugged a shawl around her shoulders to protect herself from the Midwestern winter permeating the cracks in the house.

She was getting along just fine, Mrs. Juarez told him, although it got pretty lonely. She didn't drive, and her only human contact was when her daughter brought in supper after her waitress job. She didn't eat with them in the main house because, well, her son-in-law got drunk almost every night and she didn't want to cause any trouble.

---

**THOUGHT–DISCUSSION QUESTIONS**

As seen in the scenarios above, many issues and family system dynamics were interacting with the various problems presented. If you were Pastor Johnson, how would you proceed? If you were Juan, what would be your next step?

---

Even when living independently, far from family, each older client is a part of a family system (Burlingame, 1988). This is a natural social system with properties of its own, that has evolved a set of rules, roles and power structure, forms of communication, and strategies for negotiating and problem-solving that allow various tasks to be performed. One of those tasks is elder care, but the family may be juggling that with other tasks, too. Sometimes the tasks conflict. You will find threads of universal themes in your elder's family dynamics, such as dealing with dependency, sibling rivalry, conflict and intimacy, boundary management, role assignments, sexuality, separation anxiety, and individuation. Each family has its own strengths, deficits, and unfinished business, all of which may be played out one more time during an elder's crisis.

Adult children can prove worrisome. Divorces may cut off grandchildren contacts and bring in their wake concerns about appearances, guilt, and moral behavior. Adult children may also belie their status and continue unrealistic expectations of what their aging parents can do, either by denying their increasing frailties or expecting them to be more independent than is possible. Or worse, they may begin to patronizingly parent their parents. Of course, grandchildren and great-grandchildren are important to an elder's adjustment. Many without them grieve for the loss and feel a lack of social status. Grandparenting enhances mental health, vitality, joy, and a sense of continuity but can also contribute to sadness. The gerocounselor should not make assumptions about the meaning of this relationship before checking it out first.

### Late-life Marriages

Marriages late in life may trigger many of the same stresses as younger ones that brought significant changes. The earlier tasks such as nest-building, child-raising, getting ahead, etc. have all been completed, but new ones emerge such as filling companionship needs, adjusting to retirement, coping with limited resources, dealing with new sexuality issues, managing aging and medical problems, and caregiving.

Most older couples report increased marital satisfaction, but sometimes a marriage experiences dramatic changes during this time. An estranged couple may become openly hostile as retirement-togetherness forces new intimacy. Close marital partners may disengage, preparing for widowhood ahead. Unanticipated sexual problems may arise due to medical conditions, medications, depression, or ageist views on sexuality. A marriage may develop an overadequate/underadequate pattern after a partner has a stroke or serious illness. Once established, it is difficult to revert to the old system when the crisis is over and systems intervention may be needed.

### Friends

Friends take on an added importance in later life. Having a long-term friend is often a substitute for spouse or family. When family lives away, friends and neighbors fill in during times of illness and trouble. Late-life friendships satisfy many needs. Your client may need a friend for companionship, support, assistance, sexual expression, or to feel valuable and needed by someone. A workable arrangement is often found when siblings live together sharing finances and affection, but it does not work for everyone.

> When Mabel was widowed, she moved in with her sister, Myra, to save on expenses. The pair had been congenial the past 50 years, at a distance. But with a move-in, old patterns of sibling rivalry and power struggles emerged. They fought over task assignments, finances, friends. The struggle ended in a physical fight and Mabel calling 911. Family members intervened. Mabel moved to Ellis Home where she got HUD assistance.

Friendships bring their share of problems, too. Those moving to a senior residence or nursing home must learn new social skills and overcome personality problems formerly tolerated by families. Some fear not being accepted, gossiped about, or not having enough privacy. New friendships may involve dealing with conflict and learning new assertiveness. Your older client may need help in settling a dispute, dealing with an offensive roommate, or with the manager's favoritism of another resident.

Older people identify with and hold friends in close regard, and the death of a friend (or pet) can be a major loss and cause for depression. It can create secondary losses as it may mean the loss of a life style if transportation and shared outings and other social activities were a part of the friendship. Elders worry about outliving others they love and may feel guilty for outliving another or their own usefulness.

> Janet Fergusen, age 66, had crippling arthritis since her mid-fifties. Husband Bill served as homemaker, chauffeur, and social director. One day Bill died of a massive heart attack. Janet mourned his loss and later the secondary losses of all that he provided. A home health aide, Hilda Greenwich, was assigned to Janet, who appreciated the visits and soon began to use her as a sounding board. She expressed wishes that she should be dead since he "was the healthy one." She worried that she may have been the stressor causing his untimely death. Hilda wondered how she should respond.

Those who have been loners most of their lives do not necessarily suffer poor mental health in old age; it is more likely the ones who tried to make intimate contacts and failed, or the ones who have lost their intimate contacts, who are most vulnerable to emotional problems.

# Situational Contexts

For older persons, the real underlying problems may be role loss and a diminishing sense of self—the sense of going from something familiar instead of looking forward to something new. Helping such people to solve situational, practical problems like those mentioned below, however, can be a means of dealing with these underlying troubles. One thing is certain: It is the situational types of problems that are likely to bring clients to you in the first place.

## *Health and Health Care*

Health and health care, and their cost, constitute a major concern of the elderly. Many worry about the cost, quality, availability, and accessibility of health care, where prescription drugs alone can pauperize. Different generations in immigrant families will conflict about the use of Western medicine versus traditional ethnic treatments. You will be faced with such concerns over and over again.

## *Environmental Concerns*

The environment is another important issue for the elderly. Some elders get involved in positive environmental issues, seeing the environment as a legacy they want to leave for future generations—a resource from which to draw a sense of continuity and control. On a more local note, one's neighborhood can be a source of security and pride, or of fear and helplessness. Qualms about safety and crime are expressed by elders despite the data that shows them least likely to be victimized (Hendricks & Hendricks, 1986). Many older persons gain a sense of control and self-worth by joining groups like "Neighborhood Watch," or volunteering their homes as safe houses for children in distress. In line with this, adult children should be advised to help make their elderly parents' homes safe. Moreover, older persons on minimal fixed incomes worry about rising energy rates and property taxes and need assistance with creative financial planning.

Relocation is a major issue. Whether it is leaving a family home for a condo or senior residence or moving to another state or to a nursing home, relocation is often traumatic to the older person. It can cause further regression of the mentally ill or the demented. Much careful preparation is required.

Tied into the environment problem is the question of transportation. In many places, having an available means of transportation makes the difference between independence or dependence, between a social life and isolation. Many women of older cohorts do not drive and experience virtual immobility with widowhood. Other elderly fear and/or manipulate drivers' tests to hold onto licenses as long as possible while their adult children hold their breaths, fearing accidents. Many communities have inadequate public or senior transportation offerings. The problem is greatest in rural areas.

## Work and Retirement

The full ramifications of retirement often do not hit an older person until his/her pet projects are done—painting the porch, cleaning out the basement, or some such. Then men in particular can become depressed from the loss of identity and self-esteem, which they had come to equate with their work. Their work being done, they are at a loss to find another status builder. Some seek part-time work to supplement Social Security or offset boredom, and many of them meet ageism in the workplace. Many find satisfaction through volunteer activities.

## Finances

No question, finances are a number one issue. For those who lived through the depression, financial well-being is a state never to be taken for granted. In your counseling, you must expect to spend a great deal of your time discussing your fee, Medicare payments, Social Security cuts, inflation, and taxation. Many elderly fear economic dependence on children.

## Religion, Death, and Dying

As mentioned, older people generally continue affiliations with their religious organizations and appear to be more religious than younger ones. Church-related activities outside the home diminish, but older people are more apt to read the sacred writings of their belief, pray in their homes, and listen to religious programs on the radio or TV (Moberg, 1970).

Elders may not be obsessed with death, but they do talk about it frequently. A common fear is being abandoned near the time of death, of dying alone. To alleviate this fear, ensuring a continuity of relationships is vital, and this is an area where the gerocounselor can be a major help. Encourage your clients in every way possible to form and maintain personal relationships.

Many elderly welcome death as an end to suffering and want to talk about it and participate in life review. Gerocounselors are advised to get in touch with their own concerns about such issues so that they neither avoid nor overdo these important subjects (Genevay, 1990).

This chapter has presented a method for viewing your clients in a holistic way that includes their biological, psychological, and sociological systems. Many of aging's routine and problem aspects have been identified, and you have been given clues as to what to expect and to look for in the people who will become your clients. The next chapter deals with assessments of more specific problems your clients will present.

---

**EXERCISE**

Find an elderly "doing well" person who will consent to your getting to know his/her bio-psycho-social aging. Assure him/her of confidentiality. Prepare a written 10-page paper (or oral report) about your subject, weaving in what you have learned from class discussion, video viewing, and readings.

You may offer to share some information later, but do not promise a complete report as you may not wish to share all conclusions. You may elicit cooperation by saying that this will help you learn and even be helpful to other older adults. Also, your subject may find it enjoyable to share his/her stories with an interested person. (If you use a client or a patient, be certain that you clear first with your supervisor. Sometimes a signed release is necessary.)

If you are not reading this book for a course, do the project anyway, or at least think of the elderly people you know. How are they similar and different from each other in their biological, psychological, and sociological contexts?

---

# Chapter 4

# Gero-Assessment

$G$*ero-assessment* is the systematic process of evaluating the bio-psycho-social systems of an older person to identify all available strengths, resources, and deficits in order to develop an appropriate intervention or care plan to deal with whatever is troubling the client. The intent of assessments can cover a wide range: to effect change, prevent deterioration, maintain the status quo, and much more. Other assessment goals include predicting outcomes and measuring treatment progress for future case planning and/or agency accountability. Gero-assessment asks and answers questions such as

1. What is the nature of the problem?
2. What are the available resources?
3. What is my part in the problem?

## What Is the Nature of the Problem?

Attend carefully to the specific problem content as presented—not only by the client, but also by the family and referral source. Elicit this information in clear, specific, and concrete terms. For example, after initial rapport building, you might say, "Can you tell me in your own words why you're here and how I can be of help?" Give each person in the case a chance to respond as you practice good active listening. They may have come to you as "the expert," but you must assure them, through questions, that *they* are the experts on their problems, and it is your job to listen and understand.

Clients often use ambiguous terms to state their problems or goals: "I want to be happier," or "I want my kids to pay me more respect." Words like "happy," "respect," and "better" are personal, so you, the gerocounselor, must not assume what the client is looking for. You might say, "I don't know what you mean by happy. What are signs that would show that you are happier?" Or, "How often must your grown children contact you in order for you to feel more respected?"

You will understand more as you continue to probe with questions like: How is this a problem to you? To others? How has it been handled concretely to date? What is each significant person doing to contain, handle, or resolve the problem? What has worked so far? What did not? By doing this, you will be assessing your clients' coping and problem-solving strengths and styles. As you uncover the way they live and see their lives, you will see that their accounts reveal family system dynamics and the way they operate in their worlds.

## Style

Learning more about how they have tried to solve their problems themselves will give you leads as to the counseling style to use with them. If they were direct and assertive, you'll know these clients will be comfortable with a direct approach. If they beat around the bush timidly, you may want to proceed cautiously. But eventually, by helping them to bravely and openly discuss the problem together, you will encourage closeness, foster increased problem-solving skills, and free up more energy to use on getting the problem taken care of to everyone's satisfaction.

## Timing

A good counselor not only probes to learn the precise nature of a client's problem, but also wonders "What is the underlying meaning of this request for service *now*? What was the precipitating factor? What does the timing mean to the precipitant?" Usually clients will seek help before or after a specific event: an upcoming late-life remarriage with its anticipatory anxiety, for instance, or a family death and subsequent grief. On other occasions, the timing may not be so obvious. The triggering event may be something like a pet's death, gradual memory loss, or a disagreement over going out for dinner.

## Point of View

People in a situation together often do not experience the same situation. An elderly parent may not see his minor bouts of forgetfulness as a problem, but the adult children may overreact and see them as a prelude to Alzheimer's. A client, trying to keep things the way they've always been, may deny a condition the doctor reported very clearly. The "problem" a client brings into your office may hold different meanings to each family member—it may not even be a problem to some. Before any assessment of a situation is attempted, you must uncover any perceptual differences about the problem among the participants and establish an agreement on the facts of the case. You can't make progress if you are all working from different agendas.

Sometimes the problem presented as the trouble is only the symptom. Mr. Smith is depressed, and he feels he has a problem because he is depressed. After a brief conversation, the counselor realized that a reframing of the situation was all that was needed. Smith was newly widowed and he needed to be reassured that it was normal to experience conflicting emotions in bereavement—there was no question of his going "crazy" or anything of the sort.

In other cases, a request for tangible service can be a plea for help with a more serious underlying problem. Or, the stated causes of the problem may not be the real ones. A black mood can be precipitated by an anniversary, the arrival of winter, or the December holidays. What looks trivial to some, can carry a great freight of meaning to others. A traumatic event can lead to traumas that an outsider would not be aware of. Janet Fergusen, for example, lost her husband quite suddenly. That would be bad enough, but she went on to blame herself for her husband's death because he had always been healthy and she had been the sick one. Anna's precipitating problem was also confusing.

Anna, age 76, was referred to the Counseling Center by her internist because of depression. Her daughter brought her in. Anna has lived at Elmwood Senior Home for two years following the death of her husband. After the move, Anna got a cat and found a friend, Molly Braun, who drove. The two "bummed around" to rummage sales together. In May, Molly had a stroke and was moved to a nursing home in another town. Anna dealt with these events well. Then two months ago, her cat suddenly died. Anna shut down, clung to her couch, and wanted to die. No one could understand this irrationality over a dead cat. Her daughter feared Alzheimer's disease. What is the problem here?

### THOUGHT–DISCUSSION QUESTIONS
What additional information do you need to know about Anna's condition? How will you obtain it?

## What Are the Available Resources?

Who/what can help you make proper assessments? Help is near. You can find informational resources in (a) your client and his/her family, (b) informal support resources, (3) formal support resources, and (d) yourself.

## The Client as a Resource

You must learn how an individual and/or family cope now (and have coped in the past) in order to draw upon their existing strengths. Successful coping methods sometimes break down because of aging or other changes. Your client may say, "I used to walk it out . . . talk over problems with my husband . . . work harder . . . be the smartest . . ." Now, those coping skills no longer work or no longer apply, and must either be reworked or replaced. You uncover the old coping skills by asking questions like, "How did you deal with losses before in your life?" Or, "How did you make difficult decisions in the past?" From the answer you can begin adapting the old skills to the present situation, which is easier than building entirely new ones, and is more comfortable for clients, who have only to amend what they were used to doing anyway.

There is more than coping skills involved, too. Clients' family, health, intelligence, education, finances, housing—all are vital resources that can play significant roles in your assessments. Family is the most important resource after your client, and it is the one usually turned to when all other informal supports are exhausted.

More to the point, however, your assessments and goals must reflect the realities of your clients' resources. For instance, Joan prefers Jungian counseling methods, but if her client lacks sufficient education to benefit from them, they are useless. Ernie advises everyone "to go back to school," but many find tuition too expensive. Mary tries to get her clients more involved with their families, but some families live too spread apart and find travel impossible. Good assessments must be realistic if interventions are to succeed.

## Informal Support Resources

Social supports are informational, tangible, and/or emotional. Elders with more social support sources enjoy better health and well-being than those with fewer sources. Your client's informal support system consists of neighbors, friends, significant others (landlords, beauticians, bartenders, etc.), and, as we mentioned, family. Caring neighbors are often a prime support in an elder's network. Old and new friends also rate high, sometimes higher even than family.

Midway between informal and formal supports is your client's church, mosque, or synagogue. Some think religious institutions give older persons more support than any other resource except the family. This support system is not in place for all, however; some elders are unchurched, lapsed, only passive members, or belong to organizations that for one or another reason do not meet the needs of the elderly.

## Formal Support Resources

Despite their number, formal services are often uncoordinated and puzzling to families and professionals. Use your local Area Agency on Aging, your area's elderly services network forum, and your ability to network with others to inform yourself about services available to your clients.

Formal services range from the Administration on Aging under the President to local providers. The latter includes access, community-based, in-home, institutional, nutritional, legal and medical services;

voluntary organizations; and multipurpose senior centers. Learn as much as you can about them: what services they provide, their eligibility requirements, and the quality of their care.

## The Gerocounselor as a Resource

You must always be conscious of your limitations and possible countertransference problems, but at the same time you must keep in mind the strengths you bring to your older clients. Qualities like your knowledge and skills, hope and optimism, acceptance and nonjudgment, caring and empathy are powerful resources that offer your clients the opportunity to work out their problems with someone who cares and can help.

Unless you are working in a geriatric assessment center (a multidisciplinary clinic that usually includes a social worker, nurse, and geriatrician in order to provide a comprehensive, holistic evaluation), your assessments will generally be simple and functional. They will all have to be based on information you have pieced together and analyzed, and that process is the heart of your work as a gerocounselor.

---

**THOUGHT–DISCUSSION QUESTIONS**

The requests seem simple enough, but you probably will see that there is more information that you need to know in each example. What additional data do you need regarding each client? How can it be gathered?

---

Annie Mae's resident accused her of taking a ring. This was unlike her and was something new in their relationship.

Ernie's patient, Mrs. Jackson, was exhausted, ill, and weepy. She had been caring for her husband with Parkinsons for over four years.

One of Mary's most active volunteers suddenly stopped coming to the center. The staff was alarmed.

Rabbi Goldman received a family call about a temple member who was "forgetful" and a danger to self, but would not go to a group home.

John is resident manager at Elmbrook where only "healthy, alert" seniors are eligible. Mr. Rybaka's son called asking if there was an opening for his father who has arthritis, prostate cancer, and is depressed and confused at times.

## What Is My Part of the Problem?

At this point, the reader needs some reassurance. You cannot intervene in all your clients' problems—or even be expected to know about them all. You can only know and assess that part of the problem that pertains to you, the part that the client asked you for help with. You will always have to look for more information to devise effective assessments, but there are real limitations of time, money, energy, and professional behavior that you will have to recognize.

## *Gero-Assessment Methods*

Some helpful assessment references are *The Merck Manual of Geriatrics* (Abrams & Berkow, 1990), the *Diagnostic Statistical Manual of Mental Disorders, DSM-IV* (American Psychiatric Association, 1994), *Aging and Mental Health* (Butler et al., (1991) and *Geriatric Nursing* (Matteson & McConnell, 1988). Also helpful are Kane and Kane (1989), Biegel, Shore, and Gordon (1984), Herr and Weakland (1979), and Sterns et al., (1984). Data for simple, functional assessments are usually obtained by the counseling session, contacting collaterals, and using instruments—which are covered briefly in the following discussion.

## The Counseling Session

The initial counseling session is the jewel of the assessment process. Many tasks come together: the development of rapport, the statement of the problem and expectation of service, interpretation of agency function, and more. Because there is often too much to cover in one session (many elders find the process complex and fatiguing), it is recommended that the initial counseling session be in two parts.

During the meetings, you will observe much about the client's person and demeanor. Subtly, you will gain information about your clients such as (a) time orientation, (b) history of and feelings about major complaints or problems, (c) mental set and preoccupations, (d) general appearance, attitude, and behavior, (e) manner of speaking, (f) appropriateness of mood, (g) estimated intelligence level, (h) degree of insight into own problems, (i) probable reliability as a reporter, and (j) your estimation of the severity of the present condition. A beginning gerocounselor will need assistance in this. Much information can be gathered as you do the genogram.

A *genogram* is a drawing of a family tree that records three or more generations (Figure 4.1). It serves many purposes and is a helpful get-acquainted tool in the first home visit. The elder usually enjoys talking about family and past, and this can be a beginning of life review counseling. Genogram work gives you clues about patients' memory, orientation, relationships, and other characteristics. You can construct a simple one in your lap notebook as you talk. Say that you'd like help in drawing a client or family "picture" in order to know the client better.

Format symbols are easy to learn: males are squares; females, circles, with birth and death dates in each. Dotted lines identify living-together relationships; completed lines, marriages. Lines are slashed once for separations, twice for divorces. Lives are dated. A subset under a couple denotes offspring in birth order; pregnancies are triangles. Today's elderly often generate complex genograms, with divorces, remarriages, and many generations. Still, the comings and goings of life are important in the assessment process, and the completed graphic can show you who is in and out of the elder's support system and tell you about family roles and alliances. A second genogram can be drawn in the family session. Make contact with each person as to names, ages, and other nonthreatening questions. It can be done lightly to help the family feel comfortable. Figure 4.1 illustrates Arthur and Carol Brown's genogram.

The Brown genogram depicts six generations. Arthur's and Carol's parents are deceased. Carol and Arthur have two living children, Joseph and Susan. Susan and Bill are married and have three sons. (Susan's circle is shaded to indicate an alcohol problem.) Grandson Scott is married to Heather and they have one child, Sue. Joseph is divorced from Donna and is now married to Juanita; they have one grown son, Jose. Juanita has two children, Debbie and Doug, from a previous marriage. Debbie is married to Fred, and they have one child, Tony. Therefore, Arthur and Carol have two children, one son-in-law and one daughter-in-law, one step-grandson, one ex-daughter-in-law, four grandchildren, one granddaughter-in-law, two step-grandchildren, one great-grandchild, and one step-great-grandchild.

## Collateral Contacts

It is important to have clear, precise communication with your referral sources to know their understandings about the problem and

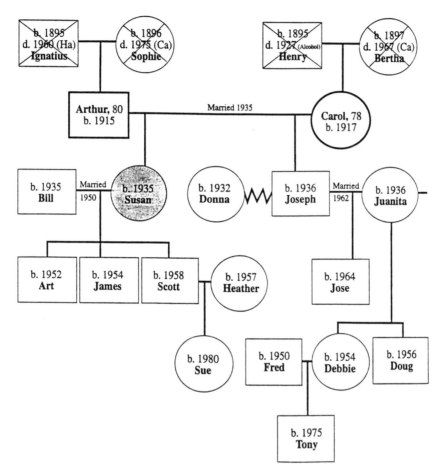

FIGURE 4.1  Four-generational genogram on Arthur and Carol Brown, January 1, 1995.

what is being asked of you. Medicare requires that the primary physician be informed of any reimbursed counseling services but, even if there is no payment involved, it is good practice to contact your clients' physicians about significant medical problems. Do not be shy to call. You and your clients' physicians will be resources to each other. If you are effective and communicate well, you will be a time-saver in the physician's or nurse's busy schedules.

Other collateral sources include members of the client's informal and formal support systems. They will be helpful sources of information in assessment and as possible intervention resources. But again a word of warning: *Do not contact any collateral resources without your client's written permission.*

---
## *Assessment Instruments*
---

Counseling sessions are the foundation of gero-assessment, but judicious use of appropriate instruments enhances the process. Test results add objective data about a client's problem and aid in treatment planning and progress monitoring. To familiarize yourself with the procedures, you first may wish to test out a counseling approach or do a before-and-after measurement with a group.

Test instruments should be chosen, used, and interpreted carefully. Consult the descriptive literature and ask: (a) Does it test what it purports to test? (validity); (b) Does it test similarly over time? (reliability); (c) Is it relevant to the elderly population? and (d) Am I qualified to administer it? Remember a test should be used for a specific reason and not routinely. Testing for testing's sake is wasteful of time, energy, and money, and may prove harmful. It can create anxiety if the elder is hurried or given material that is too difficult. The test could be demeaning if it appears simplistic. Over-testing can diminish a client's ability to respond accurately. We cannot cover here the growing array of assessments for elderly clients. A few instruments that work well with the elderly and their families in the Gero-Chi Model are discussed below.

## Assessment in the Gero-Chi Model

Most attempts to construct multipurpose instruments have not been successful due to problems with validity and reliability. It is hard to make one instrument do triple-duty, and therefore we recommend using several measures of functioning to gain an overall picture of your client's status.

### *The Ebersole and Hess Assessment*

Ebersole and Hess (1990) devised an elder assessment related to Maslow's hierarchy of human needs: self-actualization, self-esteem, belonging, safety and security, and biologic integrity. Each goal, if unmet, may present symptoms that indicate problems, which create needs that must be met, normally by assessment, goal-setting, and appropriate interventions.

For example, *problems* (social clocks, routinized life, self-fulfilling prophesies) may show *symptoms* (apathy, rigidity, boredom, ennui) which may indicate an unmet Maslovian *need* (self-actualization) which in turn may result in *goals* (self-expression, new situations, self-transcendence, stimulation) which may be helped by assessing the situation properly, setting reasonable goals, and planning appropriate *interventions* (creative pursuits, mediation, reflection, fantasy, teaching/learning, relaxation).

## The OARS Assessment

OARS, the Older Americans Research and Service Center Instrument (Duke University, 1978), measures functional abilities regarding social and economic resources, mental and physical health, and activities of daily living (ADL) in 105 questions.

## Psycho-Social Task System Assessments

Erikson (1950) elaborated a model of psychosocial tasks that lead the self to the final developmental stage, wisdom (viewing one's life events and self-involvements with a sense of integrity instead of despair). Tasks, completed by balancing two opposite conditions, become the building blocks of self. Table 4.1 illustrates Erikson's Psychosocial Development system (1950). Kivnick (1993) mapped the tasks in a 64-box schema to assess where a particular elder placed on each goal.

TABLE 4.1   Psychosocial Development

| Stages | Dynamic Tasks to Balance | Goals |
|---|---|---|
| Infancy | Trust vs. Mistrust | Hope |
| Toddler | Autonomy vs. Shame | Will |
| Play Age | Initiative vs. Guilt | Purpose |
| School Age | Industry vs. Inferiority | Competence |
| Adolescence | Indentity vs. Diffusion | Fidelity |
| Young Adult | Intimacy vs. Isolation | Love |
| Middle Adult | Generativity vs. Stagnation | Care |
| Older Adult | Integrity vs. Despair | Wisdom |

*Note*: Adapted from Kivnick (1993).

Completion of a goal is not a pass/fail event, but rather each older person is situated at different levels. A client could score high on hope but need continued work on will (assertiveness), as was the case with Charles Jones in Chapter Three. Kivnick included a Life Strengths Interview Guide to be used for assessment and goal-setting.

### Other Developmental Tasks

A Tasks of Aging for Assessment/Goal-Setting/Intervention tool can be seen in Figure 4.2 (See also Chapter 5.)

## The Major Subset Systems: Assessing the Biological System

The responsibility for diagnosing the biological or medical condition of the older person lies with the medical profession. Gerocounselors, however, will need to interpret these assessments to help clients more efficiently. There are also some biological assessments that gerocounselors can perform.

### General Physical Health Assessments

If you are a nonmedical gerocounselor, a medical manual can help you interpret medical reports. You will also receive a description of ailments and medications from your clients. Several recording forms have been constructed for your convenience.

The *Health Inventory* (Figure 4.3) records your client's medical problems at the appropriate body location. Add date of onset, severity, physician, and other pertinent data. The *Drug Inventory* (Table 4.2) includes data about all prescription and over-the-counter (OTC) drugs and traditional herbal medicines being taken. The *Nutritional Assessment* (Table 4.3), developed by the Nutritional Screening Initiative (1993), is used with elders, as many are nutritionally at risk. Although the elderly need fewer calories, a daily balanced diet is critical. Culprits causing poor nutrition are often sensory changes, periodontal disease and loss of teeth, social isolation, and prior poor eating habits.

### Activities of Daily Living Assessments

Subjective assessment of a person's functional abilities can be unreliable, but evaluations based on practical tasks offer a clearer

NAME ———————————————————— D.O.B. ——————— DATE ——————

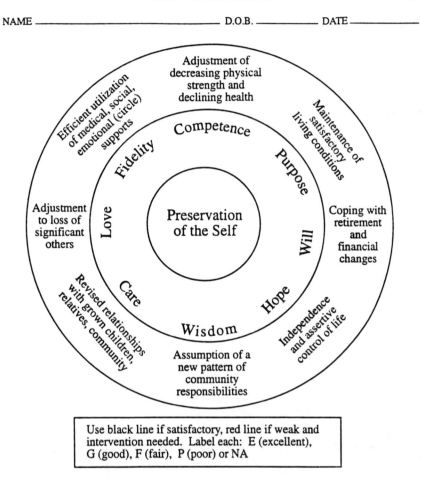

Adjustment of decreasing physical strength and declining health

Efficient utilization of medical, social, emotional (circle) supports

Maintenance of satisfactory living conditions

Competence

Fidelity

Purpose

Adjustment to loss of significant others

Love

Preservation of the Self

Will

Coping with retirement and financial changes

Care

Hope

Revised relationships with grown children, relatives, community

Wisdom

Independence and assertive control of life

Assumption of a new pattern of community responsibilities

Use black line if satisfactory, red line if weak and intervention needed. Label each: E (excellent), G (good), F (fair), P (poor) or NA

FIGURE 4.2   Tasks of aging for assessment/goal-setting/intervention.

picture. Activities of Daily Living (ADL) and Instrumental Activities of Daily Living (IADL) are used by professionals and caregivers to aid in immediate planning and in future evaluations of progress.

ADL scales include functional assessments of dressing, bathing, toileting, transfer, feeding, and, often, mobility and bowel and bladder control. The Katz Index (1963; Table 4.4) is one of the most used and researched. More complex, the IADL scales include money management, telephoning, meal preparation, laundry, housework, routine and special health, and being alone. Examples are the Lawton (1972) and the OARS (Duke University, 1978).

NAME ——————————————————— D.O.B. ——————— DATE ———————

## NORMAL AGING

**CLIENT'S PHYSICAL STATUS**

**Memory**
Fades slightly at midlife.

**Personality**
No major changes unless dementia.

**Pituitary Gland/Hypothalmus**
Growth hormone secretion declines causing shrinking muscles, fat increase.

**Sight**
Nearby objects harder to see. Fine detail lessens in 70s.

**Smell**
Declines at 45, more after 65.

**Hearing**
Declines at 20, males worse.

**Thymus**
Begins shrinking at puberty. Slow immune response.

**Bones**
Weaken at 40, females worse.

**Lungs**
40% decrease in breathing capacity between ages 20 to 70.

**Heart**
After 40, 20% decline in max. rate after exercise; Less responsive to stimuli from nervous system.

**Muscles**
Loss of 20-40% of mass from 20 to 90 years if exercise is lacking.

**Adrenal Glands**
DHEA (secretion that slows cancer, boosts immunity) declines after 30; Stress hormone cortisol production is up after 70.

**Ovaries**
Estrogen down after 50.

**Skin**
Collagen changes cause skin to lose elasticity.

**Blood Vessels**
Diameter narrows, arterial walls stiffen. BP increases.

**Nerves**
Message speed drops 10% from age 40 and 80.

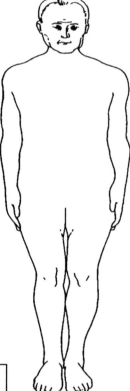

Record significant health problems at the appropriate body space above.

FIGURE 4.3   Health inventory.

TABLE 4.2   Drug Inventory

Name _____ d.o.b. _____
Date _____

| MD Date | Prescribed, OTC, Herbal Medications | Date Started | Dose | Frequency | Comments (Include Costs) |
|---|---|---|---|---|---|
| | | | | | |
| | | | | | |
| | | | | | |
| | | | | | |
| | | | | | |
| | | | | | |
| | | | | | |
| | | | | | |
| | | | | | |
| | | | | | |
| | | | | | |
| | | | | | |
| | | | | | |
| | | | | | |

| Alcohol consumption per day: |
|---|
| Illegal drug consumption per day: |
| Caffeine consumption per day: |
| Tobacco consumption per day: |

Scores indicate the degree of independence in each function with and without corrective devices, and they take into consideration timing, quality of performance, and other testing factors. Since many of the IADLs measure home tasks, they are difficult to administer in institutions and are biased in favor of women. An elder's mental states, such as anxiety or depression, can also influence scores.

## Assessing the Psychological System

Psychological assessments of older persons have many applications. Both cognitive and affective disorders can diminish self-care abili-

TABLE 4.3   Determine Your Nutritional Health

The WARNING signs of poor nutritional health care are often overlooked. Use this checklist to find out if you or someone you know is at nutritional risk.

Read the statements below. Circle the number in the YES column for those that apply to you or someone you know. For each YES answer, score the number in the box. Total your nutritional score.

| | |
|---|---|
| I have an illness or condition that made me change the kind and/or amount of food I eat. | 2 |
| I eat fewer than 2 meals per day. | 3 |
| I eat few fruits or vegetables, or milk products. | 2 |
| I have 3 or more drinks of beer, liquor or wine almost every day. | 2 |
| I have tooth or mouth problems that make it hard for me to eat. | 2 |
| I don't always have enough money to buy the food I need. | 4 |
| I eat alone most of the time. | 1 |
| I take 3 or more different prescribed or over-the-counter drugs a day. | 1 |
| Without wanting to, I have lost or gained 10 pounds in the last 6 months. | 2 |
| I am not always physically able to shop, cook and/or feed myself. | 2 |
| TOTAL | |

Total your nutritional score. If it's:

1-2      Good! Recheck your nutritional score in 6 months.

3-5      You are at moderate nutritional risk. See what can be done to improve your eating habits and lifestyle. Your office on aging, senior nutrition program, senior citizens center, or health department can help. Recheck your nutritional score in 3 months.

6 or more   You are at high nutritional risk. Bring this checklist the next time you see your doctor, dietitian, or other qualified health or social service professional. Talk with them about any problems you may have. Ask for help to improve your nutritional health.

*Source*: Reprinted with kind permission of the Nutrition Screening Initiative, a project of the American Academy of Family Physicians, The American Dietetic Association, and the National Council on the Aging, Inc., and funded in part by a grant from Ross Laboratories, a division of Abbott Laboratories.

TABLE 4.4   Katz Index of Activities of Daily Living

1. Bathing (sponge, shower, or tub):
   I* Receives no assistance (gets in and out of tub if that is usual means of bathing)
   A Receives assistance in bathing only one part of the body (such as the back or a leg)
   D Receives assistance in bathing more than one part of the body (or not bathed)

2. Dressing:
   I Gets clothes and gets completely dressed without assistance
   A Gets clothes and gets dressed without assistance except in tying shoes
   D Receives assistance in getting clothes or in getting dressed or stays partly or completely undressed

3. Toileting:
   I Goes to "toilet room," cleans self, and arranges clothes without assistance (may use object for support such as cane, walker, or wheelchair and may manage night bedpan or commode, emptying it in the morning)
   A Receives assistance in going to "toilet room" or in cleansing self or in arranging clothes after elimination or in use of night bedpan or commode
   D Doesn't go to room termed "toilet" for the elimination process

4. Transfer:
   I Moves in and out of bed as well as in and out of chair without assistance (may be using object for support such as cane or walker)
   A Moves in and out of bed or chair with assistance
   D Doesn't get out of bed

5. Continence:
   I Controls urination and bowel movement completely by self
   A Has occasional "accidents"
   D Supervision helps keep urine or bowel control; catheter is used, or is incontinent

6. Feeding:
   I Feeds self without assistance
   A Feeds self except for getting assistance in cutting meat or buttering bread
   D Receives assistance in feeding or is fed partly or completely by using tubes or intravenous fluids

*Abbreviations: I = Independent A = Assistance D = Dependent

Source: Adapted with kind permission from the *Journal of the American Medical Association*. Katz, S., Ford, A., Moskowitz, R., Jackson, B., & Joffe, M. Studies of illness in the aged, pp. 94–99, Copyright 1963, September 21. American Medical Association.

ties and must be investigated for long-term planning. Sometimes a psychotic condition must be determined before other assessments are made. Decisions about guardianships and institutional eligibility, difficult when there are multiple problems, are facilitated by assessment. Initial assessments also help to document progress, change, or deterioration.

Psychological assessments are made from examination; from a list of symptoms, behaviors, or changes; and from using measurement tools such as unstructured mental status exams, self-questionnaires, observer ratings, and other formal psychological tests. Assessments of normal and abnormal states include personality functioning, cognition, and affective states.

## Personality Functioning Assessments

Older peoples' personalities and mental health status reveal life-long patterns of decision-making, personal living style, and reaction to stress, and they are often assessed in conjunction with qualities such as adaptation, morale, and life satisfaction. Personality disorders (inflexible and maladaptive traits that cause significant impairment in social or occupational functioning or subjective distress) are detected in instruments such as the Minnesota Multiphasic Personality Inventory (MMPI) and in clinical observations based on DSM IV criteria. Prevailing through life, these disorders are not as acute in old age.

## Cognitive Functioning Assessments

*Clinical assessments* are used for cognitive conditions that include primary degenerative dementia of the Alzheimer's type, multi-infarct dementia, and other organized syndromes or disorders to assess impairments in orientation, memory, comprehension, calculation, learning capacity, and judgment. Also investigated are shallowness or lability of affect, lowered ethical standards, exaggeration of personality traits, and lessened capacity for independent decision. After reversible conditions are ruled out, such a person should have physical, neurological, and psychiatric evaluations. Lab tests include computerized tomography, electroencephalography, and studies of spinal fluid, blood, and metabolism. Conclusions are weighed with the medical history, mental status, and course of illness. A true diagnosis of Alzheimer's disease, many believe, is made only at autopsy.

*Intelligence tests* were mostly developed for youths and younger adults and are not always suitable for the elderly. Still, the short form of the Wechsler Adults Intelligence Scale (WAIS) is often used with appropriate older adults. Because orientation and memory are important to most geriatric assessments, quicker, shorter forms have been developed. They are used to identify the need for more complete assessment.

The MMS: The Mini-Mental State Examination, designed by Folstein, Folstein, and McHugh (1975), covers memory, orientation, attention, ability to name and follow verbal and written directions, writing a sentence spontaneously, and copying figures. A perfect score is 30; 21 or less is seen in patients with dementia, schizophrenia, delirium, or affective disorders. Its oral or written 5– 10-minute administration is simple, and it allows for on-the-spot scoring. Its validity and reliability are considered high with elderly persons, but it depends on good tester–taker rapport (see Table 4.5).

The Oars Short Portable Mental Status Questionnaire (SPMSQ; Duke University, 1978) is considered a universally useful community-based assessment tool. It is reliable, simple to administer, and has available norms.

## Affective Functioning Assessments

*Affect* (an immediately expressed and observed emotion) and *mood* (a pervasive, sustained emotion) become flatter in old age and are difficult to assess in the elderly. Even more difficult to assess is full-fledged *depression* (a gloomy mood state with profound affective disturbances which include lethargy, psychosomatic complaints, sleep, appetite and sexual disorders, feelings of worthlessness, hopelessness and helplessness, crying jags, and suicidal thoughts). The DSM IV criteria has many subclassifications that do not always relate to elders' depressions. Unfortunately, despair and discouragement about some very real aspects of aging may be regarded as "normal" affect and therefore not treated (Blazer, 1980). Irritability and other unsubstantiated somatic complaints may be overlooked in the diagnosis of depression also.

A few assessment instruments encompass a Gero-Chi Model and are used for depression (Doherty, Baird, & Becker, 1987; Engel, 1977). Other popular scales that measure depression in the elderly can be found in the literature (Beck, 1967; Kasniak & Allender, 1985;

TABLE 4.5   The Mini-Mental State

Maximum Score

ORIENTATION

5 (   )   What is the (year) (season) (day) (month)?

5 (   )   Where are we (state) (county) (town) (hospital) (floor)?

REGISTRATION

5 (   )   Name 3 objects: one second to say each. Then ask the patient all 3 after you have said them. Give 1 point for each answer. Then repeat them until he learns all 3. Count trials and record.
(   ) Trials

ATTENTION AND CALCULATION

5 (   )   Serial 7's. 1 point for each correct. Stop after 5 answers. Alternatively spell "world" backwards.

RECALL

3 (   )   Ask for the 3 objects repeated above. Give 1 point for each correct.

LANGUAGE

9 (   )   Name a pencil, and watch (2 points).
Repeat the following: "No ifs, ands, or buts." (1 point)
Follow a 3-stage command:
"Take a paper in your right hand, fold it in half, and put it on the floor." (3 points)
Read and obey the following:
Close your eyes. (1 point)
Write a sentence. (1 point)
Copy design. (1 point)

(   )   TOTAL SCORE
Assess level of consciousness along a continuum.

| Alert | Drowsy | Stupor | Coma |

*Source*: From the *Journal of Psychiatric Research, 12*. Folstein, M. F., Folstein, S. E, & McHugh, P. R. 'Mini-Mental State,' a practical method for grading the cognitive state of patients for the clinician, 189–198, © 1975. Used with kind permission from Pergamon Press, Ltd., Headington Hill Hall, Oxford OX3 OBW, UK.

and Hamilton, 1967). The Geriatric Depression Scale (Yesavage et al., 1983), shown below, is the only one to date that considers elders' somatic complaints (see Table 4.6). Gerocounselors should also be able to differentiate between normal bereavement and clinical depression. The following is an adaptation from Wolfelt, 1988 (Table 4.7).

TABLE 4.6  Geriatric Depression Scale

| | |
|---|---|
| Name _____ | d. o. b. _____ |
| Date _____ Interviewer _____ | Score _____ |

Score 1 for CAPS - 0 for lower case

Score (1 / 0)

| | |
|---|---|
| 1. Are you basically satisfied with your life? | yes / NO |
| 2. Have you dropped many of your activities and interests? | YES / no |
| 3. Do you feel that your life is empty? | YES / no |
| 4. Do you often get bored? | YES / no |
| 5. Are you hopeful about the future? | yes / NO |
| 6. Are you bothered by thoughts that you can't get out of your head? | YES / no |
| 7. Are you in good spirits most of the time? | yes / NO |
| 8. Are you afraid that something bad is going to happen to you? | YES / no |
| 9. Do you feel happy most of the time? | yes / NO |
| 10. Do you often feel helpless? | YES / no |
| 11. Do you often get restless and fidgety? | YES / no |
| 12. Do you prefer to stay at home rather than going out and doing new things? | YES / no |
| 13. Do you frequently worry about the future? | YES / no |
| 14. Do you feel you have more problems with memory than most? | YES/ no |
| 15. Do you think it is wonderful to be alive now? | yes / NO |
| 16. Do you often feel downhearted and blue? | YES / no |
| 17. Do you feel pretty worthless the way you are now? | YES / no |
| 18. Do you worry a lot about the past? | YES / no |
| 19. Do you find life very exciting? | yes / NO |
| 20. Is it hard for you to get started on new projects? | YES / no |
| 21. Do you feel full of energy? | yes / NO |
| 22. Do you feel that your situation is hopeless? | YES / no |
| 23. Do you think that most people are better off than you are? | YES / no |
| 24. Do you frequently get upset over little things? | YES / no |
| 25. Do you frequently feel like crying? | YES / no |
| 26. Do you have trouble concentrating? | YES / no |
| 27. Do you enjoy getting up in the morning? | yes / NO |
| 28. Do you prefer to avoid social gatherings? | YES / no |
| 29. Is it easy for you to make decisions? | yes / NO |
| 30. Is your mind as clear as it used to be? | yes / NO |

Scoring: 15 items—5 or more—probable depression
          30 items—0 to 10—normal
          11 or more—probable depression

*Source*: From the *Journal of Psychiatric Research 17*, Yesavage, J. A., Brink, T. L., Rose, T. L., Lum, O., Huang, V., Adey, M., & Leirer, V. Development of a geriatric depression screening scale: A preliminary report, 37–49, © 1983. Used with kind permission from Elsevier Science Ltd., The Boulevard, Langford Lane, Kidlington OX5 1GB, UK.

TABLE 4.7  Bereavement versus Depression

| Normal Grief Person | Clinical Depression Person |
| --- | --- |
| Responds to comfort, support | Does not accept support |
| Is often openly angry | Is irritable but does not express anger |
| Can relate grief to loss | Does not relate mood to life event |
| Displays sadness and feeling of emptiness | Projects hopelessness and emptiness |
| Has transient physical complaints | Has chronic physical complaints |
| Has guilt concerning some specifics | Has generalized guilt |
| Has temporary loss of self-esteem | Has self-esteem loss of great duration |
| Experiences cognitive impairment | Experiences cognitive impairment |
| Needs support, time, a chance to grieve | Needs referral for meds, psychotherapy |

*Source*: Adapted from Wolfelt, A. D., *Death and Grief: A Guide for Clergy* © 1988. Reprinted with the kind permission of Accelerated Development, Inc. Publishers, Muncie, IN.

### Suicidal Intent Assessments

Talk or threats of suicide are symptoms that must be viewed seriously. MacDonald and Haney (1988) listed 14 indicators of suicide, but, briefly, if there are verbal indicators of suicide and if there are no immediate supports who can ensure the client's safety, then you must get help. Alert the family, a psychiatrist, a clinical psychologist, or an emergency agency (police/paramedics) about the immediate need for protective hospitalization. Suicidal indicators are verbal expressions of

1. Feelings of the hopelessness of one's life,
2. Feelings of helplessness of the person,
3. Resolution of problems through death,
4. A specific suicidal plan, and/or
5. No specifiable concrete reason to NOT attempt suicide.

## Assessing the Sociological System

Three kinds of assessments are helpful when considering clients' sociological systems: social support assessments, family assessments, and environmental assessments.

## Social Support Assessments

In social support assessments, Biegel et al. (1984) suggested investigations of strengths (kinds of services provided to meet the older person's daily needs and quality of life), weaknesses (unmet needs), and potential weaknesses (e.g., the future geographic move of a support person, undue stress on caregiver). They devised a circular diagram which can be used for this purpose. Others use the Area Agencies on Aging support inventory form or the Katz ADL (1963).

Following is a Simple Support System Assessment (Figure 4.4) form which can be a record of important persons to contact (with permission or in an emergency) in your elder's network. It can be used for assessment and goal-setting.

## Family Assessments

A clear assessment of the family system is critical in gerocounseling. A family usually consults a counselor about a member's problem. The family's goal is for continued homeostasis (internal stability), and the problem has disrupted the stability. After clarifying the problem and gaining some resolution and return of stability, the counselor may shift the focus away from the individual (called "identified patient" or IP) and on to the family system. That is because the family counselor often conceptualizes the problem as a family system event and not only an individual one. Assessment of several family system components (structure, communication, coping styles and behavioral styles) as healthy or dysfunctional is ongoing during this process.

*Family structure* includes membership, boundaries, and hierarchies.

*Family membership* becomes evident as you plan the first family session. Sometimes non-kin will be included because they perform family-like roles. You may encounter some opposition to the inclusion of certain family members. This may make your goal of trying to include everyone more difficult, but such information gives you data about who is in and who is out. At the first session, the family genogram will contribute a wealth of information as will your question to each one, "What do you think is the

NAME —————————————— D.O.B. —————— DATE —————

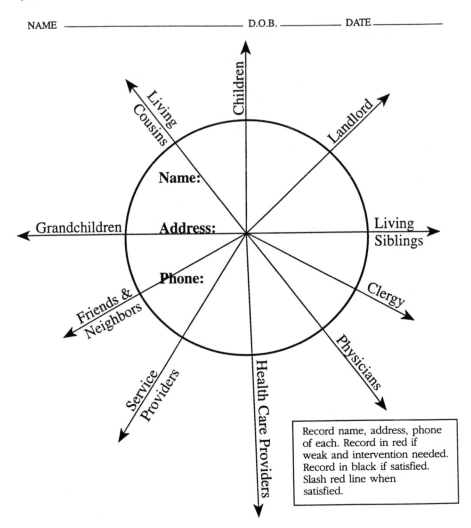

FIGURE 4.4  Simple support system assessment.

problem that needs to be resolved in regard to . . . ?" Each answer clarifies the problem and gives you a glimpse of external boundaries and the internal hierarchy.

*Family boundaries* (Figure 4.5) identify a family and have invisible gates that let you in or lock you out. They range from a surname, a defined geographic locale, an ancestry, or admittance to family secrets. Some boundaries are transgenerational; others may have emerged only recently. Three major forms emerge from external boundaries: the family with permeable boundaries, the enmeshed family, and the disengaged family.

1. *Functional families* have permeable boundaries; that is, they allow spaces (open gates) in their external boundaries that provide for both closeness and individuation. Family members and others are free to come in and go out of the system, thus keeping the system alive.
2. *Enmeshed families* have impermeable boundaries. Members are, in effect, too close. New energy cannot come into or go from the system to keep it going, and eventually such a system is subject to destruction.
3. *Disengaged families* are those with weak or no external boundaries. They are merely a set of individuals sharing a domicile and/or maybe a last name, but they have few cohesive factors keeping them together.

*Family hierarchies* (Figure 4.5) are internal boundaries. Functional families have clearly defined intergenerational boundaries in appropriate hierarchies. Above is the grandparents' system—not because they rule the roost, but because they came first, and, it is hoped, they are deserving of this respect. Next comes the parents' system and, lastly, the children's system. In late-life families, there will be several grandchildren's systems, lengthening the hierarchy considerably. They are important to note because often a grandchild is a valuable support to the grandparent.

A family may become dysfunctional when a generational boundary is violated. Adult children may disrespectfully begin to "parent their parent," thus depriving each of potentially satisfying roles. Or, a grandparent may cross a generational boundary and become parent to the grandchild, thus denying parents and child of their normal rights, and robbing the child of a usual grandparent relationship.

*Family communication patterns* are also important in family assessment. (Chapter 2 discussed good communication skills in detail.) Not only are there one-on-one communications between you and each family member to keep track of, but there are interactive patterns in the system at large, too. In family sessions, one must become aware of communicating with an invisible entity: the system, which is more than the sum of its parts. Communicat-

**BOUNDARIES**

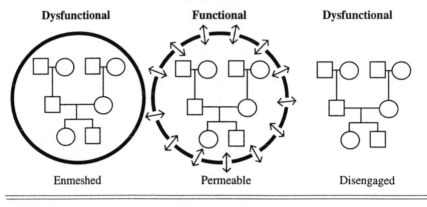

| Dysfunctional | Functional | Dysfunctional |
|---|---|---|
| Enmeshed | Permeable | Disengaged |

**FUNCTIONAL GENERATIONAL HIERARCHY & FAMILY BOUNDARY**

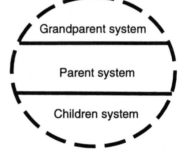

Clearly-defined hierarchy with permeable boundary

**DYSFUNCTIONAL GENERATIONAL HIERARCHIES**

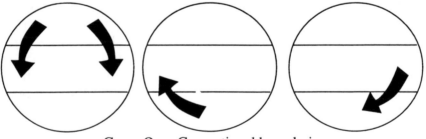

Cross-Over Generational boundaries

FIGURE 4.5    Family boundaries and hierarchies.

ing on a systems level is the most powerful and, many believe, the only method of communication that works in such situations.

Family rules (overt or covert) govern family communications, and they can make or break your counseling goals. You should be asking yourself during the process questions like: Who speaks for whom? Who speaks through whom? Who is silent? and Who is verbose? Your answers tell you about the power, control, intimacy, problem-solving skills, and other characteristics of each family system as it struggles to maintain its homeostasis. The answers also tell you how to access the system in order to be effective within its boundaries.

A word of caution. Do not take all communication at face value. Sometimes the unsaid is more significant than the said. Does the member speak only of the past and not the present or future? Are subjects avoided? Also, do not be deceived about verbosity and power. Sometimes the most silent member (or "weak" one in tears) exercises the most control. A family's good naturedness may be evidence of a covert rule that says, "Everything will be pleasant at all times in the family." This precludes acceptance and solution of any problem. And do not be deceived about a member's ready acceptance of "blame"; such an approach may be no more than a device to end discussion of the subject.

Family therapists use various instruments to assess communication in relationships. Initially, such tools assessed the first level of communication, those patterns readily discernible. These tools are used in conjoint counseling to enhance relationships. Lately, family therapists are studying deeper transactional levels which are beyond the scope of this book.

*Family coping styles* affect a family's problem-solving abilities and how you will be able to intervene with proffered solutions. Family coping styles do not lend themselves to easy assessment. In an article for the journal, *The Counseling Psychologist*, Sterns, Weis, and Perkins (1984) adapted five levels of human functioning into a model for family assessment of late-life families. They are mastery, coping, striving, inertia, and panic levels of functioning. Please refer to Chapter 8 for a summary of each of these levels.

*Family behavioral styles* have been identified and labeled differently by the many schools of family therapy. They are usually called the functional marriage and/or family style, the overadequate/underadequate marriage and/or family style, the conflictual marriage and/or family style, and the pseudomutual marriage and/or family style. Their titles are self-explanatory.

---

**THOUGHT–DISCUSSION QUESTIONS**
Apply the family therapy theories discussed above to late-life families. When is one likely to see generational cross-over? Is this good? Bad? Why are permeable external boundaries and clear distinct generational-hierarchial boundaries in the best interest of the adult children and/or the grandchildren? Can you think of times when they would not be in the elder's or family's best interests?

---

## Environmental Assessments

Good gero-assessment includes an evaluation of the client's environment. A home visit is essential, as you will want to know if it is sanitary, safe, secure, and accessible. Are there hazardous conditions because of your client's physical or mental disabilities? Other factors besides the external environment that are important to consider include internal layout, safety, and comfort.

The *external environment* is very important to safety and well-being. Is the neighborhood safe with respect to crime and security? Is the housing accessible to transportation or otherwise accessible to mail, shopping, medical services, and social contacts? Are there sidewalks? Is parking available near the housing? Are supportive neighbors nearby?

The *internal layout* is critical. What indoor space does the elder occupy most of the day? Is it readily accessible to food, toileting, telephone, a life alert system, or another adult? Can the elder reach other parts of the dwelling (on his/her own, with a walker, with a wheelchair)? Are stairs too steep or too long? Can the elderly person exit the place easily and alone in an emergency?

*Safety* is another assessment issue. Are devices like smoke detectors, fire extinguishers, or life alert systems available, in working order, and appropriate to the person's condition? Is lighting sufficient for an elderly person with weakened vision? Do the doorbell and telephone ring loudly enough? Are there enough electri-cal outlets? If extension cords are used, are they well-insulated and laid out? Does the cook stove have safety mechanisms if needed?

Are floor coverings safe (no throw rugs, ripped carpets, slippery tiles, threatening thresholds)? Are there grip bars at the bath, shower, toilet? What about possible climatic extremes and the temperature needs of older persons? Are heating and cooling systems adequate (temperature at 70 to 75 degrees with cross ventilation and heater ventilation)? Is an inadequate heater or oven used for added warmth?

*Home comforts,* in evidence, will give you some inkling of the elder's quality of life. Is there a place for privacy and comfort? For socialization? Are taken-for-granted appliances such as radio, television, microwave, telephone available? Are favorite pictures, artifacts, and personal furniture in evidence?

If your environmental assessment rates low but the older person desires to remain at home, your next question will be, "Is it possible to make the home adaptable, accessible, affordable, and therefore acceptable?" References on improving an older person's environment can be obtained from the National Institute on Aging (NIA), the American Association of Retired Persons (AARP), The Older Women's League (OWL), and your local Area Agency on Aging. Remnet (1989) provides experiential approaches to learning about assessing the environments of elders.

---

**EXERCISE**

Create an environmental assessment schedule. Use it when you make a home visit to an elder whom you know. How can you help this older person create a supportive home environment that will provide optimum bio-psycho-social functioning? Or, think about some of the elders' homes you have visited. How did these homes stack up to the points listed above? Are there also other factors about the external environment to take into consideration.

---

This chapter has discussed various areas of an older person's life that the gerocounselor may be called upon to assess. Examples of assessments were presented as an introductory overview. The question was raised, "Does the gerocounselor have to know and assess everything?" The answer, of course, was no. You will devise an assessment plan that is adapted to your particular service, remembering that a small change in one part will evoke changes in all other parts.

---

**THOUGHT–DISCUSSION QUESTION**

What particular assessment areas and tools discussed in this chapter apply to the work you do with elder persons and their families?

---

# Chapter 5

# *Gerocounseling Goals*

Both you and your client will have goals in the counseling process. Though you must strive to keep them in sync, you will, of course, be influenced by your own inherent goals concerning ethics, relationship, and communication principles and what you consider good mental health to be. Your gerocounseling goals will also be based on your psychological orientation in regard to aging and your beliefs regarding how (and if) elders and their families can change.

As stated, Freud was pessimistic about the psychoanalytic treatment of older persons because he believed that they were incapable of change. Through most of the 20th century, gerocounseling adopted versions of Freud's negative determinism (which assumed that the more advanced the age, the more unlikely a person is to respond well to therapy), and, for the most part, limited its treatment goals to offering support and concrete services, seldom opting to work for "change."

Despite this, as early as 1925, Jelliffe wrote that the age of the neurosis was more important than the age of the patient. He and others devoted considerable time to treating older patients based on the belief that elders could indeed benefit from psychotherapy. Butler et al. (1991) wrote that while Freud saw only younger patients, Jung's practice was two-thirds middle- and old-aged persons. Today there is more acceptance of the fact that older persons can learn, take charge, and change. The goal of such counseling has been called empowerment (Waters & Goodman, 1990).

Your initial goal in gerocounseling is to get to know your elder client and the client's unique views and values, attitudes, coping procedures, thinking and learning styles, and also feelings about self and others. They may be quite different from yours.

Naturally, the first thing that you will ask your new client or family is, "How can I be of help to you?" Their answer will initiate the goal-setting in process. Listen to it carefully. It will probably need refining as you work together, but their initial statement tells you why the client or family are there and what they want from you.

You may see a dozen other problems begging to be solved, but remember that that probably reflects *your* priorities. It is important to sort out right away what is yours—in terms of values and professional know-how—and what is the client's. The client's goal, if appropriate, is the important one and should determine the counseling direction. You will begin working on establishing goals together directly after the problem has been clarified. Again, this does not happen in a linear progression. Goal-setting begins immediately at the first encounter.

## General Principles of Goal-Setting

Counseling is a circular, goal-focused process, with the goal the result of planned steps. Good goal-setting has many therapeutic values. It clarifies why counseling is taking place, it helps the individual and family agree and sort out the plan for attaining the goals, and it validates your estimation of the clients' resources and strengths.

## Goals of Goals

Goals, as informal contracts, help to define the limits and limitations of the gerocounseling. Defining clearly what is to be expected from the counseling helps to prevent unrealistic expectations, fantasies, and future problems for both client and counselor. These limits also indicate that there will be an end to the counseling. It is always helpful to have an agreed-upon task and time limit; it makes for much less stress on both sides when termination time comes.

Goals can also be yardsticks for the measurement of progress. Even partial success adds to feelings of empowerment, control, and self-esteem. Its opposite can lead to feelings of failure if the goal was set too high. When a realistic goal is not attained, it may be diagnostically significant as an indication of ambivalence, lack of motivation, or faulty assessment, and that needs to be examined. Finally, goal-setting and measurement can give evidence of the counseling's effectiveness and aid in future program planning.

## Types of Goals

Goals may be short-term (to solve a current situational problem) or long-term (to effect a significant change such as recovery from illness, a personality adjustment, or a personal growth and fulfillment). Goal-setting also frequently involves efforts to harmonize the problems with individual clients' goals, family goals, and/or society's goals.

There are distinct differences in the ways that goals are developed and used by counselors. Chapter 1 discussed some of the counseling orientations—psychodynamic, humanist, family systems, and other styles—and showed how various approaches can be used. Many counselors, for example, make assessments as outlined in the second half of Chapter 4, which is in keeping with the medical model and is necessary for third-party reimbursement. In this situation, the assessment results in a diagnosis made by the "expert" counselor who determines the goals and direction of the counseling. The diagnosis is the important part. The goals are often a reversal of the diagnosis (to become un-depressed, for instance), and they are usually achieved through the removal of symptoms and uncovering causes through insight, trying new behaviors, relationship therapy, and/or medication. It can be a lengthy process, and the amount of reimbursement depends on how "sick" the patient is and how grandiose the goals.

A second counseling model, the *brief therapy school*, is primarily goal-focused. Here, you help your client, the "voluntary consumer," the expert, to define and decide what is wanted from the counseling. This is planned to take only one to six sessions. It is a get-in-and-get-out process, solution achieved. Usually there is no diagnosis made; diagnosis is considered a limiting handicap that gets consumer and counselor "off track" from the goal of achieving a defined solution. Many brief counselors do not even use the term "problem-solving" because that focuses on and reinforces the problem and not the solution. The new brief therapies were designed because their creators believe that the approach of working with limited, short-term goals is more effective and relevant to the needs of clients and the times.

The mechanics of short-term, pragmatic goal-setting are discussed below. Following will be a discussion of long-term goals and their philosophical underpinnings. You may want to consider both viewpoints in your goal-setting objectives.

## *Short-Term Goals*

Chapter Two's section on active questioning explored some solution-focused, brief therapy ideas applicable to gerocounseling. You may also incorporate some of this model's goal-setting techniques into more traditional frameworks.

Butler et al. (1991) wrote that life was not static, but more like a movie in process. Walter and Peller (1992) used a similar analogy: "We like to think that the therapy process is similar to creating a movie" (p. 51). The therapist helps the client direct and act in the client's own cinema. They used the movie metaphor to establish their six criteria for well-defined goals, as seen in Table 5.1.

### Defining a Positive Goal

Walter and Peller (1992) suggest that you express a goal in positive terms and with respect to what the client hopes to be doing or thinking (instead of not doing or thinking). This gives the client a mental image of the desired goal which is then rehearsed. (It is virtually impossible to imagine or rehearse not doing or feeling something.) Moreover, stating a solution negatively keeps the focus on the problem instead of on the solution and leads to rehearsing what is to be stopped rather than what is to be done.

For example, Arthur, our golfer, is coached by the pro to say, "I will keep my head down and concentrate on the ball before I hit it," instead of, "I will not raise my head before I hit the ball." Carol, in trying to get Arthur to spend less time on the golf course, will be coached to say, "I will practice being happy and busy when Arthur comes in from golf," instead of, "I will not nag Arthur when he comes in from his golf game."

TABLE 5.1  Criteria for a Well-Defined Goal Worksheet

| Criteria | Key Words | Sample Questions |
|---|---|---|
| 1. In the positive | "Instead" | "What will you be doing instead?" |
| 2. In a process form | "How" "-ing" | "How will you be doing this?" |
| 3. In the here-and-now | "On track" | "As you leave here today, and you are on track, what will you be doing differently or saying differently to yourself?" |
| 4. As specific as possible | "Specifically" | "How specifically will you be doing this?" |
| 5. In the client's control | "You" | What will you be doing when that happens?" |
| 6. In the client's language | Use the client's words | |

*Source*: From J. Walter & J. Peller, *Becoming solution-focused in brief therapy*, p. 60. © 1992. Used with kind permission from Brunner/Mazel, Inc., 19 Union Square West, New York, NY, 10003, and the authors.

## Using a Process Form

When the client sticks to a negative version, Walter and Peller (1992) suggest that the client can be coached with the word "how" to evoke *ing* gerunds and to indicate that it is a process. The pro asks Arthur, "How will you improve your swing?" Arthur is encouraged to reply, "I will be keep*ing* my head down." Carol will be coached to say, "I will be keep*ing* busy."

> **THOUGHT–DISCUSSION EXERCISE**
> Turn to the case examples at the end of Chapter 2. Assume that you know enough of the facts. Help each client formulate a beginning goal that is positively defined as discussed above. Then try it using a process form.

## Staying in the Present

Express goals in the present tense because the future is too remote and out of one's control. The present tense puts the solution immediately into play. Walter and Peller (1992) suggest coaching with the question, "If you are to be 'on track' for getting this accomplished *now*, what would you be doing?"

Janet Fergusen, for example, told Hilda, her home health aide, that she wanted to make a decision about remaining in her house or moving to a condo. Hilda suggested that Janet start toward making that decision immediately. What should she be doing *now* about it? Janet said that she would be calling the realtor today for information. Alicia Perez told Mary, her support group leader, that most of her anxiety was due to her insecurities about monthly bills. She knew that she needed a budget. Mary advised Alicia to get to it pronto; how could she start *now*? Alicia said she would be calling the budget counselor at Family Service today for an appointment.

---

**THOUGHT–DISCUSSION EXERCISE**

Turn to the case examples at the end of Chapter 2. Assume that you know enough of the facts. Help each client formulate a beginning goal that is in the present tense as described above.

---

## Being Specific

Be direct in helping the client speak in behavioral instead of vague feeling terms. As stated, we don't know what others mean by "feeling good," and the like. Carol Brown said, "I just want to be happier." The counselor helped her reframe that to, "I will feel happier by doing one nice thing for myself each day and smiling more." When Mabel Petsky said, "I don't remember anymore," Mary helped her rephrase that to, "I will be paying more attention when I meet someone so I remember more about him."

---

**THOUGHT–DISCUSSION EXERCISE**

Turn to the case examples at the end of Chapter 2. Assume that you know enough of the facts. Help each client formulate a beginning goal that is specific.

---

## Staying Within the Client's Control

Setting goals too high or overestimating a client's ability to change can spell failure and a loss of self-esteem. Herr and Weakland (1979) suggest that a counselor help the client narrow goals to achievable proportions.

Instead of asking oneself, "What will I need to change in my life so that all my problems are solved?" the client is coached to ask instead, "What is the smallest amount of change that could occur in my life that would give me a sense of progress in solving this major problem?" Butler et al. (1991) warned, ". . . in the emotional or psychological domain, we recognize that 'cure' is a continuing and never fully completed process" (p. 412).

Avoid making your goals too ambitious. As gerocounselors, you do not have to change values, psychopathology, or character disorders. Instead, by helping clients deal more effectively with specific problems that confront them, you will be lessening the pathology. There will also be times when the situation will not change, as in cases of death, divorce, or a medical diagnosis. In those instances, your goal will be to help the person to learn new coping skills, to lessen the sense of defeatism, and to accept the fact that some relief is better than none.

There is an old saying, "We can't change other people, we can only change ourselves." Often clients will complain about others and wish to change them. Carol Brown's goal, for instance, was to get Arthur to be more attentive. This was reworked to, "I will start doing something nice for Arthur every time he is around . . . starting today." (Who knows, by changing herself, maybe Arthur will change too, and want to stay around more.)

Sometimes such relationship goals may involve the client and counselor. Juan, case manager, was frustrated with his client, Meg, who negated every suggestion that he made. His goal was to change her attitude, and he finally argued with her. As you recall, Meg fired Juan as her case manager. He might have been more successful if he had asked himself how he could change his approach with Meg to make her less resistant. If he had reframed and validated her anger and saw it as a means of maintaining control and independence, he might have improved their rapport.

---

**THOUGHT–DISCUSSION EXERCISE**

Turn to the case examples at the end of Chapter 2. Assume that you know enough facts. Help each client formulate a beginning goal that is within the client's control.

## Using the Client's Language

In our zeal to help, we run the risk of imposing our standards on our clients. One way to avoid this is to write down exactly what the client or family say they want. Sometimes a flip chart is useful for this as you then rework the goal to everyone's agreement and in their own language.

> The Lee family haggled over their goals. Amy Lee, the daughter, wanted her father to "concentrate on the positive aspects of his stroke recovery instead of crying all the time." Lijun Lee, the wife, wanted the counselor to help Mr. Lee "act happier and be his old self." Wen Fu Lee wanted his family to stop nagging him and appreciate how hard he worked and how hard this was for him. Joan, the counselor, helped them first to acknowledge "how hard this was" for all and complimented them on "how hard they all had been working." She suggested that their first goal could be to start learning more about Mr. Lee's stroke process and depression so that he will begin to concentrate more on the positive aspects, that is, to be more like his old self, and so Mr. Lee will, in turn, feel more understood and less nagged.

Sometimes it helps to describe the problem and the goal in a client's personal, unique metaphor. For example, if you are talking to a nurse, you might want to use medical terms to summarize the situation. "Your emotional thermometer has informed you that your relationship with your mother has become unwell and you are trying to find 'medicine' to make it healthy again. What specifically do you mean by a 'healthy relationship'?" Or, you might use mechanical terms with a blue-collar worker and his family, "It is obvious, as you say, that the four generations of your family are not meshing at the present time, despite all your good tinkering. What can we do in terms of oiling the nuts and bolts, changing the gears, or giving the machine some added gas, to get it working again?" Or, you might use golfing terms with Arthur Brown.

---

**THOUGHT–DISCUSSION EXERCISE**

Again, turn to the case examples at the end of Chapter 2. Assume that you know enough facts. Help each client formulate a beginning goal using the client's own language insofar as possible as discussed above.

---

Ideally, your final goal should be acceptable, attainable, and affordable to all. Some believe that it is important to accomplish the goal-setting at the first session, but with elderly clients who have much history and information to relate, you may only be able to set a tentative goal. Sometimes, the first goal will be to get more information for assessment and final goal-setting. At the end of the final goal-setting, it is important to go over the problem statement and your mutual decisions about long- and short-term goals. While you may have several goals, it is wise to begin with one short, simple one, explaining that you will just be spinning your wheels if you attempt to do everything at once.

## Long-Term Goals

Today, most counselors who do long-term counseling do set goals, but the goals are often more global and less specific and mutually agreed upon than the Walter–Peller goals. A problem is that sometimes the psychotherapy goals (and their success) may be viewed quite differently by the client, the society, and the counselor.

## The Client's Goals

If "goaling" may be said to be the focus of some brief therapy schools, "goallessness" may be seen as the aim of some psychoanalytic long-term work. Wolberg (1977), in addressing the differences, cited therapists on both sides of the fence—those who relied on goals for good psychotherapy and those who didn't. He believed that most psychotherapy goals were for the modification of the person's goals because improvement in mental functioning and adjustment to reality called for the lowering of one's expectations to more modest goals. Also, complete, idealistic goals for cures in a sick society cannot exist. Probably the most that a patient could get from therapy, he wrote, was relief from anxiety, inferiority feelings and other destructive elements, and the ability to cope with life's difficulties.

Many people go to counseling for symptomatic relief, but this as a goal may be harmful. Giving up a symptom may mean relinquishing some vital aspect of the personality, may exacerbate certain neurotic drives, or may result in substitute symptoms of a more serious nature. At other times, a client's goal may be to develop certain traits that will come closer to an ideal that is unrealistic. Or the client may come asking for help in learning how to tolerate what you believe is an extremely destructive life situation for him or her. Or a client may want to patch up a marriage that was over many years ago. In any of these cases, when such goals are unmet, the client may view the counseling as unsuccessful and blame the counselor.

## Society's Goals

Family members or others in society may have their own goals for your client's gerocounseling, too. When that occurs, it is wise to hold such goals suspect. We have cited many illustrations of this throughout the book. Arthur Brown, for example, wanted the group counseling to change Carol. The Lee family wanted the counselor to help Mr. Lee change his attitude and be his old self again, and so on. At the end of this chapter, you will read about Dr. Woo, a physician who, desiring the best for his father, wants the counselor to help him convince his father to give up traditional Chinese medicine.

Sometimes such goal differences interfere with the ethic of autonomy, with a person's religious or cultural preferences, or even with the person's mental health. Each goal in conflict raises the questions: Who is the client? and Where does the counselor's fidelity belong?

Such decisions become sticky when the question boils down to whether the group (e.g., family goal) or the individual goal should predominate, or whether the goal of the young should have preference over the goal of the old. Examples are when the elder wants to move in with the family but other family members do not want this to happen, or when as a nation we must decide if money should be spent on measles shots for the children or life-extending procedures for the very old. Mediation, compromise, reframing, appealing to fairness, and win-win efforts are recommended, but, when they do not work, the decisions are always hard to make and never perfect. At such stressful times, all the gerocounselor can do is to empower the client and family with the best information available and then point out alternatives and consequences so that they can come to (and live with) a decision themselves.

# The Gerocounselor's Goals

As a gerocounselor, you, too, will have a set of goals. Often they will relate to concepts of normality and what constitutes good mental health for older people and what is normal behavior for a functional family. Sometimes the goals may be influenced by your own value system and countertransference as discussed earlier.

Your global gerocounseling goals will evolve from your general knowledge about older persons: how they age, how they change, what you think they need, and how you think they can be helped. As the Walter–Peller goal techniques can be used for short- or long-term counseling, some of the following global goals apply to both as well.

## Goals of Aging

Each developmental stage has its own prescribed tasks to accomplish, and aging is no exception. Tobin (1988) saw the goal of aging as "preservation of the self" and Erikson (1950) said it was to gain a sense of integrity, instead of despair, about one's life that would lead to wisdom. Ebersole (1990) used Maslow's hierarchy of needs to develop goals for aging clients. There are other more practical tasks to accomplish as one journeys from young-old, to old, to old-old. Several of the most important are discussed below. (See also, Figure 4.2.)

**Supports.** The client's efficient utilization of medical, social, and emotional supports is a task that you will be assessing as you compile information. Have needed medical tests been completed? If not, why not? Is this something that can be facilitated through referral or will more counseling be necessary around the issues of obtaining sound medical advice? Are denial, ignorance, fear, financial concerns, cultural or religious reasons, or the unavailability of services prohibiting the access of services? These various prohibiting circumstances may call for education, reassurance, referral, granting autonomy, or your advocacy.

Necessary social supports may not be in place because the client does not know that they are needed, that they could be helpful, that he/she is eligible for them, or that funding is available for them. Members of some ethnic groups feel shameful or suspicious about seeking help outside the family. One of the gerocounselor's functions is to be a resource person, dispensing such information, making referrals, and following through to see that it succeeded if possible. This might be considered the gerocounselor's first (and only) goal.

The goal of finding and using needed emotional supports may be more long-term and require individual, family, or group counseling. Or, it may just involve referral to a group or information about the closest senior center. Sometimes the gerocounselor temporarily becomes the client's only emotional support, but in such cases the building of an outside support network should then be an underlying goal.

***Adjustment.*** Adjustment to decreasing physical strength and declining health is often another developmental task or goal. Each age change results in ripple effects that create new losses: When Anna became seriously arthritic, she could no longer "walk off" her problems. And, as her eyesight diminished, she had to give up her needlework, a favorite activity (see Chapter 8). Similarly, when Mr. Smith's advanced diabetes resulted in a leg amputation, the consequences were enormous.

Each change, each loss (and its ripple effects) call for adjustment, accommodation, and some kind of acceptance or assertion if one is to maintain emotional health and optimum self-care. Often it is the gerocounselor's goal to help with these tasks.

***Living conditions.*** The maintenance of satisfactory living arrangements is another task of aging that you might convert into a goal. You will need to know about the various levels of care and housing options in your community and eligibility criteria for each. But that is only the beginning.

The second part of that challenge is creating the "fit" between your clients' needs and their means. What are your client's abilities, needs, and desires? How can you create that fit in accord with the principles of environmental press? (See Chapter 7.) After a Gero-Chi assessment that also includes a financial inventory, you will, it is hoped, be able to find a fit between existing available facilities and your client's needs. (However, this is not always the case.)

The next most important question is "What does your client desire?" What is your client's goal now? Such goal resolution does not come easy. Whether it is trying to decide about giving up one's family home or having to decide on a nursing home, relocation, when you are old, is never easy. There will be tugs from every side. Even when the move represents an upward step, such as moving out of a high-crime area or leaving a white-elephant house, the move is liable to be traumatic. Sometimes it involves giving away (or putting to sleep) a beloved pet, and always it means the scaling down and giving up treasured belongings. Ambivalence, indecision, and regression can be expected. And you, the gerocounselor, may be asked to provide information and support and to assist in resolving some of these sentimental and practical issues. Many free, helpful publications are available.

*Responsibilities.* Assumption of a new pattern of community responsibilities is another task/goal. It appears often in early retirement years when there are role and identity substitutions to make. It can also appear with declining health when the elder can no longer participate in meaningful activities. Helping the client to find new ways to contribute, to feel productive, to value self, and to keep in touch with the world may be your treatment goal then.

*Relationships.* Revision of relationships with grown children, relatives, and the community is a goal that resembles the above goal of responsibilities. The point has been made that healthy families need to maintain and respect traditional family hierarchies; that is, adult children are not supposed to parent their parents (as some of the literature suggests). Help families to maintain this stratum of need and respect. If the problem is the reverse (the grandparents usurping the parental role of the parents), your goal may be to mediate there.

At other times, it may be the gerocounselor's goal to help the frail elder make attitudinal changes that will allow for more dependence on family and others. We mistakenly over-stress independence in our society and elder network. Older persons can be helped to see that independence is an adolescent goal and that maturity requires *interdependence*. We need to be able to take as well as to give. The NASW poster in my office reads, "Return the Gift of Caring." A goal can be to help older persons graciously allow others to give back to them at this time of need. The other side of this coin is that it may be a time for elders to find novel ways of continuing to give (storytelling, family history, love and support, money, etc.).

***Loss.*** Adjustment to loss of significant others will be a frequent goal in your gerocounseling. It will be discussed in Chapters 8 and 9.

***Retirement concerns.*** Coping with retirement and financial changes encompasses such tasks/goals as forging new identities, creating pleasurable use of leisure time, restructuring schedules, finding new meanings, developing new social skills and relationships, making marital readjustments, and dealing with newly found loneliness.

The financial woes of retirement range from concerns about whether the Dow rose or dropped today to whether one should spend one's remaining money on food or medicine. Many retired clients seek help on decisions about a second or third "career," or what to do when one finds new health problems rendering impossible a part-time job that was to provide a necessary income supplement to Social Security.

***Life control.*** The maintenance of assertive control of life runs through all of the above goals. It can be achieved by empowering the client with information, by pointing out options and alternatives, by letting the client make the decisions, by teaching assertiveness skills, by suggesting that the client lobby and advocate for his/her own concerns, and by listening attentively to what the client is saying.

## Tobin's Goal for Aging

Sometimes "life control" means helping the staff and family accept the older person's anger as real and legitimate—maybe even therapeutic. Tobin (1988) reported that "nasty folks," among the old, fare better at surviving stress. "Elderly persons who are non-passive and mobilized tend not to blame themselves for unavoidable losses, thus avoiding depression. . . . Aggressiveness, therefore, is a way to cope with stress . . ." (p. 552). Also important, he wrote, is the enhancement of magical coping, that is, the inflating of a patient's belief in his/her own mastery of current problems and thereby not accepting present limitations and/or disability. Preserving the self amidst the countless losses of self being endured is therefore the task or goal of the very old. "Do not go gentle into that good night."

This is a common gerocounseling issue. Recently, a physician consulted me about his aged mother who complained bitterly in his nightly phone calls to her. It gave him a sense of helplessness, intense guilt feelings, and stomach pain. Because his mother had serious medical problems and he was the responsible son, she needed an opportunity to complain to him before she could be positive. He was, in fact, playing out an important role. I suggested that he see this not as a rescue mission he could not accomplish but as a gift to his mother because she knew he would listen intelligently. He agreed to make a deal with her: he would listen to her complaints if she would end each talk on a positive note. Reframing the goal helped him feel less helpless and more positive.

## Erikson's Goal for Aging

During the process of assessment, you may have placed your client at various achievement levels on Erikson's psycho-social task schema. As no person succeeds 100 percent at any stage, by the time the elder becomes your client, his/her psycho-social outcomes could be anywhere within a range of 64 boxes (Kivnick, 1993). Your client may score high on trust, middle-high on fidelity, but low on will. Using Kivnick's schema, if your client, Charles Jones, was too meek with his overly controlling daughters, your goal for him might be increased assertiveness (will).

At Elmbrook Senior Home, John noted that Sam Rybaka, a retired landscape artist, was having a problem fitting into the group. When Sam told John that he never felt he belonged anywhere, John set the development of fidelity as a goal in his informal counseling with him. He encouraged Sam to take over the planning of a new garden for the east wing. Such an intervention soon helped Sam to identify with and feel more at home at Elmbrook. Mary used the Erikson–Kivnick psycho-social life theme schedule as part of her reminiscence work with her group. Members identified some of their strengths (and deficits) and set some appropriate goals accordingly.

## Ebersole's Goal for Aging

Chapter 4 discussed the Ebersole and Hess (1990) adaptation of Maslow's hierarchy of needs to an assessment schema. Relating the clients' problems and symptoms to the Maslovian needs hierarchy, Ebersole then converted them to goals which in turn led to interventions. Let us look at two examples.

Martha, a retired teacher and Annie Mae's patient on One West, had problems with the dull routine of the nursing home. She soon developed symptoms of apathy, rigidity, boredom, and ennui. "What Martha needs," Annie told the activity director, "are some opportunities for self-expression, new situations, and some all-around stimulation." The goal? Self-actualization. The interventions? The Activity Department involved Martha in some creative pursuits (such as starting a nursing home newsletter) where she could write, learn new things, and teach others.

Sam had problems with losses all his life. The son of an army colonel, Sam's childhood consisted of a move to a new army base every two years. Faithfulness (or fidelity) to a place was not high on Sam's list. Also, when he gave up his home to move to Elmbrook, it reminded him of earlier displacements and he again felt alienated and lonely. John recognized Sam's need for some group affiliation but also a need for a sense of his "own territory." The goal? Fidelity through a feeling of belonging. The intervention? John put Sam in charge of something he could contribute to the facility.

---

### THOUGHT–DISCUSSION EXERCISE
Devise some gerocounseling goals (based on the various underlying goals described in the last section) for the clients described at the end of Chapter 2. (Assume that you know all the facts.)

---

## Family Therapy Goals

As the tasks of aging are converted into goals, the tasks of family life also can become underlying goals for family counselors. These classical goals are the continuation of the species, socialization of the children, provision of emotional support of the members, acquisition of and sharing goods for survival, adjustment to retirement, provision of physical care for the elderly, and attendance to death. When any of these are in conflict (e.g., if the socialization of the children is in conflict with the provision of physical care for the elderly), the counselor's goal is to help the family reframe goal priorities and to develop appropriate strategies.

A basic goal of family counseling is to replace dysfunctional relationships among members with healthier forms of relating and problem-solving. Sometimes a goal may be to alter boundaries, change hierarchy, probe the keeping of secrets, or expose catastrophic expectations that are hindering family members' abilities to love—and to fight fairly.

In some families, necessary goals are balancing the needs for independence and dependence, separation and individuation, closeness and autonomy. Improved communication, enhanced intimacy, and the successful management of conflict are also common, appropriate goals in family counseling. All the family goals mentioned are relevant to counseling late-life families. Dealing with losses, role changes, and generational differences are especially so. Sometimes there are even cultural conflicts within the very same family.

Robert Woo came to California from Northern China to attend medical school in 1967. In his last year of a radiology residency, he married a fellow student. The couple was able to find promising jobs, gain citizenship, and settle in the Bay area. There, they enjoyed a comfortable life style, raised two sons, and made significant contributions in their respective areas of medical research.

The Woos visited their families in China every other year except during the Cultural Revolution when travel was unsafe for them.

Dr. Woo's father, Herman Woo, a retired chemical worker, lived in Hanchow with his wife in a small, plain apartment in a senior housing settlement designated for retired government workers. They enjoyed playing croquet, mah-jongg, and Chinese checkers at the Senior Center and visiting with friends and family. Occasionally they would take the train to West Lake or to Shanghai. Life was simple and comfortable but not as luxurious as their doctor son's life in America.

Dr. Woo thought about this contrast often with much regret, especially during the Cultural Revolution when freedom was curtailed. There was a ten-year period during which his parents were unable to see and enjoy their grandsons. He worried about their comfort and safety.

In 1993, Dr. Woo learned that his father had developed lung cancer, the very area of his own research. Coming from a family of heavy smokers, he was not surprised to hear of his father's fate. He also knew that as a retired government worker, Mr. Woo would be getting some of the best medical care in China, but he feared that his parents leaned more toward Eastern traditional medical regimes and did not always blend the two. "That was all right for headaches," Dr. Woo told himself, "but not for cancer."

After pulling many strings and much coaxing of his parents (he used the grandchildren as the convincing point), Dr. Woo was able to bring his parents to California. They settled in the Berkeley area close to the Woo residence and the hospital. Mr. Woo was set up for an oncology appointment during the very first week.

But the Woos were not happy in their new home. Language and other cultural ways inhibited them from connecting with their neighbors; they thought that the Chinese Societies were too "clannish." Mrs. Woo had expected to see a lot of her grandsons but learned that American grandchildren were not as attentive as those in China. Although they tried to be as considerate as possible, the Drs. Woo were busy with their practices and the two grandsons were busy with school and activities. The senior Woos smiled appreciatively at their American family, but Dr. Woo knew there was much unhappiness beneath the smiles.

Dr. Woo consulted their priest, Father Casey, for help. Despite his Irish background, Father Casey spoke several Chinese dialects and helped many Chinese immigrants assimilate in the U.S. He made frequent home visits to the Woos. He noted Mr. Woo's gradual weight loss and the couple's social isolation. He was able to help Mrs. Woo join a Chinese Woman's Society, and she slowly began to make new friends.

Mr. Woo refused to participate. His world seemed to be absorbed in the medical center where he was having radiation therapy. But Father Casey noticed that he was just mechanically involved and that Mr. Woo expressed little faith in its success. Still, he was grateful for all that his son was doing for him.

Father Casey worked hard to get Mr. Woo to broaden his world beyond the confines of the apartment and the hospital. Although he brought in Communion, he tried to get Mr. Woo to attend Mass. But he was unsuccessful at everything that he tried. Dr. Woo and the sons took some time off to take Mr. Woo fishing, but it was of too short a duration. Dr. Martin, the oncologist, finally prescribed an antidepressant medication which helped with appetite and sleep.

In March, Mr. Woo seemed to experience an incredible psychiatric recovery. His mood state improved and he began to visit Chinatown almost daily. He joined a Chinese Society and had a new lift to his walk. Dr. Woo and his wife were relieved. They loved the father and were worried that they had made a mistake in bringing him away from all he had known. The doctors could now go back to their heavy research schedules with the realization that Dr. Woo's parents were happy and safe.

In the fall, Dr. Woo received a call from his father's oncologist. Breaking an ethical principle because they were colleagues, Dr. Martin related that Mr. Woo's cancer had advanced. Mr. Woo had told him that he had discontinued his cancer medication last spring. Dr. Martin suspected that Mr. Woo had gone back to practicing Chinese herbal medicine for his cancer cure.

Dr. Woo was shocked. Untrue to his culture and character, he angrily confronted his father. Here, he had provided his parents with every possible American comfort and the best medical help in the world. How could his father do that to him? Mr. Woo fell silent, humiliated that his son would address him in such a manner. He had given up everything in China to do this for his son.

Father Casey was called in again. He said that he felt like the Pacific Ocean between the East and the West. He could not achieve a reconciliation or even compromise between the two diverse mindsets. Frustrated and feeling that he had failed, he finally referred them to a Catholic Social Service Agency in the Chinese section of San Francisco that was staffed with Chinese-American counselors. Elizabeth Li was assigned to the case.

Certainly important general cultural themes prevail in this case. These themes probably could also be found in a Puerto Rican family in New York City, a Hispanic family in Dallas, or a Native American family in Arizona.

---

**THOUGHT–DISCUSSION QUESTIONS**
What seem to be the goals of each actor in the above scenario? Why aren't they in sync? What factors influenced the goal-setting of each individual? How can the goals be reconciled to what is called a practical goal (or goals)? What do you think Elizabeth Li's goals will be?

---

## Attainable Goals

Some clients, because of damaging early life experiences, have so much psychopathology that they are incapable of much or any change. Other clients, due to organic intellectual deficits, will require limited goals, too. Sometimes a person cannot escape from negative circumstances, and you will not want to help that person alter neurotic defenses that are the very coping mechanisms his/her situation requires. Sometimes the problems of aging are such that neurotic defenses may be saving graces.

There are other clients who lack the incentive for change or do not have sufficient ego strengths to bring it about. Others lack sufficient time or money for extended counseling. Often the amount of insurance coverage will help to determine your goals. Wolberg (1977) defined a practical goal as "the achievement by the patient of optimal functioning within the limitations of his financial circumstances, his existing motivations, his ego resources, and the reality situation" (p. 749). Maintaining a balance between dealing with that reality and still striving for excellence is delicate, tricky, and, often, necessary.

---

**THOUGHT–DISCUSSION QUESTIONS**
Think of some of the older persons you have known or with whom you have worked. What were some of your goals with them? After reading this chapter, would you revise any of those earlier goals? How? Why?

---

## Goal Grading

As you work together with your clients, you will be assessing your goals often. This is done subjectively from the client's self-reports or from statements from the family, physician, and others. Appearance, body language, and voice quality can also help you assess progress. As mentioned, the couple who is now sitting together on the same sofa is indirectly reporting that their relationship is improved. It is very important to record and ask about the specified goal each meeting. Clients are proud of their accomplishments and want to share them with you. You can utilize behavior modification by rewarding the success or good efforts with your attention.

The Goal Attainment Scale (Kiresuk & Sherman, 1968) is a flexible scale that facilitates goal setting by guiding the establishment of goals, pointing out obstacles, clarifying tasks, focusing on one goal at a time, and indicating probable outcomes of intervention. It credits partial success and fits a multidisciplinary team approach.

Working under the medical model, my own clinic (Southeastern Wisconsin Medical and Social Services) has an efficient treatment plan/contract that is developed at intake. It gives attention to the formation of treatment goals that correspond with the diagnosis and to the creation of objective/measurable outcome criteria for these goals. It concludes with the patient's signature which indicates agreement to participate in the goals of the treatment plan (see Figure 5.1). What are some of the behaviorally specific goals and

**OUTPATIENT TREATMENT PLAN**
❑ INITIAL ❑ UPDATED

\*\* All Items Must Be Completed and Legible \*\* Patient No.: _____

Intake Date: ___/___/___   Insurance Name: _____  ❑ HMO ❑ Commercial ❑ HMO/T-19 ❑ PPO ❑ Other

Patient Name: (Last) _____ (First) _____ (MI) _____ Male ❑ Female ❑ DOB: ___/___/___

**CLINICAL EVALUATION/RISK ASSESSMENT**
Suicide Potential Assessed ❑ Present ❑ Absent ❑
Homicide Potential Assessed ❑ Present ❑ Absent ❑
Substance Abuse Assessment: Indicated ❑ Not Indicated ❑
Psychiatric Evaluation Date: _____
Medication: _____
Prescribing Physician: _____
**CURRENT SYMPTOMS (SUBSTANTIATING A DIAGNOSIS)**
_____
_____
_____
_____

**CURRENT DISABILITY**

❑ Mental Health

❑ Alcohol/Drug

**TREATMENT HISTORY (for updates only)**
Outpatient ❑        Dates: _____

Number of Sessions to Date: _____

Inpatient ❑        Dates: _____

| PROGRESS TO DATE: | |
|---|---|
| Regressed | ❑ |
| None | ❑ |
| Improving | ❑ |
| Achieved | ❑ |

| **PRIMARY DIAGNOSIS** | **SECONDARY DIAGNOSIS** |
|---|---|

DSM III-R AXES: I. _____    I. _____
II. _____    _____
III. _____    _____
IV. _____    _____
V.(CURRENT)_____ (PAST YEAR)_____    _____

**A. TREATMENT GOALS (to reflect DSM III-R symptoms)** | **B. OBJECTIVE/MEASURABLE OUTCOME CRITERIA**

1. _____   1. _____
2. _____   2. _____
3. _____   3. _____
4. _____   4. _____
5. _____   5. _____
6. _____   6. _____
7. _____   7. _____

| MODALITY OF TREATMENT | NO. OF SESSIONS/HRS. | MH/AODA | | FREQUENCY #/MONTH | PROVIDER NAME/DISCIPLINE | TOTAL COST ESTIMATE |
|---|---|---|---|---|---|---|
| Intake/Evaluation | | | | | | $ |
| Individual Psychotherapy | | | | | | $ |
| Couple/Family Psychotherapy | | | | | | $ |
| Group Psychotherapy | | | | | | $ |
| Psychiatric Assessment/Evaluation | | | | | | $ |
| Medication Management | | | | | | $ |
| Other | | | | | | $ |
| Psychological Testing | | | | | | $ |
| Day Treatment | | | | | | $ |
| Drinking Check-Up | | | | | | $ |
| TOTALS | | | | | | $ |

I agree to participate in the above treatment plan with the staff of Southeastern Wisconsin Medical and Social Services, Inc., or their authorized provider. I certify that I have been given copies of patient rights and patient information brochure.

_____  Date:___/___/___
(Patient's Signature/Guardian if patient is a minor)

Provider Signature: _____  Date:___/___/___

FIGURE 5.1   Southeastern Wisconsin Medical & Social Services, Inc., Outpatient Treatment Plan.

*Source*: From Southeastern Wisconsin Medical & Social Services, Inc. form, © 1994. Reprinted with kind permission from Southeastern Wisconsin Medical and Social Services, 10335 W. Oklahoma Avenue, Milwaukee, Wisconsin 53227.

objective measurable outcome criteria one is liable to find in such a treatment plan? Examples may be

## Goal and Outcome Criteria

GOAL: Improved socialization patterns
CRITERIA: Attending social functions once per week

GOAL: Controlled anxiety
CRITERIA: Participating in desired activities (with no disruptions or avoidance) for 2 weeks

GOAL: Improved emotional control
CRITERIA: Substituting socially acceptable behavior (e.g., exercise) to displace temper and other disruptive displays for 2 weeks

GOAL: Improved self-esteem
CRITERIA: Rating self 7 or above on Self-Esteem Scale of 1–10.

GOAL: Altered alcohol-related dysfunctional behavior
CRITERIA: Attending 3 AA meetings per week; calling sponsor or friend when cravings occur

GOAL: Improved sleep
CRITERIA: Sleeping restfully 6–8 hours per night for 2 weeks

GOAL: Improved communication
CRITERIA: Using "I" messages with spouse for 2 weeks

GOAL: Improved medication compliance
CRITERIA: Taking medication as directed for 2 weeks

GOAL: Assertiveness
CRITERIA: Saying "no" (for 2 weeks) when a proposed activity or request is not desired

# Chapter 6

# Gerocounseling Modalities

When Joan gets a referral at the Counseling Center, she schedules individual and/or family sessions and seeks out (with written permission) necessary information from collateral sources. Together with her clients, she is establishing a therapeutic alliance, making the necessary assessments and establishing goals. Again, these functions are not in linear order but are interactive as in the Gero-Chi Counseling model. Also, despite the specific function of her agency, Joan is thinking about her client in the total Gero-Chi model.

Goal-setting leads her to consider interventions and to ask what counseling modalities will best fit this client and problem. If she has the professional luxury to choose, she will be considering one, two, or all of the basic counseling modalities, individual, conjoint, or group counseling.

## Individual Counseling

Although a family system approach is recommended for most gerocounseling, the actual bulk of the counseling is done individually. Goals of autonomy, independence, self-sufficiency, confidentiality, misguided expediency, and other aims often supersede goals of community and interdependence until the grave crisis of dependency occurs. This practice prevails among clients, families, and service providers. Joan sometimes had problems with the family emphasis, too. Although a trained family therapist, she often saw elders alone. Soon to be retired, she was in therapy herself to work on future goals of self-actualization, and she would have resented her counselor calling in family to assist with what she considered some individual issues.

Individual gerocounseling is defined as the one-on-one counseling of an individual older person.

Despite your preference and orientation, you will find yourself often seeing clients individually just as Joan does, and as she desires for herself personally. She has reconciled this by knowing that even when seeing a person alone, she is mindful of the invisible family system sitting there with them, and, to the best of her ability, she includes that system in her work.

Most early gero-mental health approaches were custodial; the mentally ill were tucked away in asylums, old people's homes, or mental hospitals, often far from the person's community and support systems. Institutionalization was attributed to breakdowns in the local systems. In the 1960s, a trend toward deinstitutionalization took place in the U.S. This return-to-the-community movement resulted in a problem of homelessness for many mentally ill elders (and others) and a rapid growth of nursing homes.

In 1975, a program of federal block grants to the states mandated community mental health centers (CMHCs) to supply a full range of diagnostic treatment, liaison, and follow-up services. Although current funding specifies the elderly as a priority group and also emphasizes preventive efforts, the elderly, and especially the minority elderly, continue to be an underserved clientele. In 1990, Medicare expanded mental health coverage and included social workers as providers, but the focus was still on inpatient and nursing home treatment.

Defenders of CMHCs and services point to the reluctance of older persons to use counseling, but the charge resembles a blame-the-victim defense. True, elders stay away because of generational attitudes, ethnic injunctions, economic realities, and misinformation about the goals and methods of counseling despite the many stressors of old age. But CMHCs do not allocate enough services to meet the needs of older adults, and creative programs to reach minorities have been minimal. Most counselors are untrained in gerontology—possibly because of the professionals' own fears and denials about aging as well as other forms of ageism. Perhaps gerocounseling was also slow in getting started because many still believe that older persons are incapable of change or are untreatable. There are others who believe that the elderly should not be set apart as a separate age group.

As with the life-span versus life-stage controversy about younger age groups, there is also debate regarding the discontinuity versus continuity theories of old age. *Life span* advocates do not separate the elderly from other age groups. Rather, they believe that one evolves throughout the life span and that old age is just the last chance for development. Others, *life stage* advocates, see the normative changes of aging as life transition processes. Using a life planning approach, the gerocounseling goal is to negotiate the transitions of aging before they become the crises of aging.

Individual gerocounseling in the private sector occurs in family service agencies, senior centers, religious organizations, hospitals and clinics, and other topic-specific settings such as employment agencies and volunteer organizations such as AARP. Some writers, pessimistic about drawing older persons to counseling, recommend that transition counseling be taught to specific helpers in the community such as beauticians, barbers, or retailers. Peer counseling programs, which were developed to offset fiscal cutbacks in mental health services, have also been found to be effective in many communities.

---

**THOUGHT–DISCUSSION QUESTIONS**

Be Joan. You are indecisive about your retirement planning, and the subject makes you depressed, anxious, or at other times pleasantly excited about your new life ahead. You've decided to see a counselor. Should you consult a gerocounselor or a life transition specialist? How might it matter? Are there times where you would want your son or daughter to be present in the counseling?

---

## *Family Gerocounseling*

When indicated and possible, a family approach is to be considered the treatment of choice for our elderly clients. The case of Arthur and Carol Brown is an example.

Arthur Brown was born in Russia in 1915 and immigrated to America at age two with his parents. He married Carol (who was born in Chicago in 1917) in 1935. They had two children, Joseph, born in 1936, and Susan, born in 1935. (See genogram on page 83.) Arthur enlisted in the Air Force in World War II to get into "some of the action," even though he had a deferment. On the surface, the Browns appeared to have a fairly functional marriage from outward appearances until their children hit the teen years.

Prior to this, Arthur devoted his time and attention to being a dynamo at work, a leader in community activities, and a star on the golf course. Carol was angry about Arthur's lack of attention to her and overcompensated in her role as mother. Setting up an alliance with the children, Dad was often "left out," which enabled him to distance himself even more from the family. Carol's role with the children vacillated between over-protection and displacement of the anger she felt toward Arthur. So the children grew up with ambivalence toward mother and a yearning for their absent though idealized father.

When the children reached adolescence, Carol was in midlife and menopause. The children were demanding emancipation: Susan, in arguments with her mother about teenage issues around drinking and sex, and Joseph in his under-achievement in school. In her senior year, Susan became pregnant, and the family entered into family counseling, a new form of counseling that included whole families.

In family counseling sessions, Carol pleaded for more help and attention from Arthur. He verbally agreed to this, but his old habits were set; he believed that Carol should attend to the internal matters of the family, and he frankly had come to find Carol boring and unexciting.

The family limped through various separation issues and events with the children (college, moving out, marriages, Joseph's divorce, etc.) and the years were especially stressful for Carol. Susan had three boys in three years, temporarily separated from Bill, and returned home, an alcoholic. Joseph went to the Korean War. Carol had many gastrointestinal complaints and after many medical tests and treatments was diagnosed depressive disorder with somatization.

Carol was referred to the Counseling Center in 1975 at age 58. For the next ten years, she saw a therapist on and off, tried several support groups, and was on both anti-anxiety and anti-depressant medications at various times. However, her list of medical symptoms grew and the marriage continued to be a source of disappointment to her. A goal of counseling was increased assertiveness, but this often came out as merely demanding and aggressive, turning her husband and children even further away from her.

When Arthur retired at age 65, Carol expected that he would have more time for her, but this was not the case. Additionally, because of her many physical problems and complaints, her friendships had dwindled and her children also were spending as little time as possible with her. When they did, they complained that she "laid a guilt trip" on them. Even the grandchildren did not enjoy their grandmother because she criticized their life styles. Carol could not cope with the antics of her great-grandchildren, either. As a result, they were kept from her, and Carol was quite socially and emotionally isolated.

At age 78, Carol fell into a major depression, attempted suicide, and was hospitalized. She was treated with psychological and drug therapies. The family was called in for counseling about depression, their mother's needs and treatment, and to do planning for her post-hospitalization.

The family counselor noted that there were many unresolved, long-standing issues still in operation which could maintain Carol's illness. Outpatient family therapy was recommended. Arthur also agreed to accompany Carol to the support group at the Senior Center.

There are many teaching points in the Brown case. It is a lengthy story because late-life families present a long history to learn, and three or four generations to know and to enlist in the proceedings. Unlike normal group counseling, families with their histories and group structures create a powerful, bonded system that is sometimes difficult for the gerocounselor to access.

As seen in the Brown case, family counseling and family therapy are different. In the hospital, the Browns participated in family counseling to help them mobilize their resources to assist in Carol's recovery. Such family gerocounseling included education, cognitive restructuring (by reframing and clarification), planning and networking resources and support. The counseling was focused on the here-and-now immediate planning. The family appeared to be at a striving level of functioning described by Sterns et al. (1984):

Families operating at the striving level have some control over long-term aspects of their environment and are attempting to gain more control. Although their behavior is planned and basically goal-oriented, they fail to deal effectively with the issues and problems in the family. The family is reluctant to face the reality of the situation and often employs delaying tactics in making needed decisions. The issues of aging often become detrimental to the functioning and interpersonal relationships in the family. There are periods of extreme emotional discomfort and, therefore, the tendency to move from crisis to crisis. (p. 58)

## The Family

A *family constellation* is a person-to-person, biologic or non-biologic mutual aid system that is intended to provide a variety of functions such as the provision of emotional support to its members and the assurance of economic and physical survival on a sustained basis. A healthy family is characterized by intimacy, commitment to the family, continuity and intensity of the relationships over time and throughout change.

A *family system* is a term that defines this critical unit operationally. As a constellation of persons, the Brown family is also seen as a single emotional unit with a life of its own. Like a mobile with interdependent units that interact together to constitute a separate whole, each person's behaviors and reactions affect the others and create the system. (What Arthur does affects and influences Carol; what Carol feels and says affects Susan, which affects Joseph and Arthur, etc.)

The Brown family interactions are an endless series of chain reactions, and causality is circular. Therefore, there is seldom one cause to a problem but rather a ripple pattern of behaviors that maintains the systemic events. One may say that Carol had a dysthymic personality since childhood (from genetic and familial influences), but if she hadn't married Arthur, who displayed indifference to her, and if the course of Susan's life had gone more smoothly, and Joseph had not gone to war, for example, Carol's problems may have been less severe.

## Family Therapy

Family therapy is a psychotherapeutic technique that attempts to shift the pathogenic relating among family members so that new forms of relating become possible. The supportive or intensive psychotherapy session is usually attended by multiple family members based on a belief in the relationship between symptoms of the identified patient and family interaction and the belief that the family is the most powerful influence in any person's life. It is considered an efficient and effective method as it strives to enlist cooperation of those in the family system and to prevent sabotage by any of its members.

Let us hypothesize about the Browns. Perhaps one of the secondary gains that Susan receives from her current stress is, finally, some attention from her idealized father. As the family therapist works to strengthen the bond between Carol and Arthur, Susan's condition may worsen in an unconscious attempt to maintain her new inroads with Arthur. The therapist, aware of such dynamics, may encourage Arthur and Carol to work together as a co-parent system to assist Susan, and also move to aid Susan, through referral, to strengthen her marriage and to develop a peer support system of her own. In this, the therapist's goal is to strengthen the generational boundaries which, in turn, will satisfy some of Carol's needs and be a more satisfactory solution to Susan in the long run.

### *History of Family Therapy*

The family therapy movement (FM), as we know it, seems to have surfaced at mid-century because of certain issues in society, academe, and the mental health professions that led to the formation of its underlying concept. That concept held—and holds—that family relationships (systems) are as important to the personalities, behaviors, and experiences of people as are their intrapsychic events. This concept has been embraced in the theories, research, and therapies of multidisciplinary groups.

In 1957, many new ideas were shared at the Orthopsychiatry national conference and elsewhere. This was a revolutionary time as the new ideas were in conflict with the accepted and sacred principle of transference in psychotherapy. This principle ruled that the inclusion of relatives contaminated therapy and the practice was not allowed.

Competing schools of family therapy were soon established, and the new theory made its way across the seas, creating new schools in Europe and elsewhere. Soon they began to share their novel ideas with the Americans. Basic cybernetics and systems principles prevailed, and the different schools seemed only to be tipping the kaleidoscope at slightly different angles. In the 1980s, newer schools (problem-oriented, solution-focused, brief family therapy, etc.) emerged, building on former models and accommodating the demands of contemporary society. Today conjoint work for educational, supportive, and therapeutic treatment is an accepted and recommended practice among most disciplines, particularly gerocounseling.

## Managing Problems in Families

Most of the family counseling you will be doing will be informational, supportive, or for the purpose of solving practical problems and making decisions about long-term care. The goal of the therapy with the Browns was to discourage their dysfunctional patterns of relating so that the family could more effectively work to solve Carol's illness. Although many families need an explanation of a systems' approach—and may even request that the "identified patient" be seen alone—usually you will find most families to be receptive to and appreciative of a family approach.

A word of caution. Most gerocounselors, as mentioned, are not equipped to do intensive family therapy and should not attempt it. You will, however, be working with families, and you will want to know about family systems, what constitutes a healthy family system, and when you will need to refer a family for more intensive help than you can offer.

Earlier, we defined a healthy family system as one with permeable external boundaries and an appropriate internal hierarchy. Such a system includes all those persons, kin or non-kin, who perform family roles and therefore, ideally, all are included in the family therapy sessions. Usually it is advisable to hold the meeting on the older person's own turf, the counselor's office, or some neutral place. This is especially wise if there is a crossing of generational boundaries or pronounced sibling rivalry. Such settings and planning demonstrate a respect for the family hierarchy. If there are family conflicts, do not meet at the home of one of the adversaries. It is also preferable for you or the elder to do the actual inviting, for similar reasons.

In addition to boundaries and hierarchy, you will be looking at overt and covert family rules that influence the problem and its resolution. Often covert rules are based on catastrophic expectations and, when surfaced and examined, can be modified. The gerocounselor may ask, "What's the worst thing that could happen if . . ." By facing the "worst," the family or person often sees its improbability or that, even if it occurred, it could be handled without the sky falling down. Examples of some other covert rules in late-life families might be: "We can't talk to Grandma about Grandpa in the nursing home because it may make her sad." Or, "We don't discuss death in our family even though Dad is dying and seems to want to talk about it." Or, "Grandpa has a bad heart and we shouldn't confront him about anything even though his fly is always open and it is embarrassing to his twelve-year-old granddaughter."

Healthy families must know how to love and to fight, but the ability to do this can be blocked by catastrophic expectations. Some families are afraid to show love because of the catastrophic expectations of rejection. Carol's family labeled her a "complainer," and in her desire not to be rejected as a nag, she began to internalize her legitimate complaints about her husband's negligence. Such suppression of anger could have been a contributor to its early displacement onto her children and her later major depression. Likewise, as angry as the family would get about Susan's drinking, they fell into co-dependent roles, fearing any confrontation would make her drink more or become suicidal. Such catastrophic expectations need to be analyzed and revised.

In other family counseling situations, family members are helped to find new ways of interacting with each other in order to increase autonomy while maintaining emotional closeness. This can be seen when a caregiver must relinquish some of the help (and control) exercised over a stroke patient in order to encourage more independence. The emergency of the stroke may have induced an overadequate/underadequate (or co-dependent) relationship system in which the sick person came to depend on the help given by the well one and the well one came to depend on the self-esteem (or power) of being necessary to the sick person. In such cases, as the sick person improves, the need for help diminishes and unnecessary help can be detrimental to recovery or demeaning to the patient. Likewise, as time evolves, the satisfying role of helper becomes a burden and the caregiver feels put upon.

Despite the negative consequences of this system, it is difficult to change once it has been established. The family therapist's goal will be to encourage the couple to exchange the dependence—independence imbalance for more long-term satisfaction of its members and to help them achieve closeness and autonomy in new ways. This is a common systems problem in late-life families.

### Dealing with Labeling in Families

Labeling also occurs. It can begin anytime—early in family formation—or even in previous generations. An example may be, "Men in our family are . . ." In late-life families, labeling can be associated with ageism and/or misinformation about the aging process. It can then become a self-fulfilling prophecy and create new problems. An example may be, "Old people are senile and forgetful. Grandmother is old and forgets; therefore we shall treat her as if she were senile." Ultimately, with such treatment, Grandmother responds in like manner.

## Triangulation in Families

Triangulation is the procedure whereby two people in a marital or family conflict gang up (triangulate) to scapegoat a third party. This is generally an attempt to displace feelings they have about each other on to a third party, thereby avoiding a catastrophic expectation.

> Susan and Bill are in conflict about sex, but are afraid to discuss it because they fear conflict will lead to divorce. They therefore displace that anger on their involuntary involvement in family therapy for Carol's problems. They scapegoat and triangulate Carol instead of dealing with the real issues between them.

Triangulation and scapegoating can be a cause of elder abuse as two family members, frustrated and angry about another circumstance, displace and take it out on an innocent though burdensome elder. Family gerocounselors are warned to be cautious about triangulation. Family members who are repressing anger about the increasing dependency of an elder may displace such anger onto the service provider and sabotage the service. It is important to recognize triangulation when it occurs so that it can be avoided, discussed, and handled.

## Issues in Late-Family Counseling

Although most older persons live alone, families are usually involved, if only through "intimacy at a distance," using mail and telephone to stay connected. Help to parents appears to be motivated by responsibility, keeping up appearances, duty, guilt, concern, and/or love. Daughters, programmed in caregiving roles, appear to be of more help than sons. Family conflicts may emerge from perceived imbalances in the sharing of responsibilities for elder care. Although a generation gap exists, generational conflict in late-life families appears to be low. Seven out of ten elders report helping their family members on a regular basis, indicating that an interdependence or reciprocity still exists in late-life families.

Many societal messages and practices contribute to ageism in families, such as unpaid work with no benefits for caregivers, false and unflattering media representations of older people, trivial conceptions of grandparenting, disdain of dependency, the overstressed value of independence, and the unrealistic expectation that once one's kids are grown, the midlifers will be free of responsibilities. Negative or ambivalent feelings and behaviors toward elders can result. Elder abuse and/or wishful or actual "granny dumping" in families is also seen. Many persons are unprepared for the burdens of yet another dependency as they find their older relatives living longer. If that relationship was not a healthy one in prior years, the consequences of imposed elder care are destined to be problematic. An empathic, non-blaming approach to all family members in these cases is critical to a successful outcome. Despite demographic and sociological changes, families continue to work on their classical themes and tasks and, when they are in conflict, the family in therapy is helped to establish priorities and new strategies.

---

### THOUGHT–DISCUSSION QUESTIONS

Grandfather, with early stage Alzheimer's, moved in with his adult son, Jim, and his family. Jim was critical of his father's behavior and forgetfulness and would blow up often, then feel guilty, then remorseful. A recovering alcoholic, Jim soon resumed drinking. In drunken states, he would verbally attack his teenage son, Mac, for various normal teen behaviors. Confused and angry, Mac began cutting classes when his homework was incomplete. Blue slips arrived from school and Jim yelled even more. Mother sided with Mac and began fighting with Jim. The couple could not resolve their conflict, and, finally, mother threatened to move out with Mac. She blamed and verbally abused grandfather for ruining the family. What is going on here? How would you, a family counselor, deal with these problems?

## *Group Gerocounseling*

Mary's senior support group meets at the Senior Center every Tuesday afternoon. This discussion will examine Mary's group in relation to other counseling groups. Different from the family, a group is a set of individuals, usually biologically unrelated, who assemble around a common need or interest. Group gerocounseling is a modality that uses the setting, structure and process of a group and is usually facilitated by a professional leader to achieve a therapeutic, educational, or social goal. Such groups are often conducted in hospitals, clinics, social service agencies, churches, senior centers, senior residences, or other places. They utilize principles from individual psychotherapy, group process, and gerontology.

## History of Group Counseling

Group counseling began as a historical necessity and opportunity. In England, during World War II, group therapy became popular in the military because the war created a concentration of psychiatric and family problems and also a concentration of psychiatric creative talents that developed new theories and methods to meet the emergency. It was slow to spread nevertheless. Butler et al. (1991) reported that Silver conducted group therapy (using a party mode—music, milk and cookies) with elderly dementia patients with severe memory and attention deficits in 1950. That same year, remotivation therapy was started by an English hospital volunteer. In 1967, large numbers of nurses and direct care personnel were trained in remotivation work in the U.S.

Despite such early efforts, the group counseling field initially paid little attention to the problems of the elderly. In the 1950s, a few group therapy programs and reality-orientation and reminiscence groups were offered. Most were conducted in institutions and with the frail elderly. Community-based groups have not been popular, probably because of privacy issues, but this is likely to change as new cohorts emerge. Senior center group utilization has been low except with the more gregarious elders. Most group gerocounseling is probably done by nurses for patient education.

## Goals and Values of Group Gerocounseling

While each member of Mary's Senior Center group has a particular goal and each gains differently from group participation, there are certain common characteristics that members share. They are all over 65, and they are discovering that many of the aspects of human aging they previously worried about are in fact normal. Such discoveries reassure them. Motivated to keep up and remain healthy, they are learning appropriate health maintenance measures. They are also learning new social skills.

Despite situational and personality differences, many share recent role changes, such as retirement, widowhood or relocation—with their attendant identity gaps. The elders are helping each other to replace losses and to conquer loneliness by forming new roles and gaining experience in relating to more than one person. The group, then, is like a laboratory where members learn and practice communication and relationship skills.

The group has learning and other curative benefits too. Arthur Brown is gradually accepting the idea that there is more than one way to look at an issue. It has made him more tolerant of his wife's problems. Group members also share information about resources. Mary introduced Mr. Smith to Meals-on-Wheels, and some women shared cooking-for-one tips. Carol Brown, burdened with self-centeredness and depression, is learning the value of altruism as she observes Marge Addams who seems to stay vibrant because of her service to others. With new information about aging and cognition, and learning that others have minor memory problems, Mabel is less anxious about her memory loss. Alicia Perez has more hope and optimism as she sees group members survive on comparable budgets. Sara Crimmings says that just talking about her burden gives her inspiration to "hang in there." Such inherent values of group counseling have been put in more technical terms by Yalom (1985) and others, but you see them in action in Mary's group. The overall goal is maintenance of or increased competence and self-esteem of each member.

## Types of Gerocounseling Groups

Counseling groups range from educationally oriented discussion groups for the general population to psychiatrically oriented therapy groups for mentally ill patients. Gerocounseling groups can be used for (a) socialization, education, and recreation, (b) service and advocacy, (c) support, (d) therapy, and (e) family and caregiver assistance.

## Social, Educational, Recreational Groups

These groups are formed for the enjoyment, stimulation, learning, growth and/or development of their members. The leader provides structure and facilitates programs that reflect the goals. Members bond through common interests and activities, and membership can be diverse except that participants should share a similar skill level. Communication is usually instrumental, verbal or nonverbal, and related to activities. There are two types in this category.

**Enrichment groups**. Enrichment or preventive mental health groups are used with seniors to provide informal discussions, new directions, knowledge about community resources, and a clarification of values.

**Topic specific groups.** Senior topic groups are growing in popularity. Some feature the arts or creative activities such as singing, music listening, or prose and poetry writing. Topic groups are also organized for patient information and support around a particular illness; others may treat topics of interest to elders like retirement and the like.

## Service Advocacy Groups

These group members unite to accomplish a task for the benefit of others. A coordinator or officer facilitates organization and action and the focus is on the task. Members are bonded by a sense of common purpose, and membership can be large and diverse.

## Support Groups

The growth of support groups is another gerocounseling trend. Here the goal and focus are to help members cope with shared stressful events. The leader facilitates mutual support and help, and members are bonded by their common problems such as medical problems or grief. Communication is highly interactive, open, and member-to-member.

## Therapy Groups

As therapy groups exist to help members change attitudes and behaviors and to rehabilitate themselves, the focus is on members' problems, concerns, and/or goals. Depending on their orientations, leaders are either authoritative or facilitative. While the membership can be homogeneous or diverse, group bonding is emphasized. Communication is leader-to-member, member-to-member, or both. This category includes some of the following types.

***Intensive psychotherapy groups.*** These groups are run by professionally trained therapists at or above the masters' level with additional training and supervision in group process. Although intensive group psychotherapy deals with subjects similar to group counseling, the approach has more depth. Unconscious processes are uncovered and changed for more effective functioning and control of affect.

***Remotivation therapy groups.*** This group method, used primarily in institutions, encourages communication and aims to stimulate mental processes about present and future events. Members are asked to describe themselves realistically and concretely and to avoid personal and family problems. A five-step procedure for remotivation therapy was sketched by Waters and Goodman (1990):

1. Establish an atmosphere of acceptance and rapport,
2. encourage a bridge to reality by having the members read articles aloud,
3. use visual props to discuss the world, and other topics,
4. discuss positive aspects of work and its relationship to their lives, and
5. conclude with an appreciation of positive group involvement and future planning.

***Reality orientation groups.*** These small educational groups, designed to increase overall functioning, provide support to disoriented, institutionalized persons and orient patients as to time, place, and other aspects of shared reality. They are led by trained nurses, counselors, and paraprofessionals. Caregivers are trained to reinforce group progress (Burnside, 1984).

*Reminiscence groups.* Reminiscence or life review groups are popular in both institutional and community settings. Based on Butler's life review theory (1974), and developed by Ebersole (1978), this activity involves a progressive return to consciousness of past experiences to help the elder survey, resolve, and integrate old conflicts. Butler saw it as a normal and universal process. Through the recall of memories, the older person can complete unfinished business. This can be a final stage of growth and a preparatory act toward the acceptance of death. Along with its cathartic values, reminiscence is a useful tool for bonding with others and raising self-esteem.

*Caregiver assistance groups.* These groups help families function in caregiver roles. The focus is on caregivers' needs, the care receiver, and the caregiving stressors. The leader acts as educator, supporter, enabler, and/or advocate. Members are often homogeneous in gender and function, and the mutual bonding is the caregiver role. Communication is member-to-member and leader-to-leader.

*Self-actualization groups.* Such groups combine nontraditional therapies (e.g., yoga, meditation, dream analysis) with traditional forms of peer support and group process.

## Techniques of Group Gerocounseling

Mary wanted to help her Senior Center members deal with aging issues through a support group. An organized person, she realized that a good group began with careful advance planning. She considered individual and group goals and reviewed the first part of this chapter. Then she had to decide on the type of group, recruitment and selection of members, style of leadership, use of group process, program planning, temporal limits, and termination.

### Goals

After subjectively assessing the needs of her center membership, Mary decided that the diverse members could profit from a group that offered enrichment through creative, social, and educational activities with emotional support. But she realized that that was her agenda. She knew that each group member would have his or her own need, and she must focus on each individually expressed goal. She also wanted to offer a safe place to express feelings, but she knew that the members initially would want an educational agenda. If she planned to respect autonomy (and keep them coming), she would have to put their goals first. Anyway, feelings were bound to come out.

Polling the group for goals, she learned about their diversities. Arthur Brown wanted new learning; Alicia Perez wanted to master her finances; Mabel wanted to become more assertive; Sara wanted support; Bill Smith wanted to make some life changes; and Marge just wanted to have a good time. Carol? Well, Carol had so many needs and ambivalences, she didn't know where to begin. The group decided her first goal would be goal definition.

### Membership

Mary read that an ideal group size was from six to eight members, but she took Bumagin and Hirn's (1990) advice to recruit twice as many in order to insure a constant viable number. Many say yes but don't come, drop out, miss sessions, or travel periodically. The group loses vitality and morale if too few attend. She sent out flyers and advertised in the newspaper and at the center.

Mary screened applicants in person to make sure that they were appropriate and could profit from the group. They were persons capable of interaction and with somewhat common concerns. She also looked for those who expressed a commitment to stay in the group. Her contract was that they were free to leave the group, if they so chose, but only after several sessions and a good-bye to the group. Mary was also prepared to guide out of the group (and into some other form of assistance) those persons who were cognitively impaired, aggressively hostile, or depressed and suicidal.

### Group Process

Mary wanted to be a facilitative leader but also a member of the group. By sharing some of her thoughts and feelings, she might role model the same for others. Still, she remembered that in group process, a group was usually dependent on a leader-expert at first. Then, as it gradually achieved competence and confidence, it eventually rejected the dependency on the leader and established its own identity and generated its own directions. So she decided to take a middle ground and to share personally only at special times.

As in individual counseling, Mary was careful to be clear and reach agreement about the group's goals. Next she asked, "What do we want to see in the group as a whole? How can we accomplish this at the next meeting?" To avoid personal confrontations, she asked members to concentrate on the group and not on individuals. To be on the safe side, she used a written questionnaire at first. As the group developed, she continued to be supportive but would confront at times and ask for group feedback to an individual's comment. While group feedback was less than honest at first, it became more open and helpful. Always she would point out their connections and commonalities and validate their feelings.

Because it was hard for Mary and the members to leave the individual approach and focus on group process, Mary had a few useful techniques. At the end of each session, she processed the group dynamics with questions about what members perceived happening in the group:

1. *Communication and interaction patterns.* (Were we lively today? Were we enjoying group?)
2. *Cohesion.* (Are we getting closer? Is everyone interacting?) On this, Mary was careful to gently discourage too much self-disclosure at first and to reduce conflict and competition early on.
3. *Social control mechanisms.* (Did we give everyone a chance to talk?) Mary and the group established group norms that were written out and read at the beginning of each group. (See the Group Meeting Agenda, Table 6.1.)
4. *The group environment.* (Are we safe and comfortable here?)

## Programs

Mary found an abundance of program ideas from a number of sources. She sent for *Age Pages*, an informative newsletter from the National Institute of Aging (NIA), and she found many valuable materials and videos from AARP. Other sources included Waters and Goodman (1990), and Jacobs (1987).

TABLE 6.1   Group Meeting Agenda

1. The group meets on Tuesdays promptly at 1:30–3:30 P.M. at the Senior Center, 935 Jones Avenue, Springfield. Mary Loomis, Facilitator (945-6234).

2. We begin with a stress management exercise.

3. We next read the group purpose:
   The purpose of this group is to provide consultation for its members through the skills of the counselor and group support of its members. This method includes stress management, setting goals, sharing concerns, feelings and support, new information, reminiscence, journal writing (at home), some spirituality, and some fun.

4. We read and keep the group rules each time:
   A. Everything that comes here stays here (confidentiality).
   B. Only one person talks at a time (good listening skills).
   C. Nothing said is scorned or made fun of (respect).
   D. We do homework assignments, call if we must miss, and we are on time (group responsibility).
   E. We set and try to keep goals (we help ourselves).
   F. We don't quit group unless a good-bye is said (we care about commitment, losses, and feelings).
   G. We welcome new members. We call the member who misses. (We care.)

5. Each time we introduce ourselves and say how we are feeling, how our goals are coming, and why. "Hello, I'm _____, and today I feel _____ (mad, sad, happy, afraid, hurt, ashamed) because _____. My goals are going to be: _____."

6. Next, we learn something new about a topic.

7. Next, we share reminiscence.

8. Next, we read the homework questions for our journals.

9. A group member shares a spiritual thought.

10. Next, we share our plans for the coming week, review for next time, and end with a bit of humor.

## Termination

Mary began talking about termination from the beginning, for she knew that most seniors were especially vulnerable to losses. A group rule was that if any members quit, they would say good-bye first. Since she structured the group in ten sessions (instead of having an open-ended format), she began each session saying, for example, "This is our second session. We have eight left." About midway through the sessions, she urged members to begin planning what they would do when group terminated. They unanimously voted to meet for breakfast once a week and to continue to support one another.

To ritualize the termination, a mock graduation was planned with diplomas that were both humorous and inspirational, and members brought in a potluck lunch. Each person read a goal for continued growth after the group ended. Mary, through her self-disclosure, helped to evoke group members' feelings of sadness about the termination, which they were able to express.

## Efficacy of Group Gerocounseling

Marodoyan and Weis (1981) wrote that group gerocounseling is superior to one-on-one counseling because it diffuses the generational gaps between counselor and counselee and "provides a unique opportunity to use the dynamic interaction of group members as a therapeutic tool." This interaction helps elders to find appropriate social roles for successful aging, encourages supportive sharing, promotes a healthy cohort effect, and helps clients renew social interaction skills when social support systems are weakest (p. 162).

My own personal experience with gerocounseling groups on an outpatient, private practice level is that while I agree with the above (and I also think group gerocounseling is more cost-effective, but it shouldn't be planned for that reason alone), I have found it difficult to engage older clients in groups. Perhaps because of previously mentioned counseling biases, lack of sophistication, or my own methods, elders are more likely to prefer one-on-one counseling. I also believe that older persons with various medical and emotional problems would benefit from group-guided imagery techniques and journal therapy, but I have had limited success with both, also. Some gerocounselors get around these biases by calling the groups "classes or workshops" and utilizing cognitive formats. More research is needed.

---

**EXERCISE**

Simulate a gerocounseling group using Mary's planning guidelines. Describe the type of group that it will be and why you chose it for your clients' particular needs.

---

# Chapter 7

# *Gerocounseling Interventions*

$A$ny intervention, the act of interceding in the problem of a client, should be chosen on the basis of assessments you and the clients have made of the situation and goals you have mutually accepted, as discussed in previous chapters. The style advocated here for any such interventions can best be summed up in the pop phrase, "different strokes for different folks," meaning that any intervention or care plan should be specifically tailored for the individual client, family, and problem. This chapter will look at these "different strokes" or interventions. Chapter 8 will discuss how they apply to "different folks."

## *Principles Guiding Choice of Interventions*

Several principles guide the choice of possible interventions: environmental press, parsimony, values, learning styles, gentleness, and a systems outlook.

### Environmental Press

Lawton and Nahemow's (1973) concept of finding a fit between an individual's competency and the environmental press is a helpful guideline for planning any intervention. Competency is the theoretical upper limits of a person's abilities to function physically, cognitively, and socially (problem-solving, learning, ADLs, etc.). Environmental press refers to the social and physical demands made by the person's environment (home, neighborhood, community, etc.). Such presses or demands necessitate response, adaptation, and/or change.

Persons perform at maximum levels of competence when the environmental press slightly exceeds the level at which they adapt. If the press is too great, the person may become overwhelmed, fail, or give up. If the press is too small, apathy, boredom, learned helplessness, and dependency can occur. Some services for older persons can minimize the press (demands) and maximize the supports, thereby creating an unstimulating or unchallenging environment. You do not want to overprotect older clients, do too much for them, or make it too easy for them. Elders need a nice balance, a "fit," between challenge and support to maintain their level of competence and self-esteem. This requires frequent reassessments, as competency levels change often.

## Parsimony

Parsimony is the principle stating that the least intervention is the best intervention. The slogan, "start low, go slow," is a rule in medical treatment and should also apply to gerocounseling. This approach can also be diagnostic, as you go about testing and measuring to find the minimum amount of help needed to create an equilibrium with the adjusted environmental press. For example, before you suggest a significant change, such as a move to a nursing home, you should try out various levels of assisted home care and family interventions to determine if placement is preventable.

## Values

The values principle states that interventions should be chosen with an understanding of the client's value system, the system developed from the client's moral outlook, religion, culture, class norms, gender attitudes, and other factors. Bumagin and Hirn (1990) remind us that counseling interventions should help clients achieve a fit between what is available and, in addition, what is acceptable to them. Your client's values may not be your own. As a sex therapist, for example, you may know of an effective intervention that works with dysfunctional couples, but if it does not "fit" your late-life couple's values, the intervention will not work and you may also lose your clients.

## Learning Styles

As much of gerocounseling uses a cognitive approach, it is helpful to know about your clients' learning styles. Some learners must challenge before they can accept a new idea. Other learners, because of antipathy towards control or authority, will reject anything that is presented in an authoritative manner. Passive dependent learners will superficially accept anything anyone says. True learning means honestly accepting and integrating knowledge and making it one's own.

The above is relevant to the presentation style of your interventions. With most clarifications or interpretations, for instance, you can expect your clients to put up some resistance. Then it is best not to argue but let it drop. You can pick up the idea later. The same kind of resistance can come from homework assignments. Some clients will need indirect tasks such as, "I wonder if you would feel less lonely if you called a friend each day?" Others may want the idea to come from them, "What do you think you could do this week to lessen your loneliness?"

Telling stories, Bible parables, classical myths, and experiences of others often works with people who find it difficult to talk about themselves. They are people who say "we" and "you" instead of "I." They can take advice if it is framed in a story about someone else. Bibliotherapy also works well with certain clients who are readers, and many clients will request books that enlighten counseling issues. Sometimes a gerocounselor will recommend a current movie that deals with the client's themes for later discussion.

Do not be alarmed by initial resistance to your interventions. It is to be expected, and, despite the resistance, you have planted a seed that will germinate at a later date. Some clients need to chew on an idea a long time before they will accept it as their own. Then they will tell you about it as if they just discovered it anew. Of course you will act impressed with their self-help and increased self-esteem.

## Gentleness

Although we live in an era of informed consent and openness with patients, we also risk bringing about depression and/or the stripping of hope when we discuss hard, cruel facts with, say, cancer patients struggling to "whip the thing" or with the early state dementias. Sometimes neurotic defenses are needed by older persons. When harsh facts are provided, they should be in the context of "possibilities, restitution, and resolution" (Butler et al., 1991). "Too much harsh or painful reality implanted too quickly can lead to overwhelming panic or emotional devastation," they added (p. 412). Defenses should be lowered compassionately and realistically and not by attacking them overtly. Denial, for example, can be a healthy protective mechanism that helps us to cope and manage life during intense emotional pain. Do not disarm indiscriminately.

## A Systems Outlook

This book stresses the use of a circular, holistic, interactive approach (Gero-chi model) with elderly clients and their families. Sometimes you may think that an intervention is needed to help a system regain equilibrium, but you are uncertain where to intervene.

> Carol Brown and daughter Susan have been in conflict for over a year. When Carol complains that Susan does not call, Susan feels guilty, misunderstood, and angry. She retaliates with more avoidance, which makes Carol complain more, which makes Susan neglect her more . . . and so the system goes. Both complained to their counselor, Joan, that the relationship was becoming unbearable.

---

**THOUGHT–DISCUSSION QUESTIONS**
If you were the family counselor, how would you help reconcile this conflict? Who is to blame? Where would you intervene?

---

Again, a helpful systems axiom is that a change in one part will effect changes in all other parts. So it doesn't really matter where Joan intervenes. If Carol stopped nagging, Susan may call . . . if Susan called more, Carol may nag less.

Because most people respect fairness, after diagramming the system, try to get both to negotiate a system change. If Carol is too fatigued, Susan may be encouraged to take on the burden of system change alone. Then explain to the stronger or more motivated person that she is not being chosen because it is her fault but because successful intervention is more possible through her. Such system change may energize Carol.

## *Using Modalities*

Chapter 6 presented an overview of the three major counseling modalities: individual, conjoint, and group. Each can be considered a form as well as a forum for intervention. A referral for individual counseling, for example, conveys hope of ending a dysfunctional situation. Assembling a family on behalf of an elder intervenes to strengthen that family's solidarity. Having the elder assist in the family session planning affirms the hierarchy and relieves an overburdened member. Joining a group alleviates the fear of sustained loneliness. Two additional modalities, accessing resources and case management, which also double as interventions, can be added.

### Accessing Resources

Accessing resources means working with the service delivery system and others to help the client or family access tangible or intangible resources or services. Successful aging often depends on accessing and utilizing formal and informal supports. Sometimes your only help will be environmental—for example, finding a senior residence or center, obtaining Medicaid information, providing respite care. It should be noted that even then, your emotional support and gerocounseling skills will be in use. This modality also includes advocacy, which is helping others become aware of and responsive to the needs of clients and to institute appropriate services for them.

### Case Management

Case management is a comprehensive and continuous process of interventions which includes developing, coordinating, and sustaining multiple services as needed by an older person in order to remain in the least restrictive environment as long as possible. In public agencies, the casemanager determines clients' eligibility for funded programs and authorizes payment for purchased care. Such programs are not necessarily more cost-effective, but higher life satisfaction was reported when case management services were available. They are especially valuable when the client has no available family.

The scope of case management is wide and varied and can be emotionally draining on casemanagers who are susceptible to burnout. Casemanagers are often nurses or, like Juan, are social workers. Both integrate their services with a social work counseling model.

Juan's job at the County Human Services Department is to serve clients through the administration of the Wisconsin Community Options Program (Community Options). It provides assessment, planning, funding, and coordination of services as an option to those frail elderly clients who wish to remain in their own homes but who without additional services may otherwise require a nursing home.

Mrs. Mabel Petsky, age 80, was referred to Juan in the Community Options Program by Mary, Director of the Senior Center, because of her increased frailty. Missing group several times, she had complained of dizziness and fear of falling. After a medical check-up, she was started on heart medication and told that she could not remain at Ellis Home unless she got more daily assistance. This was upsetting because she did not wish to leave her new home. She became depressed anticipating the loss.

After completing the necessary assessment process, which included eligibility screening, ADLs, the Mini-Mental Test, and the Geriatric Depression Test, Juan concluded that except for her medical condition, which was now under control, and her situational depression, Mabel could function at home with some help. He called a family meeting and several members, after alluding to long-standing friction, agreed to look in on her. A granddaughter volunteered to do weekly shopping, and Meals on Wheels was arranged. A home health aide would come in two mornings a week to assist with personal care and some housework. A life alert system was installed.

Friends and neighbors agreed to look in on her, too, despite the fact that Mabel had been pushing them away in anticipation of separation. She then projected that they were rejecting her. Juan gently helped her to reframe the vicious cycle she was in and to accept the help being offered her. Mabel cried, so pleased to be able to remain home. Juan was happy it worked out, too, but he realized that her status must be reassessed regularly to see if more help was needed and if Mabel was safe and able to "hold her own" in independent living.

The Community Options Program provided continued life satisfaction for Mabel, which may in the long run reduce future medical costs. Also, the additional services offered to her at home would cost the county considerably less than a nursing home.

---

**THOUGHT–DISCUSSION QUESTIONS**
Reread the case example of Juan's work with Mrs. Petsky. What principles of intervention discussed in this chapter are in evidence?

---

## Using Time

As your chosen modality will be an intervention or mode of intervention, so too will be your gerocounseling time frame. Unless it was for environmental manipulation, most early counseling was long-term because the work focused on uncovering aspects of the past and using transference in a corrective emotional experience. Most counselors operated on the theory that the more therapy, the better. Later, counseling methods from the behaviorist and family systems orientations were more specific, task-focused, and often of a shorter duration. Since the 1980s, there has been a movement toward brief counseling because of growing acceptance of faster systems and cognitive methods, which work well and meet new societal demands.

Brief therapy will probably never replace long-term counseling completely. There will always be frailties—chronic psychiatric and social problems requiring ongoing care, such as with some psychotic and developmentally disabled persons. There will also be those clients suffering certain personality disorders who will negotiate for long-term treatment.

There will also be many frail elders, living longer, who will fall into the long-term category because many of their bio-psycho-social problems do not get better and, at best, will need to be managed on an ongoing basis to prevent further deterioration. Others will suffer from progressive problem states, and the long-term gerocounselor, like Juan, will probably count on remaining with the elder client until that client's death or referral to a higher level of care.

Still, the long-term and the brief model gerocounselors have much in common. Both consider the relationship long-term even though it may not be on a daily basis. The brief counselor will help solve the presenting problem and close the case, but that does not mean closed forever. Rather, the brief counselor practices much like the family doctor, seeing the client from crisis to crisis, transition to transition, and making him or herself available as an ongoing resource. Many of the brief counseling methods can have application to the counseling of older persons. Instead of looking for hidden pathology to correct, strengths and resources are evoked to work on the problem at hand. Hoyt (1993, page 2) listed eight characteristics of brief therapy under the managed care model. They are

1. *specific problem-solving* (client identifies and targets specific symptoms and goals),
2. *rapid response and intervention* (counselor intervenes immediately before problems worsen or develop secondary effects),
3. *clear definition of patient and therapist responsibilities* (counselor structures treatment contract, chooses particular interventions, involves family or others; client actively participates, does homework, makes changes outside of sessions),
4. *creative and flexible use of time* (client and counselor challenge traditional weekly 50-minute sessions format),
5. *interdisciplinary cooperation* (medications may be used as well as services of other health specialists),
6. *multiple formats and modalities,*
7. *intermittent treatment* (patient can return when needed), and
8. *results oriented* (counselor focuses on accountability, measured outcome, and does only what works).

## Crisis Intervention

Unfortunately, many gerocounselors must do a great deal of intensive emergency counseling. Often people do not seek help until a crisis arises, and many acute problems of the elderly do not give advance warnings. Some crisis interventions (below) resemble the brief model.

1. *Use timing.* Make intensive, frequent visits the first 4 to 6 weeks.

2. *Use a family approach.* Help support the stability of the family because it is needed to support the member in crisis; make home visits.

3. *Use the present.* Do not focus on the past; avoid dependency.

4. *Use short-term teaching.* Use intensive short-term education to facilitate understanding of problem and coping models and to foster mastery.

5. *Use outside support.* Social supports are more helpful than a focus on causes or personalities. Enlist help from formal and informal support networks.

6. *Use immediate goals.* Make coping and adjustment, not cure, the immediate goal.

## *Using Different "Strokes"*

We have established that each client and each client's problem is unique, and that therefore, interventions in the treatment or care plans must be individually crafted. This is called "individualized treatment" based on a differential diagnosis. We have already discussed interventions such as systems change, environmental manipulation, accessing resources, and building support networks. Other important gerocounseling interventions fall into the category of direct treatment. They are important because they permeate all the other interventions mentioned above. Some of these "different strokes" that have been found to be effective with older clients can be divided into (a) cognitive interventions and (b) emotional/supportive interventions, but there is much overlap. Both can be viewed as forms of empowerment, and they provide a framework for counseling older adults.

## Using Cognitive Interventions

Knowledge, the first half of empowerment (the second half is discussed under "Using Emotional/Supportive Interventions" later in the chapter), gives testimony to the fact that older adults "can learn, can change, and can take charge of their lives" (Walters & Goodman,

1990, p. 4). Cognitive approaches include clarification and education through didactic, Socratic, and experiential learning. We have already discussed bibliotherapy, the offering of reading materials on selective, relevant topics. Cognitive approaches also include reframing, training, and retraining.

The goal of cognitive counseling is to find solutions to definable, reality-based problems through the means above. Described by Beck (1967), it has been useful with well-motivated older persons who may be depressed but have few or no physically based mental impairments. (Also see Gallagher & Thompson, 1981).

Beck (1967) believes, for example, that depressed clients need to re-evaluate and correct their thinking because their depression is based on distorted, negative views of themselves, the world, and/or the future. A 1985 study by the National Institute of Mental Health found that the therapeutic effects from cognitive and interpersonal psychotherapy were comparable to effects from a popular anti-depressant drug. This should have significance to elderly clients who must make medication cutbacks.

## Didactic Interventions

In order to deal with a crisis, make decisions, consider options, problem-solve, and learn about your service, the client must first be armed with relevant information. The way to solve a problem is first to become an expert on that problem—forewarned is forearmed. Much of your teaching, therefore, will be didactic, a presentation of informative material followed by discussion. This is efficient when a new health regime is taught, eligibility requirements are explained, benefit assistance is offered, and in many other situations. With most older persons, you will talk slowly, in a moderate tone, and in terms that are concrete and meaningful to their situation. As many older clients are used to classes rather than therapy sessions, many counseling groups begin with didactic approaches and even refer to sessions as classes or consultations.

Educational interventions are helpful in providing family members with information necessary for helping aged members. They are advisable with families of the mastery or coping levels of functioning (see Chapter 8). A group mode is recommended to allow for interactions and discussion, but it should be planned to meet the unique needs of the participants. It should be led by a person knowledgeable in the interest area, and the size should be limited by the leader's ability to communicate and allow for group discussion. Common topics are institutionalization, retirement, diabetes, widowhood, and Alzheimer's disease. Families can use the material as needed; the knowledge empowers them to action.

### Socratic Interventions

Socratic teaching techniques involve the use of questions to develop ideas or elicit admissions that are latent in the client. They are considered an effective way to make learning personal. Questions can be prompted from shared audiovisual aids, genealogies, or life reviews. Chapter 2 discussed how active questioning can teach systems theory to a family.

### Experiential Interventions

Knowledge gained from practice and experience rather than from didactic approaches is often considered the most effective. This experiential approach not only teaches facts, skills and problem-solving, but also can instill empathy and confidence. It includes role-playing, stimulations, games, audiovisuals, and homework assignments. Asking clients to try out a new behavior or to try something different for a week teaches them that there are many ways to solve a problem, and also includes the learning benefit of practice. Homework extends the treatment beyond the counseling hour.

***Reframing interventions.*** Reframing, a much-used intervention, suggests that the client look at an issue from another perspective. Aptly labeled, it resembles putting an old picture in a new frame and seeing it in a fresh, new way. Often this can assist a client or family to become unstuck in their problem solving or to cease a self-blaming or scapegoating pattern. It only works if the new meaning is as appropriate and convincing as the old one.

Often family therapists will effectively reframe around developmental issues, helping a family to see that "he's not bad, he's just going through some rough adolescent years." It is unfortunate that this intervention has often been harmful to older persons. It is not unusual to hear, "You're not senile (or in need of assessment), you're just getting old." While this form of reframing has good intent, it may also have denied important medical help.

Reframing can clarify normality. Often persons will be depressed about being depressed or they feel they're crazy because they are bouncing back and forth in the grief cycle. Reframing that to, "You're not crazy; you're just understandably depressed," can be a solace. Reframing is also helpful in interpersonal relations. A sensitive person may see a casual gesture as a snub or a rejection and need help reframing that to a more positive perception. A "no" answer to a sexual overture may mean something different to a male than to a female. To her, she's not in the mood; to him, it's "You don't love me." Reframing can be a way of putting it in proper perspective and getting into the other's shoes.

***Training and retraining interventions.*** Sometimes an elder will need more than a cognitive approach; retraining may be in order. Training implies developing or forming new patterns or habits of behavior. An example might be an assertiveness training group where a combination of didactic and experiential exercises are offered. Other training or retraining groups used with elders include *reality orientation training* (to encourage an awareness of present time and place), *remotivation* (to remotivate patients' interests in the world about them), and *operant conditioning* (to get people to change their behaviors by changing the consequences of their current behavior). Physical, occupational, and speech rehabilitation therapists, for example, also use cognitive training and counseling supportive interventions along with their specific skills.

## Using Emotional/Supportive Interventions

The second half of empowerment is helping older persons cope with feelings engendered by the transitions and losses of aging. Emotional support is the temporary coping crutch that helps a person through a difficult time until one's former or new coping mechanisms appear. Supportive approaches include understanding, guidance, environmental manipulation, reassurance, and catharsis. Often it is supportive to have one's problems normalized and/or universalized. Another intervention is the externalization of interests, that is, the encouragement to pull out of withdrawal through the resumption of meaningful activities.

The goals of supportive approaches include strengthening existing defenses, finding new or better means of maintaining control, and restoring equilibrium and/or making adaptations, all of which help the person find symptom relief. The present is usually emphasized (unless you are probing for previously used coping mechanisms), positive transference is encouraged and used, and strengths are maximized.

Supportive counseling does not attempt to change personality, although this may happen serendipitously. It also may not attempt to change a situation. Often with older clients, the situation cannot be changed, as in cases with a terminal diagnosis, the loss of a spouse, or the amputation of a leg. The supportive work then will be to stand by, to listen, to bear witness, and sometimes just to be there for the person in grief. *Catharsis*, the discharge of pent-up feelings, has many curative values. It releases tension, softens inhibitions, and exposes suppressed ideas and attitudes so that they may be examined objectively. Emotional support is usually all that is needed when a person's ego is relatively strong but may have been weakened by a major or stressful event or a series of such events.

Peer support groups are used extensively with elders and their families. Those providing support are usually persons who have worked through similar concerns. But they are not for everyone. The Widowed Persons League (AARP, 1990) recommends that the newly bereaved do better at first with one-on-one supportive peer contact before referral to a group.

## Reminiscence and Life Review

Two additional interventions, reminiscence and life review, which can include all of the above approaches, are salient in gerocounseling.

The tendency of older persons to look back on life events and to *reminisce* has long been observed. Sometimes it was seen as an annoying habit, and elders were chided for "living in the past." Butler (1963) saw this inner experience of reviewing one's life as universal and curative:

Probably at no time in life is there as potent a force toward self-awareness as in old age. Memory, an ego function that serves the self, entertains us, shames us; it pains us. Memory can tell us our origins; it can be explanatory and it can deceive. Presumably it can lend itself toward cure. The recovery of memories, the making the unconscious conscious, is generally regarded as one of the basic ingredients of the curative process. (p. 495)

Gerocounselors do reminiscence work often without knowing it. When you look at an elder client's pictures and ask about them or inquire about how they formerly spent a holiday, even when you are taking a social history, you are helping your client reminisce.

*Life review* is a more structured approach and was developed by Ebersol in 1978. Participants (often in groups) are asked to review their lives, to recognize unproductive coping devices, and to set goals to incorporate more effective coping mechanisms.

Gerocounselors should do memory work delicately. When there are memory blocks, they should be left to lie; the flooding of emotions or the evoking of repressed memory should be avoided. Butler warned that sometimes intense memory work can bring on mental illness. It can also be too reductionistic and judgmental if not monitored.

There have been many versions of reminiscence and life review. AARP (1989) lists 80 articles and texts dealing with the subjects. AARP's own training workbook, slides, and audiotape are helpful guides for gerocounselors in all specialties. Life review has been adapted for marriage counseling, and also for pastoral, hospice, and nursing home counseling. It is used by family members when visiting elder relatives. When people reminisce together, they create a sense of continuity and link accomplishments of the past to the present, learn interesting things about each other or a period of history, preserve family history, transmit cultural heritage, communicate family folklore and legend, build self-esteem, resolve conflicts and fears, reflect and reassess life achievements, promote intergenerational understanding, combat isolation, and encourage social interaction (AARP, 1989).

# Chapter 8

# Gerocounseling: Specific Disorder Interventions

As you saw in Chapter 7, when choosing interventions, it is necessary to take generational, cohort, ethnic, and gender characteristics into consideration. Other times, the interventions will be related to a medical or psychiatric problem. If you are using a holistic (Gero-chi) approach, as it is hoped you will, your assessment and intervention plan will be bio-psycho-social in nature. Some interventions are problem-specific. There are very definite ways of working with elders who suffer from dementia, depression, anxiety, guilt, and or systemic family problems. This chapter concentrates on treatment of these special cases—the "different strokes" for these "different folks."

## Organic Mental Disorders

Gerocounselors often encounter clients and/or client-families who are suffering from the effects of organic mental disorders. These include Alzheimer's disease, Multi-infarct Dementia, Parkinson's dementia, Korsakoff's syndrome, Pick's disease, and others. Most of those suffering from these diseases will be supervised by a medical team, but the gerocounselor will be called upon to offer support and family counseling to facilitate acceptance, adjustment, and prevention of further deterioration and also to mobilize coping strengths for rebuilding function and relationships.

Because one of the most feared diseases of dementia is Alzheimer's disease, what we can call *Alzheimer's anxiety* is of almost epidemic proportions among the elderly. People with normal "benign" memory loss need to be reassured and helped with memory aids so they are not depressed or do not start a self-fulfilling prophecy.

## Alzheimer's Disease

Because a cure for Alzheimer's disease has not been found, efforts to assist victims of this devastating disease have centered on educational, environmental, pharmacological, supportive, family counseling, and validation interventions. Goals have focused on appropriate assessment, the prevention of secondary problems, and the slowing down of the deterioration process. Most educational interventions have been a result of the Alzheimer's Association, a national organization founded in 1979 to (a) disseminate public and professional information on Alzheimer's and other dementia disorders; (b) stimulate the formation of support groups to families with a dementia patient; and (c) promote research on dementia.

Gerocounselors working with patients and families can obtain literature and assistance by calling their 800 number. The Alzheimer's Association also directs a major thrust in the area of assessment. Sometimes dementia-like symptoms can be caused by reversible conditions such as nutrition or thyroid problems, chronic alcoholism, and depression. Other times, families may mistakenly attribute potentially serious symptoms to "aging." Evaluation for Alzheimer's disease is an involved process, and all treatable conditions must be ruled out before a tentative diagnosis can be made. A for-certain diagnosis is only obtainable at autopsy (see Chapter 4.)

Clarification of situations like the ones mentioned above will be one of the gerocounselor's first interventions. Once a diagnosis has been made, Bonjean (1988) stresses that the family will have a continued need for accurate information about the disease process throughout counseling because family members and family systems absorb such information in their own unique way and time frame.

Bonjean believes that a specific diagnosis is important to allow for "the necessary grieving of the pre-illness family identity and acceptance of a permanent change" (p. 202).

Controversy exists regarding whether or not the patient should be informed about the diagnosis. Some warn that too early a "sentence" brings on depression and exacerbates symptoms. Others argue that the patient has the right to participate in family planning, getting one's house in order, and other preparations. This course of action also helps to abate family guilt about planning for the patient. In either case, the principle of gentleness should be used as a guide.

Some cognitive therapy is attempted with early-stage dementia patients. It is done with much repetition, little new material, and focuses on affect such as smiles, hugs, hand-holding, and a warm supportive manner. Occupational, recreational, and music therapies are also desirable adjuncts to an intervention care plan. Orientation aids are used, too, such as color coding, signs, clocks, and calendars. Home or institutional adjustments are guided by simplicity and environmental press. Sometimes pharmacological treatment can help relieve accompanying symptoms such as depression, agitation, sleep disorder, paranoia, and apathy.

All of these interventions should go hand in hand with offering comfort and supportive counseling to patient, family, and, often, the neglected staff members. It has been said, "Alzheimer's is a contagious disease; everybody suffers from it." Support groups are popular with people sharing problems and solutions with each other. Others profit more from an individual or a one-family approach. Staff members should have professional support groups for themselves.

Family members need to grieve for what has happened to their loved one, and they must work to alter family roles and relationships. Caregiver support and self-care themes are indispensable interventions to prevent the breakdown of yet another family member; exhaustion, depression, illness, and even death have been known to result from the caregiving burden. Services such as respite or day-programs should be offered early in the disease course as preventive measures. Unfortunately, most wait to refer clients *after* the crisis occurs.

The following case example is true. My account is a summary of newspaper articles and my own contacts. Names are disguised but family members have turned their pain into a promise of hope for others and want their important message to be known.

Linda was the Aging Coordinator for a local agency, and one could not find a more caring, informed professional to work with the older population. As an information/referral source, she referred many elders to me for counseling. Her sister Barbara worked as a long-term-care social worker in a neighboring city and commanded a similar positive reputation.

I remember reading of the two women, both in their sixties, being adopted by their stepfather, Steven Aimes. He had raised them, and the family lovingly decided that this emotional bond should be legalized. Linda confided this was strictly for sentimental reasons. They, like their mother, Sara, had experienced nothing but love for and from Steve.

I also remember a June 1991 breakfast picnic to celebrate another year of networking in our Elderly Services Forum. Linda came late to that gathering and was shaken. Earlier, she was called by a sheriff who reported that her 86-year-old father was picked up on the Interstate, hitchhiking to Montana at 4:00 A.M. Luckily, a motorist alerted the police.

That incident was dramatic compared to the more subtle changes that the family was observing in Steven that year. Still, signs were there and the sisters blamed themselves for not catching them. Steven, seldom sick, began to blamed breathing difficulties on conditions in his home, and he made numerous alterations to the property. He developed some paranoid ideas about people "ripping him off" and "bugging his house." Muth (1993) in the *Racine Journal Times* wrote, "The proud and once strong man who used to climb power poles to make repairs in lightning storms wondered aloud, 'Who wants to live with an old man like me?'" (p. 13A).

The family realized that Steven was having mental problems and dementia (probably Alzheimer's, the daughters surmised), and they tried to get help. They were put on a waiting list for county services. The sisters visited regularly and observed Steven's frustration mounting.

On September 29, 1991, Steven's wife Sara served him pancakes using the flat side of a butcher knife rather than the spatula she usually used. A psychologist theorized that Steven may have perceived this gesture as a threat against his life. No one is certain, but at that moment Steven seized the knife and slashed Sara's throat, killing her. "We never saw it coming," said the usually aware daughters.

Steven was adjudged mentally incompetent to stand trial and was placed in a locked unit at a local care center where he remained until his death a year later. It is believed he never knew that he killed his wife.

Several years later, still working through the grief that will never end, the two daughters turned some of that energy into creating educational programs on Alzheimer's disease for community families. They began a caregiver lecture series and participated in the development of a geriatric assessment center. They shared their experiences so that others will not misinterpret a family member's change of behavior, as they believed they did.

The above is a dramatic and incredibly sad story, especially since it is true. Extreme cases, although they may be unusual, are dramatic illustrations of what this kind of disease can bring about.

---

**THOUGHT–DISCUSSION QUESTIONS**
Consider the above scenario. What interventions, before and after the tragedy, could have aided this forlorn family? Other families?

---

# Validation Techniques and Organic Mental Disorders

*Validation counseling*, used with disoriented older people to reduce anxiety, was started in 1963 by Naomi Feil while working with confused patients diagnosed with organic brain syndrome, senile dementia. Since its conception, validation techniques have been taught to over 70,000 health care workers and family caregivers world-wide (Feil, 1993). Feil wrote that validation takes no more than eight minutes of genuine open, nonjudgmental, empathetic listening daily, and can be done by anyone possessing these qualities. Certain techniques are appropriate for certain ages (old-old, e.g.) and for certain stages (malorientation, stage one; time confusion, stage two; repetitive motion, stage three; and vegetation, stage four). In her book, *The Validation Breakthrough*, Feil suggests fourteen validation techniques which we've summarized:

1. Center (caregiver focuses on own breathing to expel anger and frustration),
2. build trust (use non-threatening, factual words),
3. rephrase what person says and how said,
4. use polarity (ask the person to think of the worst examples of the complaint),
5. imagine the opposite (as if there are times when the objectionable happening doesn't happen),

6. reminisce,

7. maintain genuine, close eye contact,

8. use ambiguity (use some of the ambiguous terms used by the patient),

9. use a clear, low, loving tone of voice,

10. mirror (observe/match the person's motions, emotions),

11. link the behavior with the unmet need,

12. identify and use the preferred sense,

13. use touching,

14. use music.

## Mood Disorders (Depression)

Like organic mental disorders, depression is one of the most common but untreated problems among the elderly. Also like the dementias, depression is a "contagious disease" in that it, too, affects the family and everyone involved, particularly the caregiver. It is depressing to live with someone depressed.

Additionally, like the dementias, it is difficult to diagnose depression in the elderly because it can be assessed along a continuum from normal bereavement to major depression with or without *endogenous* (vegetative) symptoms. It is also difficult to differentiate it from anxiety states, as depression often has an anxiety component. It is further difficult to diagnose and separate depression from physical illness because many medical problems have depressive components and many depressive states are expressed in physical ailments.

There is also minimal help available (other than treatment trials themselves) for the assessment of depressed elderly clients. Many classifications do spell out differences between depression and normal bereavement but do not take age into consideration. Many elderly depressions that involve numerous somatic complaints have been overlooked. Similar faults can be found in those inventories used to assess late-life depression. Of the three used widely with the elderly, Hamilton (1967), Beck (1967), and Yesavage et al. (1983), only the Yesavage Geriatric Depression Scale (GDS) accounts for the uniqueness of elder assessment.

Like organic mental disorders, the treatment selections of depression-related disorders are many and varied—not because there is no cure as with Alzheimer's disease, but because the causes of mood disorders are many-faceted and each specialty (like the blind-folded school children defining the elephant), views and treats the illness from its own orientation.

Those who see depression as a result of a physiological or disease process or a chemical imbalance will treat it accordingly. Others who view it as the result of errors in logic will use cognitive techniques. Depression is also variously seen as the result of a failure to produce reinforcing activities, as a consequence of losses, and as a function of genetics. Still others, sometimes erroneously, attribute it to old age.

These theories are not mutually exclusive—even the old age explanation has some validity, as we know that in aging there are increased and interacting vulnerabilities in the areas of cognition, neurotransmission, ego function, and external support systems. In old age, the precipitants, clinical causes, and social consequences of these vulnerabilities and problems are different from other ages.

If there is agreement that late-life depression falls along a genetic, biochemical, psychological, and social/environmental range—and that it is a family event, too—then it is logical that interventions should have a bio-psycho-social, family-centered approach. Family can assist in assessment and treatment, and also those same family members can benefit from the preventive and supportive qualities of that assessment and treatment.

## Somatic Interventions

Depressed older patients, when treated, are often given anti-depressant medications (low dosage for older persons) with or without adjunctive counseling. Lone psychotropic medications are indicated if the elder is somatically oriented or unable to use psychotherapy. Where there is a life-threatening risk or when the severely depressed patient is not responsive to counseling and/or medication, electroconvulsive therapy (ECT) is usually recommended. Today's ECT procedures are considered safe and effective, and gerocounselors should learn about ECT in order to give accurate information to clients.

## Psychological Interventions

Interpersonal psychotherapy (ITP) and cognitive, behavioral approaches work well with depressed elderly clients. Butler et al. (1991) reported that ITP addressed four specific, disrupted areas: grief, interpersonal disputes, role transitions, and interpersonal deficits. The model included an active counseling stance, flexible session length, and attention to the client's dependency levels and social and environmental problems. It is important for the counselor to be able to tolerate the client's unsolvable social problems, possible long-standing pathology or maladaptation, and/or the clients' existential concerns.

There are some helpful guidelines for caregivers and counselors who work with depressed persons. Talk about real things and keep the conversation predictable and simple, allowing time for response. Use initiative and anticipate questions when there is no response. Don't ask for direct decisions and yes or no answers. Encourage the expression of feelings, and, of course, be nonjudgmental about them. Give realistic praise about areas in which the person does well. Talk about events, activities enjoyed in the past, and those which the person can realistically anticipate. Encourage the person to try activities that will result in success, accept the person's feelings of sadness (or fear) as real.

Caregivers can counteract feelings of worthlessness and the belief that no one cares by just being there, listening, and not judging or criticizing the depressed behavior. Caregivers should also nurture their own mental health, by being aware of their feelings, by finding a safe place to express them, and by receiving support and consciously seeking positive experiences for themselves.

Once some of the client's energy is restored, give homework assignments that break up tasks into smaller, manageable-sized ones that will bring some measure of success. Set goals that are of short duration and within the depressed elder's abilities. Support strengths and stress past successes.

With the depressed or bereaved, it is helpful to share Kübler-Ross's (1969) stages of grief model (shock and disbelief, denial and bargaining, sadness, anger, acceptance, and substitution). Conveying this kind of information to the client can serve as a catalyst to elicit feelings, as a means of normalizing and universalizing the experience, and as a window of hope that there will be a final acceptance stage. It is important to explain that the stages do not follow a strict order and that a person is not "crazy" when stages bounce back and forth.

Start with a grief assessment in *grief counseling*. This procedure assesses the quality of support at hand, how well the person copes with and perceives the loss, and the state of his/her present functioning. Retelling the death story is cathartic, especially after initial support has dwindled, and it helps the griever reframe earlier perceptions. Encourage the person to take one thing at a time, and be sure to avoid making important decisions too soon. Help the griever find concrete assistance so as to minimize feelings of helplessness. Advise the griever to seek appropriate medical intervention if symptoms warrant it. Allow expressions of grief, anger, and guilt, and do not rescue the client too soon and thereby cut off necessary expressions of feelings because of your own discomfort.

Again, a family approach is helpful. The griever not only has lost a person but a family system, as it was known. New roles and ways of relating must be established. In working with the bereaved and depressed, and with their families, do not impose your values or assume that the grieved one feels a certain way about the loss. Do not use religious explanations early, and use them only after you learned that they are within the client's cultural and religious meaning system.

There are many good references on working with the depressed and the bereaved. AARP has a helpful seminar planning guide, *Spousal Bereavement* (1990). This affordable package includes a video and information on the Widowed Persons' Service. AARP recommends a referral for individual peer support before a grief group is suggested in early bereavement days. They also warn against the dangers of psychotropic drugs for the newly bereaved, pointing out that there are safer means to accomplish the same results. The following is an example of grief counseling:

In June, Joan at the Counseling Center had a new client. Marion Kamakian brought in her mother, Anna Wells, age 70, after a referral from their family physician. Anna had been depressed six months since the death of a relatively new pet cat.

Anna appeared to have a Major Depressive Disorder with Dysphoric Mood characterized by a loss of pleasure in almost everything, a condition called anhedonia. She had six of seven symptoms necessary and listed in *DSM IV* for a major depressive disorder: poor appetite and weight loss, hypersomnia, loss of interest, loss of energy, fatigue, diminished concentration, and recent cognitive slowdown. There was some suicidal ideation as evidenced in talk about wishing to be dead. (There were no signs of hallucinations or delusions, schizophrenic disorder, organic mental disorder, or alcoholism.)

The family believed her bereavement symptoms were abnormal because of the duration of the grief and the fact that she had the cat a very short time.

At first meeting Anna, Joan asked if she wanted to come in alone or with her daughter. Knowing elderly clients were not all alike, she did not generalize about this. Some want their independence respected, while others, at first, appreciate the security blanket of a family member. (Later, when Joan was working to establish more independence, she chose to see Anna alone.)

While offering a choice, Joan hoped that Anna would opt for Marion to come in as it would help her get a glimpse of how a part of the family system operated. Does daughter speak for mother? Respect? Patronize? Dominate? Conflict? Does either one intimidate the other? What seems to be the nature of their relationship, and what is the strength of this part of Anna's support system?

Beginning a therapeutic alliance with Anna, Joan was also careful to join with Marion. One can often find a client badly in need of an anti-depressant medication or some other intervention only to go home to a family member dead set against it. Many adult children, Joan knew, wield great power over their parents. She saw the women in her support group almost cower before their adult children (future caregivers), fearing that they might "get mad at them." Joan worked on assertiveness training with these clients.

Anna stated that she wanted to be called Anna, and Joan asked her how she could be of help to her. She listened attentively to Anna's problems and concerns and did not fall into the family trap of trying to rescue and talk her out of her sad feelings about the dead cat. Joan was, in a sense, modeling behaviors she hoped Marion would adopt—to go along with Anna's feelings, and not to argue or criticize even when they seemed senseless.

After a reasonable amount of time, Joan slowly shifted the subject by telling Anna that she would like to learn about what her life was like before this problem began. She used a genogram, which gave clues about memory and cognitive functioning, coping skills, how grief was experienced before, and other aspects of life. She learned about the important comings and goings of family members, which gave her a picture of who had been important and what losses and what kinds of losses Anna had had.

Dates of events got Joan into Life Validation (Hargrave, 1992). "You grew up in the depression. What was that like for you? You must have married when World War II broke out. Did your husband go to war? Did you work in the war effort?" Such questioning supports self-esteem by asking long-term memory questions, well rehearsed, and by demonstrating before the family the thesis that Anna's life had not only personal importance but historical significance as well. Often elders feel discounted by society (and they often are). As Joan wove events in Anna's life with historical happenings, she was showing an appreciation of a life that was lived through important times, and an affirmation of a person who was struggling with preserving the self she had left.

Joan learned that Anna's last ten years were characterized by many changes caused by primary and secondary losses:

- Anna's husband was 15 years her senior and instead of the retire-ment of their dreams, he developed Alzheimer's disease, and she necessarily took on the caregiving role. Primary losses: her hus-band as she had known him, then his death. Secondary losses: social life, conversation, sex, financial security, retirement dreams, and, finally, the loss of the caregiving role that had come to define her.

- Then an arthritic condition became a greater disability. Primary losses: feeling good, some decline in ADLs and general mobility. Secondary losses: self-concept of being a "robust person," the loss of a coping device that had been to "walk it off," and losses of social contacts again.

- In the past three years, a sister out East died of colon cancer, a grandson was killed in a motorcycle accident, and her son had two major bypass operations. Then, as her arthritis worsened, she was forced to give up her home of 45 years and move to a lovely new senior residence (but it wasn't "home"). At the same time, she stopped doing her favorite craft, cross-stitching, and also driv-ing, because of a progressive eye condition.

But many good things happened, too. She got a cat and experi-enced the wonderful therapy that a pet can be for an older person. She also found a delightful new neighbor, Molly, who did drive, and she became a friendly companion and confidant to Anna. The two enjoyed many of the same interests and "bummed around" to fairs and rummage sales.

But in May, Molly had a severe stroke and was moved to a nursing home in Springfield to be closer to a son. Anna seemed to handle that well. Then six months ago, Anna's cat, Samantha, died. Anna thought someone poisoned her. Anna closed her blinds, took to her couch, withdrew from life, cried, and hadn't been the same since.

Family, friends, even her physician said, "It's silly to make so much over a dead cat." "A major depression over a cat?" Absurd—certainly not. But whether it was the final straw of a pile-up of losses or whether the cat did represent the last symbol of self she was holding onto, Anna's grief over the death of her cat was nevertheless very real and should not be trivialized or discounted.

Except for history-taking, Anna did not mention grief over previous losses. Joan did not need to act smart, to interpret this displacement for Anna, to achieve insight. Because Anna denied previous grieving, there was no need to argue and tell her that the present depression was expressing a ten-year storehouse of unresolved losses. Talking about the lost cat was, in fact, talking about all the other losses, too.

More than the losses, Anna wanted to talk about her physical symptoms: fatigue, getting to sleep but waking often, nausea, inability to eat or "hold anything down." Joan asked about her alcohol consumption (a subject often neglected with older women, thus denying them the necessary help they deserve), and polydrugs. She administered a simple nutrition test (because older single persons often suffer from malnutrition). She also asked detailed questions about suicidal ideations, and those proved too vague to be alarming. All other findings were negative.

At the second session, Anna took the Folstein Mini-Mental Test and scored only 18, which indicated possible cognitive impairment. Anna's score on the GDS was 20, indicative of depression. They discussed the scores and set goals together. Anna would agree to see the clinic psychiatrist for an evaluation for an anti-depressant medication. She would come twice a week for half a session and later would change to weekly one-hour sessions. She would bring in pictures and tell Joan about her lost loved ones. She agreed to eat two meals a day and to enroll in the Y's senior exercise program for disabled persons.

At each session, Joan worked (and it is work for both counselor and depressed patient), affirming Anna's feelings and gently guiding her through her grief. Anna brought in a picture of the cat and, later, ones of her husband and grandson. Joan normalized ("It is normal for you to be feeling this way") and universalized ("Most people would be feeling very down after all that you have gone through in the past few years.").

In about 3 weeks, Anna experienced improved sleep and some

elevated energy and enhanced mood both from counseling and from another intervention, an anti-depressant medication (low dosage for an elder).

Sometimes Anna just needed to express feeling sorry for herself and to complain. Joan did not point out the positives in Anna's life but let her "bitch." Joan just empathized. After a sufficient time of this, Joan asked, "What time of day do you feel better?" Then she used this as a prescription for an intervention. "You are less blue when your sister or friend calls you each day. Why not try this? Whenever you start feeling lonely and blue, pick up the phone and call a special person. Make a list of the special people and go down the list so you do not overdo anyone."

Once Anna said, "I feel better around four o'clock when I go downstairs for the mail." It turned out that there were two parts to feeling better: the socialization with neighbors around the mailbox and receiving a card or letter. Joan's prescription went, "I would like you to invite a neighbor in for tea once a day and also to write a letter daily to develop return mail."

Joan also did some cognitive reframing. Anna said, "After the cat died, I was so depressed, my daughter came daily. Now she comes only once a week. I was terrible to burn her out so, and she is probably mad at me." Reframing helped her to see indeed the opposite: "Your daughter is now delighted and proud that Mom is getting well. Now daughter can go back to work full-time as she needs to earn an income." Anna was able to see her getting well was helping Marion; later Marion was encouraged in a family therapy session to pay Mom some attention now to reinforce "wellness" instead of the illness.

Another intervention was to help Anna acquire new healthy defenses. Instead of internalizing her anger and sadness about losses, Anna needed to talk them out and even express anger. They worked on principles of assertiveness together.

Anna's eye problems ended the cross-stitching, and the arthritis put an end to walking off problems. Anna enrolled in a medically supervised exercise class and joined a volunteer group making placemats for nursing homes.

Anna's recovery process continued, and Joan started to think more about when and how they would terminate counseling. While she had been building an outside support system and referrals to groups to take over when counseling was not on a regular basis, Joan knew her terminating would be a delicate area for someone who had already experienced so many painful losses. Joan decided to read more about termination before she made any specific plans. This case study will be continued in Chapter 9.

---

**THOUGHT–DISCUSSION QUESTIONS**
Consider Anna's case study in relation to Joan's knowledge and skills in relationship, assessment, goal setting, choice of modalities, and interventions. What would you do differently? Why?

---

## *Anxiety Disorders*

---

Anxiety disorders constitute a major mental health problem among the elderly. Despite the fact that many are unrecorded, they are in general the most common of all psychiatric disorders in community-based studies (Myers et al., 1984). Regier et al. (1988) added that even though depression and life satisfaction are the more frequently studied indicators of psychological status of elders, "anxiety disorders are twice as prevalent . . . and affect 5.5 percent of those over age 65" (p. 977). As with the dementias and depression, many people falsely regard anxiety reactions as normal symptoms of aging. Others indict different causes. Psychodynamic counselors see anxiety as a result of id, superego, castration, or separation anxiety. Behaviorists consider it a classically conditioned response to biological arousal or trauma maintained later by avoidance. Cognitive therapists consider anxiety-producing thoughts as both the cause and result of increased original anxiety. Geriatricians find anxiety hard to diagnose because it can be both the cause and effect of many interacting somatic problems of old age. All physical symptoms, therefore, must be checked out before a psychological diagnosis of anxiety disorder can be made. Even then, it is difficult to diagnose because anxiety is often a symptom of depression.

Anxiety disorders are treated with pharmacotherapy, psychotherapy, and behavioral therapy. In psychotherapy, the focus is not on the anxiety but on solving multiple coexisting issues. Reminiscence, support, and environmental manipulation are used with somatic therapy.

In the behavioral and cognitive therapy of older persons, relaxation exercises, imagery, rehearsal, and other forms of cognitive therapy are used. The counselor assumes a direct stance to give clients confidence to face feared situations and to learn that they can effect positive changes in their environments. Such changes help them to change self-perceptions away from helpless victim roles.

Other times, belief systems are challenged and changed in order to lower standards for self and others.

With phobias, after relaxation exercises, the client is asked to create a hierarchy of concerns and responses ranging from least to most feared. The counselor then guides the client to imagine doing the least feared activity and moves upward to increasingly feared situations in order to break the association between each feared situation and the phobic anxiety. If the anxiety gets too intense, the client signals so that the counselor can return the imagery to a more comfortable state.

## Guilt Disorders

As elders work on the integrity-versus-despair task, some find themselves on the despair side of the ledger. Not only has one's life not been meaningful, but the older person may be burdened by necessary or unnecessary guilt. "Psychotherapy in old age is a therapy of atonement as well as of retribution. One cannot deny cruel and thoughtless acts, falsely reassuring that all is irrational Freudian guilt" (Butler et al. 1991, p. 410). We must not in our psychological interventions be too hasty to reassure clients who are sick with guilt.

Gerocounselors cannot grant forgiveness and mercy, but we can bear witness. Listening nonjudgmentally, providing realistic feedback, and offering alternative solutions can help in such difficult situations. Sometimes a referral to a member of the clergy in the elder's faith for a confessional experience can be helpful if the parties involved will respond as you hope. The 12-step program in Alcoholics Anonymous (AA) suggests making a list of the people one has hurt and making appropriate amends. Sometimes, if done sincerely, just helping clients rationalize that they probably did the best they could at the time may be of solace. Other supportive, cognitive work that can be of value consists of getting the client to recognize that one is never too old for new starts, second chances, and making amends.

## Family Disorders

Family therapists work both with individuals and with the family system. What does that mean? Simply put, when working with a family system, caregivers try to effect change in the system, which is seen as an entity itself, consisting of interacting parts, and all the relationships among these parts. Certain interventions specifically apply to situations involving family systems counseling.

## Boundary Interventions

A family system's boundary may be dysfunctional. Doing boundary work, the nursing home gerocounselor may try to encourage the disengaged family to visit and support their lonely relative more. Conversely, the nursing home gerocounselor may see that an enmeshed (overly close) family is visiting all the time, thus preventing the resident from attending activities and/or forming relationships with staff and other residents. The gerocounselor may then discourage so much overprotection to help the new resident make an adjustment and to help the other family members adjust to the placement.

## Hierarchy Interventions

The hierarchy of a family system may be dysfunctional. Joan has a physically impaired client who is cognitively competent, but, nonetheless, a daughter and son-in-law have taken over all decision-making, thus infantilizing the client and denying deserved autonomy. Joan's work will be to help the older client regain the appropriate level in family hierarchy. Or, the family hierarchy may be maladjusted another way. The seemingly competent but passive–dependent elder has succumbed to a child-like role with one's own children, and is feigning illness to get support and attention. Rabbi Jean Goldman counseled Mr. Schwartz to find more productive ways of "earning" time with his children.

Another time, Rabbi Goldman helped Mrs. Meyers to get more involved in Hadassah in order to meet her self-esteem needs and not be so involved with her grandchildren. The family had complained that they did want their children to be close to their grandmother, Mrs. Meyers, but that she was trying to take over all the child-care decisions, which the parents felt were theirs to make.

## Communication Interventions

There are times when the gerocounselor will intervene in the communication of a family system. Pastor Johnson noted that all the communication in the Hansen family had to go through Margaret, the oldest daughter, almost as if she were a switchboard operator. This kept all the information (power) in Margaret's hands and distanced others, who then relinquished their responsibilities for the older Mrs. Hansen's care. Subtly, Pastor Johnson began to change the way he and Mrs. Hansen planned family sessions. He even asked a middle daughter to host the December session to weaken the hold Margaret had held on such meetings.

## Coping Interventions

In Chapter 4, we discussed a handy classification of family functioning that was developed by Sterns et al. (1984). This schema set criteria for various levels of functioning and suggested corresponding interventions.

Mastery families are families in control of their environment and feelings, who demonstrate continuity and/or flexibility for change, and have clear cross-generational boundaries. They can best be assisted through educational and peer support interventions.

Coping families are families who are in control of their affect and environment and who can maintain continuity and can adapt to change, but they do so with more stress and anxiety. They are helped through educational interventions, peer support, and group counseling.

Striving families are families who have some control over long-term environmental aspects and exhibit planned and goal-oriented behaviors. They are, however, not always effective with family issues because the family fears facing the realities such as aging. They see aging as a detriment to them, and they move from one crisis to another. They are helped with peer support, group counseling, and family therapy interventions.

Inertia families are families with some control over the short term, but they deny realities and lack long-term commitment. They therefore do not support their older members. They withdraw and place responsibilities outside the family and seem unwilling to expend energy on the changing older adult. They often profit from group counseling and family therapy interventions.

Panic families are families who have lost control of the present situation and its accompanying affect. They are overwhelmed, unrealistic, irrational, and non-communicative. They need crisis intervention before any plans can be made. Later, they can use family therapy and individual counseling (Sterns et al., 1984).

# Implementing Family Intervention Methods

How are these systems interventions made? Sometimes change can be accomplished easily through a didactic approach as you teach systems and state what you observe in the family. Because such observations must be made nonjudgmentally, they could be done in a questioning way, wondering out loud if this is the most effective way to solve the problem. The gerocounselor might suggest other ways, such as role reversals, to see if members might feel better about things. A homework assignment for a week's duration can be made to try out a new behavior.

Often the family interventions will be executed less directly. If a goal is to raise the senior's level in the hierarchy, for instance, the gerocounselor may do this by asking the elder to play a leadership or co-therapist role in the session. All questions and decisions could be referred to the elder, thus modeling who is in charge.

At other times, the intervention will be accomplished through an appeal to fairness or reciprocity. One adult sibling may be carrying most of the burden, or none of the adult children may be helping the elder. You will not be able to go back in time to resolve old sibling rivalries or remove hatreds toward a previously abusive parent who now requires help from adult children, but you can assist the family in keeping the discussion in the here-and-now. The family with the lopsided division of labor may be helped through an appreciation of fairness. The family with the long-term resentments may be helped to see that they will feel better about themselves, despite the fairness matter, if they do help out rather than if they do not help.

---

**THOUGHT–DISCUSSION QUESTIONS**

Think about the gerocounseling you do or would like to do someday. What interventions have you used or what interventions would you like to try? Based on your experiences with older adults, what interventions do you believe have the most promise? Why?

# Chapter 9

# *Gerocounseling Terminations*

$T$here is no period after the word ending. . . . Like the Gero-Chi Models, endings, terminations, and deaths are circular words. Each is coupled with resurrection. There are all kinds of deaths— real and fantasized, literal and allegorical, anticipated and unexpected, primary and secondary, major and minor, and so on. And there are all kinds of resurrections. When a person is widowed or when an adult child orphaned, death opens a window to a new identity. Every funeral or good-bye demands, or offers, new forms of relating.

Because endings and beginnings are coupled, we feel ambivalent about them. Often there is a mixture of sadness, anger, and fear, but sometimes relief, hope, or happy anticipation. Such ambivalence can be seen in our gerocounseling terminations. When clients give up a dysfunctional behavior, they may feel the joy of success but also the loss from relinquishing the familiar. When our service or group ends, there is likely to be mutual pride in the achievement of goals, as well as sadness in the good-byes and fears of the unknown ahead. In like fashion, this closing chapter will first consider losses and then conclude with the findings of gerocounseling.

## *Terminations and the Gero-Chi Model*

Loss is the price tag of life, love, and ownership. As the song goes, "If nothing is forever anymore, what's the word forever for?" We must learn to view loss as a normal part of living. Grief is the concomitant or personal expression of loss, but as there are many different ways people age, there are many differences in the ways people grieve.

## The Self-System

As we grow older, we become increasingly vulnerable to multiple losses. The older person, coping with these many bio-psycho-social losses faces the task of preserving the self. Looking back at losses and gains, the elderly reminisce and reflect upon their lives, and respond with either despair or, we would rather hope, a sense of integrity and value.

## The Major Subset Systems

Losses in one subset system reverberate to create losses in other systems, as we saw in Chapter 3.

### *Biological Losses*

Losses in organ function are compounded by psychological and social losses. Because of diminished vision, Anna discontinued needlework and Mr. Smith gave up his driver's license; Arthur Brown's golf group swapped 18 holes for 9 due to cardiovascular changes among its members, and so on. Physical changes brought psychological and social ones in their wake.

### *Psychological Losses*

Because her mother had Alzheimer's Disease, Mabel Petsky believed she had it too when she experienced confusion and memory loss. Friends told her it was all in her head and she was creating her own problems. When symptoms intensified, she was angry and frightened but also pleased as it proved she had been right. Later, when she was told it was a curable depression, she had a hard time giving up the idea she had dementia. It was difficult to replace one mind set for another as well as to lose self-esteem by admitting she was wrong.

Martin Crimmings excelled academically and professionally; a successful engineer, he possessed common sense and was a master at solving family problems. His family, after three years of denying the increasing cognitive deficits Martin was displaying, finally sought medical advice after he lost his way several times. When the diagnosis eventually resulted in probable Alzheimer's disease, the family scurried for a second opinion, and a third. They could not accept the reality that they must regard him as he was now becoming. A counselor at the last assessment center finally helped them to see that Martin could always be the husband and father they loved even though, because of his increasing losses and needs, he had to be seen and cared for in new ways. The past, though now only memories, would never really be gone.

Arthur Brown encountered some psychological problems in his mid-eighties. A long-time devotee of the activity theory, Arthur prided himself in his independence and goal-oriented outlook. He broke a hip after slipping on the ice one winter day and neither a hip replacement nor months of physical therapy could restore mobility.

Confined to a wheelchair and what he viewed as unbearable dependency on others, Arthur mourned the death of his self-concept and fell into a major depression. Medicines helped to relieve the chemical manifestations of his illness, but he would not accept any gerocounseling to make attitudinal changes. Living across from a golf course, he wept as golfers went by his windows. He had dreamt of dying at the 18th hole with a final birdie.

## Sociological losses

Physical and psychological losses also create social losses and vice versa. Most social losses revolve around social roles—driver, golfer, protector, handyman, and so forth. Other losses are more external. The 1987 stock market malaise and savings and loan scandal caused many retirement funds and the financial security of many retirees to plummet. Depression, even suicides, follow such events.

Certainly retirement, with its gifts of leisure, has also been known to have its share of role, financial, and companionship losses. Many a carefully worked-out retirement plan has been sabotaged by unanticipated illness and disability or increased taxes and inflation. Relationship losses, however, create the greatest problems for most. Friends and family relocate, go to nursing homes, divorce, and die. Family or friendship feuds separate and split. Pets, such as Anna's, die unexpectedly or the old pet must be put to sleep.

Elders report more fear about the deaths of close friends and family than about their own. They also fear the unpredictability of pain and loss of dignity and self with illness. Saunders (1959), founder of the Hospice Movement, identified three interacting sources of pain in the terminally ill: (a) mental or emotional pain (anxiety and depression made less powerful through verbal expression to a concerned listener); (b) social pain (a result of the relinquishment of responsibilities); and (c) spiritual pain (from questions that ask, "Why?"). Like the related family in grief, the patient grieves the present losses and the ones that are to come.

---

**THOUGHT–DISCUSSION QUESTION**
Consider the losses that you have observed in your aging clients or friends. What ripple effects did they have?

---

## Coping With Terminations

The past coping-with-grief patterns of both client and counselor reappear in termination. If grief from previous losses is still unresolved, that termination may be painful and fraught with unexpected problems. How do we deal with losses? We grieve, we mourn, and we spend a time in bereavement. Grief is our personal expression of our loss; mourning is the process of adaptation to the loss; and bereavement denotes the time frame for adaptation.

## Grief and Mourning

Grief makes what happened outside the self, inside. Grief reactions include shock, emotional release, preoccupation with the loss, symptoms of physical distress (e.g., sleeplessness, tight throat, choking sensation, shortness of breath, sighing, digestive discomfort), emotional distress (sense of unreality, emotional distance, seeing others as shadowy or small, panic, a desire to run away), hostile reactions, guilt, depression, and withdrawal. Grief also involves re-entering relationships and seeking resolution and readjustment.

Mourning is really a healing process, similar to physical healing, with curative functions such as accepting reality, experiencing the pain, adjusting to the environment without the lost one, and reinvesting emotional energy in life (Worden, 1982). Full or impaired functioning may result. The bereavement time can be short (one or two days for a minor situational loss) or last several years or a lifetime. Grief reactions are transferred through generations as well and some, then, are ongoing.

### Complicated Bereavement

If successful grieving completes most of the tasks outlined above, it can then be called "good grief." "Bad grief" or complicated bereavement is also seen.

---

## Examples of Complicated Bereavement

---

*Avoided*: There is absent or inhibited, unexpressed grief. The mourner is too strong, coping too well and is too controlled. Feelings and symptoms are suppressed because "life must go on." Psychic numbing may cause somatic symptoms.

*Postponed*: Grief is denied until a new loss emerges. Then the mourner reacts intensively.

*Masked*: Grief is verbally unexpressed and manifested in physical, psychiatric, or behavioral symptoms, but the mourner does not make the connection. Masked grief can also be distorted or exaggerated.

*Distorted*: The grief bears little resemblance to reality, and it is fixated on one small part.

*Exaggerated*: An overly intense reaction prevails.

*Chronic*: Profound, long-lasting, and excessive grief occurs. The mourner is stuck and is no longer himself/herself. Chronic grief can also be compulsive or unresolved grief.

*Compulsive*: Constant mourning occurs with no resolution.

*Unresolved*: The mourner's tasks are incomplete, and the mourner hangs onto bereavement behaviors.

As shown, there are many ways that grief can go wrong. As you and your clients will be grieving about termination, you will notice the signs of mismanaged grief and bring attention to it. Oftentimes a grief assessment begins with, "How did you deal with such losses in the past?"—especially if the clients had previous counseling experiences.

### *Depression*

Complicated grief reactions lead to depression, a treatable affective disorder described in previous chapters. Many factors associated with aging contribute to a person's vulnerability to depression, such as physical and social changes, losses, developmental issues, illness, adverse medication effects, biological predisposition, and the idea of advancing death. Depression can also be found in gerocounselors. When complicated grief reactions and/or depression are existent and untreated, they can lead to problems in transference, countertransference, and in the ethics of gerocounseling relationship skills, particularly at termination time.

## *Terminations and Gerocounseling*

Adjustment, accommodation, and acceptance of an enormous variety of losses must be achieved at every step of the aging journey. It is a gigantic challenge that some meet more easily or willingly than others. One of the gerocounselor's goals is to soften, if not prevent, some of the elder's losses and yet, paradoxically, we create one for them ourselves. For instance, we may accept a lonely, isolated, depressed elder as our client, develop a warm, trusting, caring relationship together, and then, when the client has worked hard and achieved goals (sometimes for us and not for oneself, as hoped), we reward that client by saying it is time to terminate. Good counseling implies that the person gains entry into the client's or family's lives, joins with them, and then exits without harm to anyone. It is almost an impossible accomplishment in work with elders. Grief counselors deal with this by practicing like the family doctor. With a time-limited contract built into the client's expectations from the start, which is reinforced throughout the counseling, the clients know that they can call again when needed.

Good counseling also requires that you create your replacement early in the counseling. The question, "Who are you going to talk to after our sessions are over?" should be asked frequently. Referring some client questions to sources outside the counseling setting ("I wonder what your son would say about that?") is also helpful as are other ways to avoid excessive dependency. Referrals to self-help groups, senior centers, or other resources help to prevent your termination from becoming the last straw in a series of painful losses.

Why then terminate? Sometimes the agency or insurance plan requires termination when the immediate problem is solved. Improvement was or was not achieved, but in any case the services are no longer needed, wanted, or funded. At other times, the client may relocate to another locale or move to a different level of care. You, the gerocounselor, may be moving, transferring, or resigning. Your client may, as many in gerocounseling do, die. Good-byes are difficult for most everyone; the only question is, "How do we make these good-byes graciously?"

---

### THOUGHT–DISCUSSION QUESTIONS
Again, consider the losses that you have observed among your aging clients and friends. How did these elders cope with their losses? If you noted complicated bereavement in any way, what forms did it take?

---

## Transference and Countertransference

As mentioned, transference and countertransference were terms used by Freud to describe unconscious processes involving the arousal of the patient's or analyst's unresolved conflicts and feelings, which were prompted by the therapy process. They were considered blind spots, stumbling blocks that needed to be resolved. Today they have broader, less negative, connotations and are considered appropriate, natural, emotional responses, therapeutic tools, and the basis for empathy and understanding of both the older client's and the helper's own processes. Transference and countertransference affect how we counsel and how we terminate.

**Transference** in clients is not uncommon, and you must be aware of it to remain objective. Perhaps you made good progress in bonding and meeting goals with the Chan family, only for them to "no show" after you brought up the topic of termination. Putting aside your hurt feelings, you may remember Mrs. Chan's pattern of rejecting before being rejected, and you may call her to say you'd appreciate a good-bye session. (Your own hurt feelings may be a result of *your* countertransference and fears of rejection which need reframing. Were the Chans rejecting you, or were they feeling rejected?)

A second family, who made good progress, developed a new problem or symptom every time you talked about terminating. Instead of turning such events into an ego trip wherein you feel enormously needed, you openly recognize their fears about being on their own in the future, heap praise on them for progress to date, and help them to appreciate their strengths and readiness to venture alone.

Another client, after being praised for progress, may become hostile and devalue the counseling received. The client insists that any success was self-induced and that it happened in spite of you, not because of you. You openly recognize that the client may be angry with you for ending the counseling, as so many of his/her relationships ended in the past. The client may disagree adamantly and you do not argue. Unmasking self-deception hurts self-esteem and, who knows, maybe the client is right about your lack of helping.

Other clients, with self-devaluation patterns, may express exaggerated appreciation for your efforts and send you fruit at Thanksgiving and flowers at Christmas. You gently point out that you were only the catalyst; they were the ones who created the success. Another formerly depressed client expresses sadness about ending but also gladness because the counseling was connected to grief issues which are no longer paramount.

A client may cling to you in order to prolong the relationship even when goals are reached. This is often the dependent client, like Carol Brown, who had difficulty terminating each session and always had one more story to tell after the hour was supposedly over. It is hoped that you handled this by reassuring Carol that you were not rejecting her but that the schedule is that you must see everyone on time. "Could she make notes on her after-thoughts for next time?" This helps to pave the way for a later termination. (Such "holding-on" behaviors are usually a clue that termination will be difficult. )

As shown, clients display resistance to termination in a variety of ways. Earlier, we discussed that resistance is commonly seen in counseling, and it is best not to argue with it. Often reframing your idea in a less direct stance (or in a pessimistic style, like your client's, for example, "What will you do if you find that you can't get along without counseling in a few months?") will work. Other times, confrontation will be necessary, but go gently and use it sparingly. Many a well-meaning confrontation has resulted in a lost or harmed client. Sometimes the confrontation can be couched in a way that implies that *you* have the problem ("I'm confused, Carol. You say you are happy that the group is ending, but you are looking and sounding sad to me.").

Countertransference will also surface at termination. As a perfectionist, you may not want to terminate because you see that the goals are not yet perfectly achieved, the clients not completely cured. If there is unresolved grief over one of your deceased loved ones, you may not want to let this dear client go. Other times, if unresolved grief exists, you may terminate coldly, wanting to get it over with as soon as possible. If your personal life is wanting, you may find it hard to give up any client as it may result in increased loneliness.

You may feel repulsion about the problems of your clients (say, obesity or alcoholism, due to similar problems in your family), but because such feelings are unacceptable to your self-concept, you may go overboard in overprotecting the client, or find yourself terminating them prematurely. Your clients' problems may be those very problems that you fear may happen to you someday, such as disability, excessive dependency, sexual unattractiveness, loss of bowel and bladder control, physical suffering, and death. None of us would welcome such circumstances, but if a specific condition creates more than normal anxiety in you, you may act adversely.

Sometimes a counselor finds it difficult to accept the fact that counseling itself has limits and is not indispensable to clients. Herr and Weakland (1979) warn that you should not become a crutch to clients, that you should help them in the shortest amount of time necessary, and that you should leave something for them to work on after termination.

## Ethics and Termination

Earlier in Chapter 2, we stated that the three ethical principles of counseling—autonomy, beneficence, and fidelity—are sometimes in conflict. This can be especially true at termination. You may be firm in your belief that the client or family has not made sufficient progress to "make it on their own," but they may insist on terminating in the belief that they are ready. Again, unless the client is determined incompetent, the client's autonomy must prevail over what you deem as your beneficence. Another time a client may wish to terminate but not want a physician or family member to know about it, and here your fidelity must prevail. Still, at other times, your beneficence must win out.

> Joan, at the Counseling Center, had an ethics problem with "no shows." Because she was in private practice and did not wish to give the impression that she was trying to hold onto her "paying clients," she did not follow up on "no shows" in the belief that she was granting them autonomy. "If the Chans no longer wished counseling," she said, "that was their right." Her consultant helped her to see that in this case, beneficence should win out. Paying clients should not be treated differently from non-paying clients, and maybe Mrs. Chan's "no show" reflected a hidden agenda. Perhaps she knew termination was coming and because she experienced this as a form of rejection, her characteristic manner of dealing with this was to reject before she became rejected. Joan called the Chans and they expressed happiness about being given the opportunity to achieve a happier closure.

When a client leaves your level of care to go to another, that client must sign permission for records to follow, and that client has the right to review such records and make deletions if desired. If a terminally ill client tells you secrets in the last dying days, those secrets should remain with you forever, too. If you live in a small city, many of your clients will be around as long as you will. Long after termination, you will meet their relatives or people who knew them or you will read about them in the papers for this and that. Some may even become famous (or infamous). Your ethical principles should continue to be observed long after termination.

---

**THOUGHT–DISCUSSION QUESTIONS**

List some of the losses in your life. How did you cope with each? Do you have a particular style for dealing with losses (abrupt or slow and gradual, active or passive, you the initiator or you the one who lets things happen)? What physical, behavioral, cognitive, and emotional ways do you respond? Does your response style help or interfere with your gerocounseling work with older clients and their families? Think of a time when you were grieving personally. Did that grief impinge upon your responses to your clients? How?

# Types of Terminations

Several kinds of client circumstances require termination in gero-counseling. We terminate at the end of a session and a case. We terminate when our client relocates. And we terminate at our client's death.

## *Termination of a Session*

At the end of the first session, all parties must decide if the relationship is to continue. Despite competent intake clearance, you may discover that the presenting problem does not cover your expertise or the agency's scope. Then a proper referral is made with appropriate follow-up. This should not be seen as an inadequacy on your part; many will require specialized services, and one cannot help everyone. It is more a sign of your professional competence to refer than to accept a case about which you are unqualified.

Other times, clients may assert that they are not comfortable with your counseling style, gender, or age, and after an objective discussion you will grant those clients autonomy by arranging a referral to another. Unfortunately, this frank talk doesn't happen enough; usually a disappointed new client will just cancel or "no show" without discussion. At first session's end, ask the clients if they would like to make another appointment, thus giving them permission to say no if desired.

When terminating all sessions, let the client know that the session is coming to a close before the actual time. State the allotted time in the beginning and help the client stick to that. If the client seems reluctant, offer to continue at another specified hour and give written confirmation of time, date, place, etc. Because a client may confuse separation with rejection, make it clear that you are not trying to get rid of the client. By setting and keeping your time limits, you will be demonstrating the professional nature of your relationship as discussed in Chapter 2.

At closing, briefly recapitulate in a friendly fashion what has been discussed in terms of decisions made, questions left unanswered, and actions to be taken. Invite the client to make any revisions if necessary. You will probably close with informal talk.

## Termination of a Case

Case terminations are either planned or unplanned. It is hoped that most will fall in the former category, but occasionally a client will "no show" and stop calling, or he/she might fire you as Meg fired Juan in Chapter 2. As we grant clients autonomy, we grant them the right to not like or not desire our services. If a client no shows, you should make a follow-up phone call to ensure that there is no misunderstanding. The client may be waiting for your call and feeling abandoned by you.

If the client wishes to terminate, offer assistance with referral. In cases of a move to another state, give the name and address of the Area Agency on Aging in the new locale as a referral source. As people usually feel guilty about rejecting others, assure your client that you do not take this ending personally and will see them at a later date if needed. Planned terminations can be carefully integrated throughout the three phases of counseling.

**Phase One.** This phase, described in Chapters 1–6, involves making a therapeutic relationship, getting to know and assess your client, setting goals, and determining appropriate modalities. How and when you terminate with your client should be thought through early in phase one. It is a part of goal-setting, especially.

**Phase Two.** Chapters 7 and 8 described phase two which is sometimes called the "working through" phase. Here, interventions are matched to assessment. Again in this phase, termination should be given heavier weight than it usually is.

At first the client may relinquish some responsibility for the problem, but as stress diminishes and strengths emerge, it is gradually reclaimed. In this phase, the way to termination is paved as the client knows that the counselor is not always around but that there are others to fill in when you are on vacation, on the phone, or otherwise unavailable. It is helpful to begin each group session with, "This is group session number two; we have eight more."

Subtly, you will be terminating as you help your clients expand social networks and practice new social skills. The counselor or group should be seen as transitional objects which bridge the client with the social network outside the counseling setting. So again, do not allow yourself to become the client's entire social support.

Preparation for termination is made in the middle phase by periodically reviewing progress. Asked frequently is, "Are we approaching our goal, making progress?" Here also, you must ask, "When will we be getting close to termination?"

With depressed clients, Seligman (1975) suggests a temporary termination first. Four preparatory sessions are used. In the first, the client is warned about the counselor's coming vacation and advised that there will be a plan for continued growth and referral if necessary. At the second, there is more discussion about the client's feelings and the interim plan. At the third, separation goals and plans are again discussed. At session four, the client finishes interim planning, puts it in writing, and feelings are processed. A plan may be for the client to have written communication with the counselor during the separation.

***Phase Three***. Here, all termination work is consolidated: (a) the counseling progress is reviewed; (b) the client's readiness to end counseling is assessed; (c) unfinished issues are either resolved or referred as future tasks; (d) the client's increased self-reliance and confidence is stressed; and (e) the client–counselor relationship is brought to a close.

Complimenting the client or family for their accomplishments provides empowerment for continued work on their problem. You will also alert them to be vigilant about future slippage as progress does not always last, and family systems have a tendency to revert back to their former ways. Let them know that your counseling can and should go on without you by asking, "Now that you have some tools, what will you need or want to continue working on?"

Rituals help to solidify gains. Mary, at the Senior Center, holds a mock graduation with diplomas, a potluck, and a graduation cake. Earlier, the group decided to meet independently without her for continued self-growth. Using rituals of hugs and handshakes is also an appropriate way to say good-bye. Mary continues this show of concern and caring with a follow-up phone call some weeks later.

Termination does not have to mean the absolute end. Rather, it is a closure of a unique interpersonal relationship that may be resumed and/or applied to other relationships. As in the separation process necessary to good parenting, if the early relationship was good and the counseling successful, the separation will be less of a problem. It is always easier to say good-bye with love and appreciation than with anger and frustration.

As you will recall, Joan at the Counseling Center began seeing Anna for problems of depression after the death of Anna's cat, which was the final straw in a long series of losses in Anna's later years. The assessment and intervention processes that Joan employed with Anna were described in Chapter 8.

At the initial session, Joan instinctively considered termination risks ahead because of Anna's problems with losses. Thinking of termination was further prompted by verification of Anna's insurance coverage. She told Anna and her daughter that such hurts can take a long time to heal but if medication was indicated and if Anna responded favorably to it, counseling might last six months with intermittent follow-ups.

As Joan and Anna worked together, one goal was to redevelop Anna's social network, which had been fragmented by Molly's relocation. After she had been on medication a few weeks, Anna's energy and motivation started to reappear. Joan remembered that "good old Marge Addams" had been a wonderful resource for Mabel Petsky and asked Anna if she could have permission to call Marge to see if she would bring Anna to the group at the Senior Center. Anna was wary but agreed. The arrangement was set up and Anna joined Mary's support group.

Sometime later Anna also expressed interest in a Bible study group but lamented that she did not belong to a church. Since Anna was Lutheran, Joan discussed some of the senior activities that the local Lutheran churches had to offer. She gave Anna a list of local churches that she might visit and ministers to contact. Her daughter agreed to accompany her mother on these church visits so that Anna would not feel uncomfortable going alone. She finally decided on Pastor Johnson's church where there were not only Bible study groups but also a volunteer group where she could work on making placemats for nursing homes. She also joined a swimnastic exercise group at the YWCA.

Anna was almost too good a client. She picked up Joan's direct and indirect suggestions and always followed through. It was almost as if she were trying to please Joan more than herself. Joan was afraid that Anna was starting to hope that Joan could become that "lost friend." Joan dealt with this transference by reviewing Anna's current needs and goals, mostly the rebuilding of an outside support system so that when her daughter went back to work full-time and when counseling ended, Anna would have a fuller life and not need them anymore. This was verbalized and Anna did not object.

In June, Joan told Anna that there would be a three-week break in their counseling because she was taking a trip in August. She told Anna that there would be counselors available to see her if necessary and there would be some homework assignments so that she could continue getting well on her own. She complimented Anna's progress and said she believed that Anna was ready for this step. Anna nodded, but with some hesitation.

The next week Anna discussed her fears about Joan's absence, "What if she slipped back?" They discussed the fact that Dr. Singh, her psychiatrist, would be seeing her for a checkup during the first week and that the senior center group would be busy planning their summer picnic. Also, Anna had become friendly with Pastor Johnson and she knew she could always call on him if she felt "shaky."

At the third session, Anna stated that she was still a bit anxious but she thought that she could make it. Her daughter had invited her to her lake home for the third week of Joan's absence.

The week before Joan left, Anna and Joan put their vacation plan in writing: Anna would start a journal and partake in various pleasurable activities. She would go to her daughter's and also agreed to serve on the picnic committee at the Senior Center. Joan promised to read her journal (if Anna wished) when she returned.

The vacation from counseling went well as planned. Anna developed new confidence from making it on her own which Joan reinforced with much praise about her progress. Fall was coming and Anna signed up for some classes. They decided to see each other every other week for two months and then just once in December because Anna would be traveling to visit a son in California. Because the trip and Christmas might be stressful, they agreed to see each other again in January for two or more sessions to make sure that she was ready for termination. This occurred, and Anna expressed a readiness to terminate counseling—only with the assurance that she could return if she ever "took such a tailspin again." Joan promised and they both hugged in what was not a "good-bye" but a "till we meet again gesture."

---

**THOUGHT–DISCUSSION QUESTIONS**
Consider Joan's handling of Anna's case termination. How and why did it work out well? Would you have done anything differently?

---

## Termination and Relocation

Termination due to a client's move to another level of care can solve or arouse many problems for the elder client and for the family system and also raise some conflicting feelings in the gerocounselor.

Rabbi Goldman worked hard and long to help Sara Crimmings see that her burden of caregiving to her husband Martin had become too great. But because of an earlier commitment she had made to him (the old refrain, "I'll never put you in a nursing home"), she felt duty-bound to keep her unrealistic promise, even though her health was failing. Her adult children supported this decision and there seemed to be a massive family denial in regard to how Mr. Crimmings' condition was deteriorating and Sara's strengths waning. Rabbi Goldman feared that Sara would become a patient herself in short time. It was only after Sara broke vertebrae in her spine as she was trying to move Martin that everyone agreed. Rabbi Goldman was happy that she could help Sara and the family resolve their moral conflict and end their denial.

The Crimmings' problems did not end with Martin's placement, however. Sara and family members visited almost around the clock. While the nursing home provided an informal visiting arrangement for families, it was not meant to extend to the limits to which the Crimmings family pushed it. The family felt that one of them should supervise Martin's care at all times and not only got in the way of staff members executing their duties but also prevented Martin from relating to staff and adjusting to the new home. Martin's eldest son, a successful lawyer, was often critical of the home's administration. Martin's daughter, Marie, was overprotective of Martin, talked to him in a patronizing manner and infantilized him most of the time. Cary, another daughter, argued with Martin and was irritated when he was not acting "smart." The middle son, Tom, was the most helpful to staff and to Martin, but he was openly critical of his siblings.

Sara did not know what to do with her adult children's behaviors and, in her helplessness, withdrew. Her health continued to decline and the doctor finally told her that she could visit the nursing home only twice a week. Her three oldest children perceived her ailing and the physician's recommendations as evidence of her selfishness and lack of caring for Dad, and they turned against her. They poured even more attention on their father. Because Sara did not drive, she could not get to the nursing home unless Tom was free, but his job often took him out of town. She became increasingly depressed.

Pastor Johnson had mixed feelings about his work with Virginia Brown. In the previous year, Virginia's daughter had called from another state to complain that her mother was not handling independent living adequately. Pastor Johnson visited and reported Mrs.

Brown's clutter was a result of recent moving and cataract surgery. "She will get her act together soon," he advised the daughter in his usual optimistic manner. (Pastor Johnson prided himself on his independence and did everything he could to foster this in others.) But this did not happen. Mrs. Brown's lack of self-care and home cleanliness got worse instead of better. Complaints were made about her apartment. Pastor Johnson felt sad about having to help her give up her independence and move to a Community Care Residence Facility (CCRF). He felt that he had failed.

John, resident manager of Elmbrook (a home for healthy, alert, ambulatory seniors), was called by Mr. François' son who inquired whether his father could be admitted. Mr. François had been living alone in a large home on the lake since his wife died. He had arthritis, prostate cancer, depression and confusion and the doctor believed that he needed an environment that offered more socialization. John said that he could not make a decision based on limited information, but after confirming medical reports from Mr. François' primary physician and psychiatrist, he was confident that Mr. François would fit into Elmbrook. After an adjustment period following the move, Mr. François became less confused and depressed. John was glad that he didn't make a snap decision on Mr. François, as he fit in well.

Sisters, Linda and Barbara, lament the fact that help was not available to assess their father's mental deterioration from Alzheimer's disease. "If a professional diagnosis could have been made," they believe, "our father would have been placed in a secure facility and our family tragedy would not have taken place."

Juan, HSD Casemanager, had had Mrs. Petsky as a client since he himself started at the department. He was called in originally when there was some suspicion that Mabel's relatives were abusing her. Indeed, the family live-in situation was not good for her, and her children did not want to "take her in." After much groundwork he succeeded in wrenching Mabel from her symbiotic relationship with her sister, getting her into Ellis Home despite the long waiting list, and then making sure that she was eligible for county funding. Mabel was finally able to make the move, but her initial adjustment was wrought with problems, and it wasn't until another resident, Marge Addams, took Mabel under her wing that Mabel started to improve. The two joined Mary's group at the Senior Center.

Mabel enjoyed the group and her new relationships. However (as related in Chapter 7), she became depressed in conjunction with a heart problem that jeopardized her current living arrangement. Juan orchestrated the necessary help through the Community Options Program, and Mabel was happy that she was able to stay in the place she now called "home."

Mabel returned to her support group and other activities. However, in the senior group discussions, Mabel spoke freely of her obsessive fear that, like her mother, she was developing Alzheimer's disease. The group waffled between sympathetically reassuring her that she was all right and rudely telling her to shut up about it. They said she was creating her own problem and "driving them nuts." Mary called Juan when Mabel's disorientation and self-neglect reached frightening proportions. This time, Juan arranged for a geriatric assessment. Because of her other medical problems, the many medications she was on, her previous depression, and the fact that she lived alone, the assessment was done on an inpatient basis.

Mabel was hospitalized for six weeks. Initially, she was disruptive on the unit, but settled down and became so overly dependent on the staff that she did not want to go home to her empty apartment. A transitional day-treatment was arranged following her discharge wherein she slept at home but went to the hospital during days. Throughout this, Juan visited and helped her with homecoming. (He even supervised foster placement of Mabel's cat.) The continuity of his participation helped her to make the transitions to and from the hospital easier.

Institutionalization is usually indicated if there is physical illness; disturbances in thinking and feeling such as delusions and depression; real or potentially harmful behavior (confusion, unmanageability, medical non-compliance, violence, suicidal tendencies); psychosis that cannot be treated in the community; a need for detoxification or in-patient treatment of alcoholism, family and pharmacological inabilities to manage difficult organic brain disorder behaviors; and/or when a caregiver is unavailable or incapable of providing needed care.

Despite the fact that such placements should be motivated by beneficence, it is wise to remember how traumatic such moves are to older persons and their families. Changes in living conditions, for better or for worse, can result in "transfer mortality," that is, illness, confusion, or death. Successful moves require at least a year's preparation and should be accompanied with support and the mover's involvement when possible. When the move is to a nursing home or mental hospital, it should be done with the expectation and possibility of returning home if possible.

Although some family members feel relieved at placement, this soon turns to guilt over feeling that relief and over the notion that they may have abandoned their elder. Grief reactions are common and expected. It is almost as if the elder had died, worse rather, because of the issue of abandonment and society's negative views of that. Admissions can be facilitated by pre-visits, extended family stays, sleep-overs for family members, and volunteer work in the facility. Sensitive nursing homes welcome children and pets and provide private visiting rooms, support groups for families, and more. Admittedly, the Crimmings family overdid it, but families should be encouraged to hold quality visits often, provide transportation for home visits and outings, contribute extras, and so on.

When a nursing home is a rigid, isolated community, more interested in its own smooth management than in providing a home for its residents, then "institutional neurosis," characterized by erosion of personality, overdependence, automatic behavior, anhedonia, and lack of expression, can be seen in its residents. However, nursing homes do not have to be negative experiences for elders or their families.

Gerocounselors should look into their own countertransference feelings about nursing home placements so as not to prejudice clients and families one way or the other. There are examples of nursing home abuses, tender-loving greed, and granny dumping in some instances, to be sure, but decisions about nursing home placement and nursing homes in general should be evaluated on an individual basis and not lumped together—just as we must not lump all older persons together.

---

**THOUGHT–DISCUSSION QUESTIONS**
Consider the above case examples and the discussion on relocation. How close to the reality of your professional experiences are these messages? What can be done to make relocation easier for older clients and their families?

---

## Termination and Death

Pastor Johnson and Rabbi Goldman had much training and experience in helping elders die. Dying patients and their families seem to need wise counsel at death more than any other time. Annie Mae, as a nurse, helps terminal patients and families, too, and she often stays beyond her shift just to "be there" at that time. Mary, Senior

Director, and Joan at the Counseling Center have also counseled their share of dying clients and ailing friends. Ernie, as family "Doc," does it regularly.

As the numbers of elderly persons increase, gerocounselors will be administering more to the dying, and counseling skills for dying and bereavement must be included in the gerocounselor's repertoire. Many will encompass the same relationship skills discussed in previous chapters. Others will be new.

Several texts that relate to counseling the dying and bereaved are helpful (e.g., Rando, 1984; Worden, 1982). Good advice also comes from the Hospice Movement, a philosophy of caring and an array of services, founded in 1967 by Dr. Cicely Saunders in Great Britain. Hospice was meant to be homecare, but its principles are used in hospital settings, too. Integrating nursing and counseling models, it is another area wherein the helping professions learn and share with each other.

Rather than somatic cure, hospice uses a care model, and interventions include education, clarification, empowerment, environmental manipulation, family systems, group process, and other techniques, as well as practical medical skills. It is palliative in that the goal is to lessen pain and discomfort and to provide counseling around bereavement issues. Even if you are not directly working with the dying person, you may be counseling the family. Or you may be helping a terminally ill person and her or his family to make final decisions. In any instance, gerocounselors should understand the philosophy and provisions of hospice care. Hospice includes assistance during all phases of a terminal situation, that is, the illness, active dying, bereavement, and follow-up phases.

### The Living with Illness Phase

After a medical diagnosis and prognosis of a terminal condition, the family can be expected to experience initial stages of grief. Early on, there is shock, disbelief, denial, bargaining, and so forth. As they become more empowered with information, members regroup to provide caregiving tasks. Now, if not before, the gerocounselor can help the individual and family make decisions about advance directives and other issues such as getting the dying one's affairs in order and making appropriate arrangements in the best interests of the elder and family. In conflictual families, there is liable to be added conflict about how plans are to be made and executed.

Advance directives, such as The Living Will or Power of Attorney for Health Care, allow the terminally ill to die without aggressive medical interventions, offering only those interventions to minimize pain and maximize comfort. The patient has the right to refuse or consent to care, and family involvement should occur with the patient's previous permission. In all decision-making, the true feelings of the patient should be ascertained as clearly as possible through one-on-one and family discussions.

If a hospice is chosen, they will support and guide the patient and family through the illness, dying, and post-death phases. After a psychosocial assessment, the emphasis is on empowering the patient and family with information and support about the illness and its limitations, the strengths of the family system, and the hospice relationships. The maintenance of personal worth, hope, energy, decision-making, and normal activities within the family are paramount.

## The Active Dying Phase

The hospice counselor has many functions during the active dying phase. Cognitive, affective, and family systems interventions are utilized to support the patient and the family. They also demonstrate principles of autonomy, beneficence, and fidelity.

By allowing fears and other feelings to be expressed through nonjudgmental listening and by providing realistic information about the impending death process, the family is empowered with realistic preparation for death. The patient is included in the decision-making as long as possible, and the environment is so arranged that the person can die with dignity in his/her own personal style. Clergy is called in if desired.

Family systems work encourages the family to reconcile unresolved issues, but the counselor shows acceptance when this is impossible. The family is helped to deal with the children's issues around the death process according to their age-specific needs. All possible family members are reassured that they are giving "good care" according to their own individual abilities. The family as a whole is supported by openly recognizing its strengths and abilities.

The hospice counselor also helps the family negotiate for the provision of someone to be with the dying person during the death vigil. He/she uses people from the family support network to supplement this if necessary. The family is helped to see that dying is a process and that the dying person is still living. They are instructed that it is appropriate to continue "living" themselves while the loved one is dying, and it is acceptable to bring food, drinks, etc., into the room. The hospice worker models the maintenance of contact and communication with the dying person through touch, words, and presence. During this time, the family is encouraged to assure the dying person of remembrance, to give permission to die and say good-bye, and to express their pain and sorrow from the loss. When death is imminent, all who previously indicated a desire to be present are summoned.

### At Death

Remaining calm, reassuring, and caring, the hospice worker allows the family adequate time to be alone with the body and gives permission to touch and reposition, if requested. Mourning is encouraged and shared through tears, touch, listening, and presence.

### After Death

The family is encouraged to mutually support the physical, emotional, and practical needs of its members. Help is given for the arrangement of body removal and meaningful memory rituals. Storytelling about the last times, the good days prior to or during the illness, is encouraged. Again, the family is urged to mourn as a system and to avoid scapegoating. Other significant persons are contacted.

### Bereavement Phase

Bereavement was discussed earlier. Grief is work that needs to be processed, and there are no shortcuts. Along with making necessary adjustments and bearing painful emotions, the bereaved caregivers must make special efforts to take care of themselves physically and spiritually during this at-risk time. There is also much identity work to do. It is almost as if one must develop a new self, a self without the deceased. You will hear your clients say, "I don't know who I am anymore." Knowledge and skills will be needed and, along with your counseling advice, there are many good books and articles on ways to help the bereaved.

---

**THOUGHT–DISCUSSION QUESTIONS**

Simulate cases concerning elderly clients and/or their families who are referred to you because of (a) retirement adjustment, (b) decisions to relocate, (c) loss of a spouse, (d) conflict with a relative, or (e) diagnosis of a terminal illness. How, when/why would you plan terminations in your gerocounseling treatment or care plan?

---

## The Finds of Gerocounseling

This book began defining you as a gerocounselor and stressing the importance of knowing and developing yourself as a person and a professional. This means knowing and managing your own countertransference issues as well as developing knowledge about gerontology, geriatrics, and skills in gerocounseling.

As a gerocounselor, you are also a caregiver, but how often, when you read articles about caregiver stress, do you think of caregivers as "those other folks"? You evidence concern about caregiver burnout; you give support and advice; you guide others through bereavement, arrange respite and day care, and help others examine existential concerns. Do you offer those services to yourself? You help support family members and elders because you know they are currently at risk for morbidity and mortality, but you are at risk of potential burnout and depression, also.

Gerocounselors therefore must model good caregiver self-care. During your caregiving, you should practice good health habits, avoid overwork, and partake in pleasurable activities. You will need a supportive supervisor or consultant who can help you sort out feelings and realities, a support or "cuddle group" who will say, "Hang in there; we've been through that, too," and a confidant who says, "I care." You will need to take time to partake in the grieving rituals of your clients, to attend funerals, to talk about your grief, to ponder the imponderables, to find laughter again.

One of the final tasks of the bereaved is to transform the pain of the loss into a fuller sense of being. If you do your grieving work well, each termination will add growth to your wisdom, sensitivity, and spirituality. Each will add to your knowledge of human nature, the continuity of the generations, the power of emotions, and the meanings of human behaviors. Each will also add to your awareness of the potentials of your own and your parents' own inevitable aging processes.

To many, termination means ending. But do we ever really experience termination? Do we ever really help a person terminate "a problem"? Jung (1933) wrote:

> The serious problems of life, however, are never fully solved. If it should once appear that they are, this is the sign that something has been lost. The meaning and design of a problem seem not to lie in its solution, but in our working at it incessantly. (p. 103)

As gerocounselors, we help our clients acquire tools and then help them to practice using those tools in the ever ongoing life-problem-solving process. Therefore, we must look to care instead of cure. And we must also view gerocounseling as we do life and death, as circular and never-ending processes that can produce grief and pain, but also joy, learning, and spiritual growth. Such are the "finds" of gerocounseling.

---

**THOUGHT–DISCUSSION QUESTIONS**

What are some of the specific "finds" that you have encountered in terminations? How did they add to your continued growth? Why?

---

# References

Abrams, W., & Berkow, R. (Eds.). (1990). *The Merck manual of geriatrics.* Rahway, NJ: Merck Sharp and Dohme Research Laboratories.

Adler, A. (1927). *Understanding human nature.* Greenberg, New York: Greenberg.

American Association for Counseling and Development (1981). "What is counseling and human development?" (AACD Report). Alexandria, VA: American Association of Counseling and Development.

American Association of Retired Persons (AARP) (1989). *Reminiscence: Finding meaning in memories.* Washington, DC: Author.

American Association of Retired Persons (AARP) (1990). *Spousal bereavement and primary health care.* Washington, DC: Author.

American Psychiatric Association (1994). *Diagnostic and statistical manual of mental disorders* (4th ed.). Washington, DC: Author.

American Society on Aging (1990). *Generations, 14*(1).

Beck, A. (1967). *Depression: clinical, experimental and theoretical aspects.* New York: Harper and Row.

Beck, A. (1976). *Cognitive therapy and the emotional disorders.* New York: International University Press.

Biegel, D., Shore, B., & Gordon, E. (1984). *Building support networks for the elderly.* Beverly Hills, CA: Sage.

Birren, J. (1969). Age and decision strategies. In A. Welford & J. Birren (Eds.), *Decision making and age* (pp. 23–36). New York: S. Karger.

Birren, J., & Schaie, K. (1990). *Handbook of the psychology of aging* (2nd ed.). New York: Van Nostrand Reinhold.

Blazer II., D. (1980). The diagnosis of depression in the elderly. *Journal of the American Geriatrics Society, 28,* 52–58.

Blazer II., D. (1982). *Depression in late life.* St. Louis: C. V. Mosby.

Bonjean, M. (1991). Summarized notes from lecture and handouts. Milwaukee, WI: Unpublished.

Bonjean, M. (1988). Solution focused psychotherapy with families caring for an Alzheimer's patient. In G. Hughston, V. Christopherson, & M. Bonjean (Eds.), *Aging and family therapy* (pp. 197–210). New York: The Haworth Press.

Boszormenyi-Nagy, I., & Krasner, B. (1986). *Between give and take*. New York: Brunner/Mazel.

Boszormenyi-Nagy, I., & Stark, G. (1973). *Invisible loyalties*. Hagerstown: Harper and Row.

Bumagin, V., & Hirn, K. (1990). *Helping the aging family*. New York: Springer.

Burlingame, V. (1988). Counseling an older person. *Social Casework, 69*(9), 588–592.

Burnside, I. (Ed.). (1984). *Working with the elderly: group process and techniques* (2nd ed.). Boston: Jones & Bartlett.

Butler, R. (1964). The life review: An interpretation of reminiscence in the aged. In B. Neugarten (Ed.), *Personality in middle and late life* (pp. 486–496). New York: Atherton.

Butler, R. (1969). Ageism: another form of bigotry. *The Gerontologist, 9,* 243–246.

Butler, R. (1974). Successful aging and the role of the life review. Paper presented at the Symposium on Geriatric Medicine, Baltimore, MD, Mar. 2, 1974. In American Association of Retired Persons (Eds.), *Reminiscence* (pp. 8–14). Washington, DC: AARP (1989).

Butler, R., Lewis, M., & Sunderland, T. (1991). *Aging and mental health* (5th ed.). New York: Macmillan.

Cheng, E. (1978). *The elder Chinese*. San Diego, CA: Center on Aging, San Diego State University.

Chopra, D. (1993). *Ageless body, timeless mind*. New York: Harmony Books.

Costa, P., & McCrae, R. (1980). Still stable after all these years: Personality as a key to some issues in aging. In P. Baltes & O. Brims (Eds), *Life-span development and behavior* (Vol. 3). New York: Academic Press.

Cummings, E., & Henry, W. (1961). *Growing old: The process of disengagement*. New York: Basic Books.

Devore, W., & Schlesinger, E. (1991). *Ethnic sensitive social work practice*. New York: Macmillan.

Doherty, W., Baird, M., & Becker, L. (1987). Family medicine and the biopsychosocial model: The road toward integration. In W. Doherty, C. Christianson, & M. Sussman (Eds.), *Family medicine: The maturing of a discipline* (pp. 51–70). New York: The Haworth Press.

Dreher, B. (1987). *Communication skills for working with elders*. New York: Springer.

Duke University Center for the Study of Aging and Human Development. (1978). *Multidimensional functional assessment: the OARS methodology*. Durham, NC: Duke University.

Ebersole, P. (1978). Establishing reminiscing groups. In I. Burnside (Ed.), *Working with the elderly: Group process and techniques*. North Scituate, MA: Duxbury Press.

Ebersole, P., & Hess, P. (1990). *Toward healthy aging* (3rd ed.). St. Louis, MO: C. V. Mosby.

Ellor, J. (1990). On knowing in gerontology. *Generations, 14*(4), 5–6.

Engel, G. (1977). The need for a new medical model: A challenge for biomedicine. *Science, 196*, 129–136.

Erikson, E. (1950). *Childhood and society*. New York: W. W. Norton.

Erikson, E., Erikson, J., & Kivnick, H. (1986). *Vital involvement in old age*. New York: W. W. Norton.

Feil, N. (1993). *The validation breakthrough: Simple techniques for communicating with people with "Alzheimer's-type dementia."* Baltimore, MD: Health Professions Press.

Fitting, M. (1986). Ethical dilemmas in counseling elderly adults. *Journal of Counseling and Development, 64*, 325–327.

Flori, D. (1989). The prevalence of later life family concerns in the *Marriage and Family Journal* literature (1976–1985): A content analysis. *Journal of Marital and Family Therapy, 15*(3), 289–297.

Folstein, M., Folstein, S., & McHugh, P. (1975). Mini-mental state: A practical method for grading the cognitive state of patients for the clinician. *Journal of Psychiatric Research, 12*, 189–198.

Frankl, V. (1959). *Man's search for meaning*. New York: Washington Square Press.

Frankl, V. (1977). *The doctor and the soul: From psychotherapy to logotherapy*. New York: Vintage Books.

Freud, S. (1924). *Collected papers* (Vol. 1) London: Hogarth.

Gallagher, D., & Thompson, L. (1981). *Depression in the elderly*. San Diego: University of Southern California Press.

Gelfand, D. (1988). *The aging network*. New York: Springer.

Genevay, B., & Katz, R. (1990). *Countertransference and older clients*. Newbury Park, CA: Sage.

Goldfarb, A. (1971). Group therapy with the old and aged. In H. Kaplan & B. Sadock (Eds.), *Comprehensive group psychotherapy* (pp. 623–642). Baltimore, MD: Williams and Wilkins.

Gutmann, D. (1964). An exploration of ego configurations in middle and later life. In B. Neugarten (Ed.), *Personality in middle and late life*. New York: Atherton.

Gutmann, D. (1977). The cross-cultural perspective: Notes toward a comparative psychology of aging. In J. Birren & K. Schaie (Eds.), *Hand-*

*book of the psychology of aging* (pp. 302–326). New York: Van Nostrand Reinhold.

Hamilton, M. (1967). Development of a rating scale for primary depressive illness. *British Journal of Social and Clinical Psychology, 6,* 278–296.

Hargrave, T., & Anderson, W. (1992). *Finishing well: Intergenerational therapy with aging families.* New York: Brunner/Mazel.

Havighurst, R. (1968). Personality and patterns of aging. *The Gerontologist 8,* 20–23.

Havighurst, R., Neugarten, B., & Tobin, S. (1968). Disengagement and patterns of aging. In B. Neugarten (Ed.), *Middle age and aging.* Chicago: University of Chicago Press.

Hendricks, J., & Hendricks, C. (1986). *Aging in mass society.* Boston: Little Brown.

Herr, J., & Weakland, J. (1979). *Counseling elders and their families.* New York: Springer.

Hooyman, N., & Kiyak, H. (1993). *Social gerontology* (3rd ed.). Boston: Allyn and Bacon.

Hoyt, M. (1993, Fall). Brief therapy can be the best therapy. *The Provider, MCC Behavioral Care,* 1–3.

Hughston, G., Christopherson, V., & Bonjean, J. (Eds.). (1988). *Aging and family therapy: Practitioner perspectives on golden pond.* New York: The Haworth Press.

Jacobs, R. (1987). *Older women: Surviving and thriving.* Milwaukee, WI: Family Services of America.

James, W. (1890). *Principles of psychology* (Vol. 2). New York: Holt.

Jung, C. (1933). *Modern man in search of a soul.* San Diego: Harcourt Brace and World.

Jung, C. (1959). *Jung, collected works* (Vols. 1–9). Princeton, NJ: Princeton University Press.

Kane, R. A., & Kane, R. L. (1989). *Assessing the elderly.* Lexington, MA: Lexington Books.

Kaszniak, A., & Allender, R. (1985). Psychological assessment of depression in older adults. In G. Chaisson-Steward (Ed.), *Depression in the elderly: An interdisciplinary approach* (pp. 107–160). New York: Wiley.

Katz, R. (1990). Using our emotional reactions to older clients: A working theory. In B. Genevay & R. Katz, *Countertransference and older clients.* Newbury Park, CA: Sage.

Katz, S., Ford, A., Moskowitz, R., Jackson, B., & Jaffee, M. (1963). Studies of illness in the aged. The index of ADL: A standardized measure of biological and psychosocial function. *Journal of the American Medical Association, 185,* 914–919.

Kiresuk, T., & Sherman, R. (1968). Goal attainment scaling: A general method for evaluating comprehensive community mental health programs. *Community Mental Health Journal, 4.*

Kivnick, H. (1993). Everyday mental health: A guide to assessing life strengths. *Generations, 17*(1), 13–20.

Kübler-Ross, E. (1969). *On death and dying.* New York: Macmillan.

Lawton, M. (1972). Assessing the competence of older people. In D. Kent, R. Kastenbaum, & S. Sherwood (Eds.), *Research planning and action for the elderly,* pp. 122–143. New York: Behavioral Publications.

Lawton, M., & Nahemow, L. (1973). Ecology and the aging process. In C. Eisdorfer & M. Lawton (Eds.), *Psychology of adult development and aging* (pp. 619–674). Washington, DC: American Psychological Association.

MacDonald, P., & Haney, M. (1988). *Counseling the older adult* (2nd ed.), Lexington, MA: Lexington Books, D. C. Heath.

Mardoyan, J., & Weis, D. (1981). The efficacy of group counseling with older adults. *Personnel and Guidance Journal, 60*(3), 161–163.

Maslow, A. (1954). *Motivations and personality.* New York: Harper & Row.

Matteson, M., & McConnell, E. (1988). *Geriatric nursing.* Philadelphia, PA: W. B. Saunders.

Meichenbaum, D. (1974). Self-instructional strategy training: A cognitive prosthesis for the aged. *Human Development, 17,* 273–280.

Moberg, D. (1970). Religion in the later years. In A. Hoffman (Ed.), *The daily needs and interests of older people* (pp. 175–191). Springfield, IL: Charles C. Thomas.

Muth, K. (1993, Dec. 5). To spare others the pain. *Racine Journal Times 1A,* 13A.

Myers, J., Weissman, M., Tischler, G., Holzer, C., Leaf, P., Orvaschel, H., Anthony, J., Boyd, J., Burke, J., & Kramer, M., et al. (1984). Six-month prevalence of psychiatric disorders in three communities. *Archives of General Psychiatry, 41,* 959–967.

National Institute on Aging (1990). *Age page.* Washington, DC: U.S. Department of Health and Human Services.

Neugarten, B., Havighurst, R., & Tobin, S. (1968). Personality and patterns of aging. In B. Neugarten (Ed.), *Middle age and aging,* pp. 173–177. Chicago: University of Chicago Press.

Nutrition Screening Initiative (1993). *Determine your nutritional health checklist.* Washington, DC: *Nutrition Screening Initiative,* 1–4.

Peterson, D. (1990). Personnel to serve the aging in the field of social work: Implications for educating professionals. *Social Work, 35*(5), 412–415.

Rando, T. (1984). *Grief, dying and death: Clinical interventions for caregivers.* Champaign, IL: Research Press.

Regier, D. Boyd, J., Burke, J., Rae, D., Myers, J., Kramer, M., Robins, L., George, L., Karno, M., & Locke, B. (1988). One month prevalence of mental disorders in the United States. *Archives of General Psychiatry, 45,* 977–986.

Reik, T. (1949). *Listening with the third ear.* New York: Farrar, Straus.

Remnet, V. (1989). *Understanding older adults.* Lexington, MA: Lexington Books.

Saunders, C. (1959). *Care of the dying.* London: Macmillan.

Seligman, M. (1975). *Helplessness: On depression, development, and death.* San Francisco, CA: W. H. Freeman.

Selye, H. (1946). The general adaption syndrome and the diseases of adaption. *Journal of Clinical Endocrinology, 6,* 117–230.

Selye, H. (1970). Stress and aging. *Journal of American Geriatrics Society, 18,* 660–681.

Sherman, E. (1993). Mental health and successful adaptation in later life. *Generations, 17*(1), 43–46.

Shibutani, T., & Kwan, K. (1965). *Ethnic stratification.* New York: Macmillan.

Siegel, B. (1986). *Love, medicine and miracles.* New York: Harper & Row.

Skinner, B., & Vaughn, M. (1983). *Enjoy old age.* New York: W. W. Norton.

Sterns, H., Weis, D., & Perkins, S. (1984). A conceptual approach to counseling older adults and their families. *The Counseling Psychologist, 12*(2), 55–61.

Strelow, A., & Specht, H. (1986). *Peer counselor trainer handbook* (rev.). Minneapolis: University of Minnesota Press.

Tobin, S. (1988). Preservation of the self in old age. *Social Casework, 69*(9), 550–553.

Tornstam, L. (1992). The quo vadis of gerontology: On the scientific paradigm of gerontology. *The Gerontologist, 32*(3), 318–326.

Troll, L., Miller, S., & Atchley, R. (1979). Families in later life. Belmont, CA: Wadsworth.

Walter, J., & Peller, J. (1992). *Becoming solution-focused in brief therapy.* New York: Brunner/Mazel.

Waters, E. (1984). Building on what you know: Techniques for individual and group counseling with older people. *The Counseling Psychologist, 12*(2), 63–74.

Waters, E., & Goodman, J. (1990). *Empowering Older Adults.* San Francisco: Jossey-Bass.

Wolberg, L. (1977). *The technique of psychotherapy.* New York: Grune & Stratton.

Wolfelt, A. (1988). *Death and grief: A guide for clergy.* Muncie, IN: Accelerated Development, Inc. Publishers.

Worden, W. (1982). *Grief Counseling and Grief Therapy.* New York: Springer.

Wykle, M., & Musil, C. (1993). Mental health of older persons: Social and cultural factors. *Generations, 17*(1), 7–12.

Yalom, I. (1985). *The theory and practice of group psychotherapy* (3rd ed.). New York: Basic Books.

Yesavage, J., Brink, T., Rose, T., Lum, O., Huang, V., Adey, M., & Leirer, V. (1983). Development and validation of a geriatric depression screening scale: A preliminary report. *Journal of Psychiatric Research, 17*(1), 37–49.

# Index

## A

Active listening, in gerocounseling, 39–42
Activities of daily living assessment, 86–89
Adjustment, as goal of gerocounseling, 116
Affective functioning assessments, 93–96
Aging tasks, system of, Gero-Chi Counseling Model, 19
Alzheimer's disease, intervention, 162–166
Anxiety disorders, intervention, 174–175
Appearance, changes in with aging, 51
Assessment, 75–103
  available resources, 78–81
  client as resource, 78–79
  formal support resources, 79–80
  gerocounselor as resource, 80
  informal support resources, 79
  instruments, 84–103
    Gero-Chi Counseling Model, 84–86
    Ebersole/Hess assessment, 84–85
    OARS assessment, 85
    psycho-social task system assessments, 85–86
  issues of, overview, 75–78
  major subset systems, 86–101
    biological system assessment, 86–89

activities of daily living assessment, 86–89
    physical health assessment, 86
  environmental assessment, 102–103
  psychological system assessment, 89–96
    affective functioning assessment, 93–95
    cognitive functioning assessment, 92–93
    personality functioning assessment, 92
    suicidal intent assessment, 96
  sociological system assessment, 96–101
    family assessment, 97–101
    social support assessment, 97
  methods, 81–84
    collateral contacts, 82–84
    counseling session, 81–82
  point of view, 77–78
  style, 76
  timing, 76–77
Autonomy, in gerocounseling, 26–29

## B

Behaviorist orientation, gerocounselor, 13–14
Beneficence, in gerocounseling, 29–30
Bereavement
  complicated, termination issues, 183–184
  termination issues, 199–201

• **209** •

Biological losses, 180
Biological system
  aging and, 50–56
    appearance, changes in with
      aging, 51
    cardiovascular system, changes in
      with aging, 54
    dental system, changes in with
      aging, 54
    endocrine system, changes in
      with aging, 55
    gastrointestinal system, changes in
      with aging, 54
    medical problems, 56
    mobility, changes in with aging,
      51–52
    neurological system, changes in
      with aging, 53
    oral system, changes in with
      aging, 54
    renal system, changes in with
      aging, 55
    respiratory system, changes in
      with aging, 54
    sensory system, changes in with
      aging, 52–53
      hearing, 52
      sight, 52
      smell, 53
      taste, 52
      touch, 53
    sexuality, changes in with aging, 55
    skeletal system, changes in with
      aging, 53
  assessment of, 86–89
    activities of daily living
      assessment, 86–89
    physical health assessment, 86
Boundaries
  in interventions, 176
  and relationship skills, 31–32

**C**

Cardiovascular system, changes in
  with aging, 54
Caregiver assistance groups, 142
Case
  management intervention, 151–153
  termination of, 190–193
    phase one, 190
    phase three, 191–193
    phase two, 190–191

Client. *See* Gero-clients
  as assessment resource, 78–79
  goals of, 113–114
Cognitive functioning assessment,
  92–93
Cognitive interventions, 155–158
Cognitive orientation, gerocounselor,
  13–14
Communication interventions,
  176–177
Communication skills, 33–42
  active listening, 39–42
  active questioning, 38–39
  communication guidelines, 42–43
  environment of gerocounselor, 34–35
  humor, 36–37
  non-verbal cues, 35–36
  silence, 37
  voice quality, 37–38
Control, client's goals, staying within,
  110–111
Coping
  with aging, 59
  interventions, 177
Countertransference, and termination,
  185–187
Courtesies, relationship skills, 32–33
Crisis intervention, 154–155
Cultural contexts, of aging, 64–67
  ethnic group, 64–66
  minority/majority groups, 67
  social class, 66–67

**D**

Death
  active phase, termination issues,
    199–200
  afterwards, termination issues, 200
  termination issues, 197–201, 200
Dental system, changes in with aging,
  54
Depression
  intervention, 166–174
  and termination, 184
Didactic interventions, 156–157
Different "strokes," as intervention,
  155–160

**E**

Ebersole/Hess assessment, 84–85
Ebersole's goals for aging, 119–120

Educational groups, group counseling, 140
Emotional/supportive interventions, 158–159
Empathy, as relationship skills, 31
Endocrine system, changes in with aging, 55
Enrichment groups, 140
Environment, of gerocounselor, and communication skill, 34–35
Environmental assessment, 102–103
Environmental press, competency, balancing, intervention, 147–148
Erikson's goal for aging, 119
Ethics
  skills, gerocounseling, 24–26
  and termination, 187–188
Ethnic group, 64–66
Experiential interventions, 157–158

F

Family, 67–70
  assessment, 97–101
  disorders, intervention, 175–178
  methods, intervention, 178
  gerocounseling, 129–137
    family, 132
      managing problems in, 134–135
    family therapy, 132–137
    history of, 133
    labeling in families, dealing with, 135–136
    late-family counseling, 136–137
    triangulation, in families, 136
  systems therapy orientation, gerocounselor, 14–15
  therapy goals, of gerocounseling, 120–123
Fidelity, in gerocounseling, 30
Financial concerns, and goal of gerocounseling, 118
Formal support resources, assessment, 79–80
Friends and aging, 70–71

G

Gastrointestinal system, changes in with aging, 54
Gentleness, intervention, 150
Gero-assessment. See Assessment

Gero-Chi Counseling Model, 16–20
  assessment instruments, 84–86
    Ebersole/Hess assessment, 84–85
    OARS assessment, 85
    psycho-social task system assessments, 85–86
  counselor system, 20
  major subset systems, 18
    biological system, 18
    psychological system, 18
    sociological system, 18
  psycho-social task system, 18
  self-system, 16–18
  system of aging tasks, 19
  termination, 180–182
Gero-clients, 45–74
  aging biological system, 50–56
    appearance, changes in with aging, 51
    cardiovascular system, changes in with aging, 54
    dental system, changes in with aging, 54
    endocrine system, changes in with aging, 55
    gastrointestinal system, changes in with aging, 54
    medical problems, 56
    mobility, changes in with aging, 51–52
    neurological system, changes in with aging, 53
    oral system, changes in with aging, 54
    renal system, changes in with aging, 55
    respiratory system, changes in with aging, 54
    sensory system, changes in with aging, 52–53
      hearing, 52
      sight, 52
      smell, 53
      taste, 52
      touch, 53
    sexuality, changes in with aging, 55
    skeletal system, changes in with aging, 53
  aging psychological system, 56–62
    cognitive contexts, 60–62
    coping, 59
    life satisfaction, 58

Gero-clients (*continued*)
  mental health, 58
  personality contexts, 57–59
  stress, 59
aging sociological system, 63–74
  cultural contexts, 64–67
    ethnic group, 64–66
    minority/majority groups, 67
    racial group, 64–66
    social class, 66–67
  historical contexts, 63–64
  relationship contexts, 67–71
    family, 67–70
    friends, 70–71
    late-life marriages, 70
  situational contexts, 72–74
    death/dying, 73–74
    environmental concerns, 72–73
    finances, 73
    health/health care, 72
    retirement, 73
    work, 73
  self-system, 46–49
    gender, 47–49
  spirituality, 49–50
Gerocounseling, 21–44
  communication skills, 33–42
    active listening, 39–42
    active questioning, 38–39
    communication guidelines, 42–43
    environment of gerocounselor,
      34–35
    humor, 36–37
    non-verbal cues, 35–36
    silence, 37
    voice quality, 37–38
  goals. *See* Goals of gerocounseling
  interventions, 147–160. *See also*
    Interventions
  modalities, 127–146. *See also*
    Modalities, gerocounseling
  overview, 201–202
  relationship skills, 31–33
    boundaries, 31–32
    courtesies, 32–33
    empathy, 31
  skills, 23–30
    autonomy, 26–29
    beneficence, 29–30
    ethics skills, 24–26
    fidelity, 30
  specific disorder interventions,
    161–178

structures, 21–23
  termination, 145–146, 179–202,
    184–201. *See also* Termination
Gerocounselor, 1–20
  as assessment resource, 80
  behaviorist/cognitive orientation,
    13–14
  family systems therapy orientation,
    14–15
  Gero-Chi Counseling Model, 16–19
    major subset systems, 18
    psycho-social task system, 18
    self-system, 16–18
    system of aging tasks, 19
  goals of, 115–118
  "grandmother" orientation, 15
  humanist orientation, 13
  importance of, 2–3
  knowledge base, 6–9
  life experiences of, 4–6
  orientations, 11–15
  overview of, 3–10
  psychodynamic orientation, 11–13
  settings, 10
  skills, 9–10
  text, orientation of, 16–20
Goals of aging, 115
Goals of gerocounseling, 105–126,
    142–143
  adjustment, 116
  attainable goals, 123–124
  client's goals, 113–114
  control, client's, staying within,
    110–111
  Ebersole's goal for aging, 119–120
  Erikson's goal for aging, 119
  family therapy goals, 120–123
  financial concerns, 118
  general principles of goal-setting,
    106–108
  gerocounselor's goals, 115–118
  goals of aging, 115
  goals of goals, 106–107
  grading of goals, 124–126
  group gerocounseling, values of,
    139
  language, client's, use of, 112–113
  life control, 118
  living conditions, 116–117
  long-term goals, 113–126
  loss, issues involving, 118
  outcome criteria, 126
  positive goal, defining, 108

present, staying in, 109–110
process form, use of, 109
relationships, 117
responsibilities, 117
short-term goals, 108–113
society's goals, 114
specificity, 110
supports, 115–116
Tobin's goal for aging, 118–119
types of, 107–108
Goals of goals, 106–107
Goal-setting, general principles, 106–108
Grading of goals, 124–126
"Grandmother" orientation, gerocounselor, 15
Grief, and termination, 182–184
Group gerocounseling, 138–146
caregiver assistance groups, 142
educational, 140
efficacy, 146
enrichment groups, 140
goals, 139, 142–143
group process, 143–144
history of, 138
intensive psychotherapy groups, 141
membership, 143
programs, 144
reality orientation groups, 141
recreational, 140
reminiscence groups, 142
remotivation therapy groups, 141
self-actualization groups, 142
service advocacy groups, 140
social, 140
support groups, 140
techniques, 142–146
termination, 145–146
therapy groups, 141–142
topic-specific groups, 140
types of, 139–142
Group process, in group gerocounseling, 143–144
Guilt disorders, intervention, 175

**H**

Hearing, changes in with aging, 52
Hierarchy interventions, 176
Historical contexts, of aging, 63–64
Humanist orientation, gerocounselor, 13
Humor, as communication skill, 36–37

**I**

Illness, living with phase, and termination, 198–199
Individual counseling, 127–129
Informal support, assessment resource, 79
Instruments, assessment, 84–103
Gero-Chi Counseling Model, 84–86
Ebersole/Hess assessment, 84–85
OARS assessment, 85
psycho-social task system assessments, 85–86
Intensive psychotherapy groups, 141
Interventions
case management, 151–153
cognitive interventions, 155–158
crisis intervention, 154–155
didactic interventions, 156–157
different "strokes," utilizing, 155–160
emotional/supportive interventions, 158–159
environmental press, 147–148
experiential interventions, 157–158
gentleness, 150
learning styles, 149
modalities, usage of, 151–155
parsimony, 148
principles guiding choice of, 147–151
reframing interventions, 157–158
reminiscence, 159–160
resources, accessing, 151
Socratic interventions, 157
systems outlook, 150–151
time, usage of, 153–154
training/retraining interventions, 158
values, 148–149
Issues of assessment, overview, 75–78

**K**

Knowledge base, gerocounselor, 6–9

**L**

Labeling in families, dealing with, 135–136
Language, client's, use of, 112–113
Late-family counseling, 136–137

Late-life marriages, 70
Learning style, intervention, 149
Life control, as goal of
    gerocounseling, 118
Life experiences of gerocounselor, 4–6
Life review intervention, 159–160
Life satisfaction, and aging, 58
Listening, active, 39–42
Living conditions, and goal of
    gerocounseling, 116–117
Long-term goals, of gerocounseling,
    113–126
Loss, and goal of gerocounseling,
    118

**M**

Major subset systems assessment
    biological system assessment, 86–89
        activities of daily living
            assessment, 86–89
        physical health assessment, 86
    environmental assessment, 102–103
    psychological system assessment,
        89–96
        affective functioning assessment,
            93–95
        cognitive functioning assessment,
            92–93
        intelligence tests, 93
        personality functioning
            assessment, 92
        suicidal intent assessment, 96
    sociological system assessment,
        96–101
        family assessment, 97–101
        social support assessment, 97
    termination issues, 180–182
Marriages, late-life, 70
Medical problems, 56
Mental health, and aging, 58
Minority/majority groups, 67
Mobility, changes in with aging, 51–52
Modalities
    family gerocounseling, 129–137
        labeling, in families, dealing with,
            135–136
        late-life family counseling,
            136–137
        managing problems in, 134–135
        therapy, 132–137
            history of, 133
        triangulation, in families, 136

gerocounseling, 127–146
    group gerocounseling, 138–146
        caregiver assistance groups, 142
        efficacy, 146
        enrichment groups, 140
        goals, 139, 142–143
        group process, 143–144
        history of, 138
        intensive psychotherapy groups,
            141
        membership, 143
        programs, 144
        reality orientation groups, 141
        reminiscence groups, 142
        remotivation therapy groups,
            141
        self-actualization groups, 142
        service advocacy groups, 140
        social, 140
        support groups, 140
        techniques, 142–146
        termination, 145–146
        therapy groups, 141–142
        topic specific groups, 140
        types of, 139–142
    individual counseling, 127–129
    interventions, usage of, 151–155
Mood disorders, intervention,
    166–174
Mourning, and termination, 182–184

**N**

Neurological system, changes in with
    aging, 53
Non-verbal cues, and communication
    skills, 35–36

**O**

OARS assessment, 85
Older Americans Research and
    Service Center (Duke University).
    *See* OARS
Oral system, changes in with aging,
    54
Organic mental disorders,
    intervention, 161–166
    validation techniques, 165–166
Orientations, of gerocounselor,
    11–15
Outcome criteria, goals of
    gerocounseling, 126

**P**

Parsimony intervention, 148
Personality
 contexts, and aging, 57–59
 functioning assessment, 92
Physical health assessment, 86
Point of view, assessment, 77–78
Positive goal, of gerocounseling,
 defining, 108
Present, staying in, gerocounseling,
 109–110
Process form, use of, gerocounseling,
 109
Psychodynamic orientation,
 gerocounselor, 11–13
Psychological system and aging, 56–62
 assessment, 89–96
  affective functioning assessment,
   93–95
  cognitive functioning assessment,
   92–93
  personality functioning
   assessment, 92
  suicidal intent assessment, 96
 cognitive contexts, 60–62
 coping, 59
 interventions, 168–174
 life satisfaction, 58
 losses, 180–181
  and termination, 180–181
 mental health, 58
 personality contexts, 57–59
 stress, 59
Psycho-social task system, 18, 85–86
Psychotherapy groups, intensive, 141

**R**

Racial group, 64–66
Reality orientation groups, 141
Recreational group, gerocounseling, 140
Reframing interventions, 157–158
Relationship contexts, of aging, 67–71
 family, 67–70
 friends, 70–71
 late-life marriages, 70
Relationship skills, 31–33
 boundaries, 31–32
 courtesies, 32–33
 empathy, 31
Relationships, 117
 and goal of gerocounseling, 117
Relocation, termination and, 193–197

Reminiscence groups,
 gerocounseling, 142
Reminiscence interventions, 159–160
Remotivation therapy groups, 141
Renal system, changes in with aging, 55
Resources
 accessing, interventions, 151
 for assessment, 78–81
Respiratory system, changes in with
 aging, 54
Responsibilities, and goal of
 gerocounseling, 117
Retraining interventions, 158

**S**

Self-actualization groups,
 gerocounseling, 142
Self-system, 46–49
 gender, 47–49
 Gero-Chi counseling model, 16–18
 termination issues, 180
Sensory system, changes in with
 aging, 52–53
Service advocacy groups,
 gerocounseling, 140
Session, termination of, 189
Sexuality, changes in with aging, 55
Short-term goals, gerocounseling,
 108–113
Sight, changes in with aging, 52
Silence, and communication skills, 37
Situational contexts, of aging, 72–74
 death/dying, 73–74
 environmental concerns, 72–73
 finances, 73
 health/health care, 72
 retirement, 73
 work, 73
Skeletal system, changes in with
 aging, 53
Skills, 9–10, 23–30
 autonomy, 26–29
 beneficence, 29–30
 ethics skills, 24–26
 fidelity, 30
Smell, changes in with aging, 53
Social class, 66–67
Social group, gerocounseling, 140
Social support assessment, 97
Society's goals, gerocounseling, 114
Sociological losses, and termination,
 181–182

Sociological system and aging, 63–74
  assessment, 96–101
    family assessment, 97–101
    social support assessment, 97
  cultural contexts, 64–67
    ethnic group, 64–66
    minority/majority groups, 67
    racial group, 64–66
    social class, 66–67
  historical contexts, 63–64
  relationship contexts, 67–71
    family, 67–70
    friends, 70–71
    late-life marriages, 70
  situational contexts, 72–74
    death/dying, 73–74
    environmental concerns, 72–73
    finances, 73
    health/health care, 72
    retirement, 73
    work, 73
Socratic interventions, 157
Somatic interventions, 167
Specific disorder interventions, 161–178
  Alzheimer's disease, 162–165
  anxiety disorders, 174–175
  boundary interventions, 176
  communication interventions, 176–177
  coping interventions, 177
  family disorders, 175–178
    intervention methods, 178
  guilt disorders, 175
  hierarchy interventions, 176
  mood disorders (depression),
    166–174
  organic mental disorders, 161–166
    validation techniques, 165–166
  psychological interventions, 168–174
  somatic interventions, 167
Specificity
  in gerocounseling, 110
  goals of gerocounseling, 110
Spirituality, and gero-client, 49–50
Stress, and aging, 59
Structure
  gerocounseling, 21–23
  and gerocounselor, 10
Style, assessment, 76
Subset systems, Gero-Chi Counseling
    Model, 18
Suicidal intent assessment, 96
Support groups, gerocounseling, 140
Supportive interventions, 158–159

Supports, and goal of
    gerocounseling, 115–116
Systems outlook, in interventions,
    150–151

**T**

Taste, changes in with aging, 52
Techniques, in gerocounseling,
    142–146
Termination, 179–202
  active dying phase, 199–200
  after death, 200
  bereavement, 200–201
    complicated, 184–184
  and biological losses, 180
  of case, 190–193
    phase one, 190
    phase three, 191–193
    phase two, 190–191
  coping with, 182–184
  death, 197–201, 200
  and depression, 184
  ethics and, 187–188
  Gero-Chi Counseling Model, 180–182
  gerocounseling, 145–146, 184–201
  grief, 182–184
  living with illness phase, 198–199
  major subset systems, 180–182
  and psychological losses, 180–181
  and relocation, 193–197
  self-system, 180
  of session, 189
  and sociological losses, 181–182
  transference, 185–187
  types of, 189–193
Therapy groups, gerocounseling,
    141–142
Time, usage of, in interventions,
    153–154
Timing, assessment, 76–77
Tobin's goal for aging, 118–119
Topic-specific groups,
    gerocounseling, 140
Touch, changes in with aging, 53
Training interventions, 158
Transference, and termination, 185–187
Triangulation, in families, 136

**V**

Values, 148–149
Voice quality, and communication
    skills, 37–38